Zenobia of

Herbert Schmalz, *Queen Zenobia's Last Look upon Palmyra.*

Zenobia of Palmyra

HISTORY, MYTH AND THE
NEO-CLASSICAL IMAGINATION

Rex Winsbury

Duckworth

First published in 2010 by
Gerald Duckworth & Co. Ltd.
90-93 Cowcross Street, London EC1M 6BF
Tel: 020 7490 7300
Fax: 020 7490 0080
info@duckworth-publishers.co.uk
www.ducknet.co.uk

A catalogue record for this book is available
from the British Library

ISBN 978-0-7156-3853-8

Illustration sources

Frontispiece: from T. Blakemore, *The Art of Herbert Schmalz* (1911); pp. 13, 14, 22, 35, 44, 49, 50, 55, 64, 68, 74, 107, 113, 122, 141, 150, 153: courtesy Wikimedia Creative Commons Attribution-Share Alike license; pp. 12 and 147: Huntingdon Art Collection; pp. 33 *above* and 60: courtesy Cabinet des Médailles, Paris; p. 33 *below*: from K. Emmett, *Alexandrian Coins* (2001), based on originals in works by F. Feuardent (1872) and V. Langlois (1852); p. 58 (both photos): Meryon Bridges; p. 70: courtesy M. Gawlikowski; p. 119: from M. Rostovtzeff, *Excavations at Dura Europos, Fourth Season*, 'Graffiti' (1933). All other photographs are the author's.

Typeset by Ray Davies
Printed and bound in Great Britain by
CPI Antony Rowe, Chippenham and Eastbourne

Contents

For Jessie and Luke

The author at the Bagdad café between Damascus and Palmyra.

Preface

This book is the story of the legendary but very real queen Zenobia of Palmyra, both in history and in the imagination. It offers the reader a coherent and plausible account of her life and career but also shows how Zenobia has been treated and mistreated in art, literature and the writing of history from her lifetime right up to the present day. Contradictory and even fanciful images of her have distorted our historical judgment of the real Zenobia as a woman and, most importantly, as a ruler. Assessing Zenobia also means assessing the lives and careers of the two 'significant others' in her life, her first husband Odenathus and her battlefield opponent, the Roman emperor Aurelian. It means assessing the state of the Roman empire in her time, the seriousness of the much-debated 'third-century crisis'. So this is a political biography wrapped inside an artistic critique folded inside a study of the modern 'reception' of classical heroines. It does not offer an exhaustive (and inevitably exhausting and tedious) examination of all the detailed evidence for the lives of Zenobia, Odenathus and Aurelian. The notes and bibliography provide copious references to sources where the reader may delve further if he or she wishes. Instead, each chapter focuses on a different and essentially political question about Zenobia and her times and contemporaries, to reach a final assessment of her status, ambitions, successes and failures. The narrative is consistent with the evidence but, given the scrappy nature of that evidence, inevitably entails historical judgment at many crucial points. In the minefield of transliteration of names between Palmyrene Aramaic, Greek, Latin and English, I have opted for one version and (I hope) stuck to it. My debts to previous authors will become obvious. But I wish to name in particular Professor Michal Gawlikowski of Warsaw and Professor Fergus Millar of Oxford, without in any way implying that they are responsible for my judgments or shortcomings. I am also indebted to the library of the Institute of Classical Studies in London for its excellent research facilities: and to the library of Birkbeck College, London, for its ability to track down material on almost anything.

Note: all dates are AD unless otherwise specified.

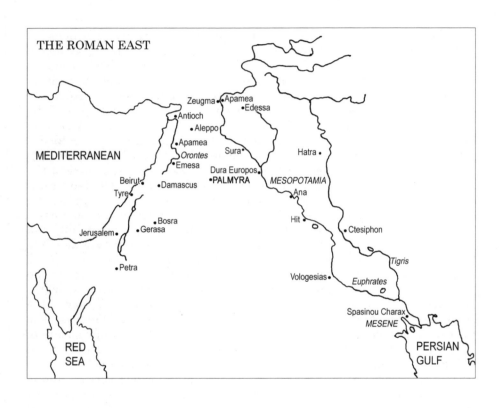

THE ROMAN EAST

Zeugma • Apamea
• Antioch • Edessa
• Aleppo

MEDITERRANEAN
• Apamea
Orontes Sura • Hatra •
• Emesa
Dura Europos •
Beirut • •PALMYRA *MESOPOTAMIA*
Tyre • • Damascus Ana
Hit • • Ctesiphon
• Bosra
Jerusalem • • Gerasa
Tigris
• Petra
Vologesias • *Euphrates*

Spasinou Charax •
MESENE

RED
SEA
PERSIAN
GULF

1

Inventing Zenobias: pen, brush and chisel

In May of 2009 a remarkable statue went on display at the Huntingdon Library and Art Collection in San Marino, California. For well over a century the statue was believed lost or destroyed until it turned up again in a sale catalogue at Sotheby's, the London fine art auctioneers. The statue is Harriet Hosmer's marble statue captioned *Zenobia in Chains*, created in Rome where Hosmer, an American, spent most of her working life in artistic exile. It is sculpted in the neo-classical style popular in the nineteenth century and stands well over life size, at 82 inches (208 cm) tall. It is therefore a fine example of the golden age of American classical sculpture. Carved on it is the inscription, appropriately in Latin, *Harriet Hosmer me sculpsit Romae* (Harriet Hosmer sculpted me at Rome).

For decades the only surviving copy of Harriet Hosmer's statue was thought to be a half-size version in the Wadsworth Atheneum in Hartford, Connecticut. The full-size original had attracted little attention when first exhibited in London in 1859 but much admiration and controversy when shown in 1864 in New York, Chicago and Boston, where 15,000 people came to see it. But then it disappeared from public view, finally reappearing at Sotheby's in November 2007. The Huntingdon then bought it using funds dedicated to the acquisition of American art. The hammer price at the auction was UK£192,500.

Sotheby's catalogue named the seller as Almon Griswold, the New York lawyer who bought the statue for US$5,000 when it was first shown in that city. So one may presume that the seller at Sotheby's was really his family or the trustees of his estate. Griswold was better known as a book collector, so it is not clear why he bought the *Zenobia*, or why he withdrew it from public view. When another neo-classical statue of the same era called *The Death of Cleopatra* by another unusual American woman sculptor working in Rome, a friend of Hosmer's called Edmonia Lewis, also turned up in a Sotheby's sale catalogue after similarly being believed lost, the owners donated it to the Smithsonian Institute in Washington in recognition of its status in American art history.

Zenobia in Chains was not only Harriet Hosmer's best-known and most admired sculpture; it also rapidly became a feminist icon for her own generation of 'emancipated' women and is now, following re-discovery, regaining that iconic status. Whether that status is due to the statue's intrinsic artistic merit is arguable. But it certainly has much to do with the remarkable life of its sculptor, and much to do with the remarkable life

Harriet Hosmer's statue of Zenobia.

1. Inventing Zenobias: pen, brush and chisel

Harriet Hosmer, 1873 engraving by Augustus Robin.

of the subject of her statue, the real-life Queen Zenobia of Palmyra in Syria. Brought together in this one statue, the combination of two remarkable female lives makes the aesthetics of the statue and its symbolic and historical values impossible to separate one from another.

Those golden chains

The statue depicts Queen Zenobia at perhaps the most famous moment in her meteoric career, being led captive in golden chains through the streets of Rome after military humiliation at the hands of the Roman emperor Aurelian in the year 274 of our era. Her head is bowed but she retains a regal bearing. We are told by one classical source that she was so weighed down by her chains and rich jewellery that her guards had to help her lift them. The pathos of her situation – if this story is true – caused *Zenobia in Chains* to become one of the visual commonplaces of nineteenth- and early twentieth-century classical history painting and sculpture, and apparently of London fashion as well. See, for example, Herbert Schmalz's *Queen Zenobia's Last Look upon Palmyra*, on the frontispiece of this book, in which Zenobia also displays her golden chains. The original is in the Art Gallery of South Australia, in Adelaide.[1] Another example is J.W. Waterhouse's 1887 neo-classical painting *Mariamne*, where (in a story told by the Roman historian Josephus) Herod's wife stands before a court of elders accused of adultery – in golden chains. In 1878 Edward Poynter also exhibited at the Royal Academy his painting *Zenobia Captive*. As late as 1897 the Duchess of Devonshire could turn up at a grand fancy-dress ball in London kitted out as Zenobia, presumably confident that her admirers would know exactly who Zenobia was.[2]

Zenobia's doomed conflict with Rome has inevitably brought comparison with Boudica, the famous British queen of the Iceni of East Anglia who came out in revolt against Roman occupation and mistreatment. Both women have earned the label of Amazon Queen because of their reputations for skill on horseback, endurance, and military leadership. Boudica became a patriotic folk hero and icon of British independence and human rights.[3] Her statue, riding a war chariot, commands the entrance to

13

Boudica's statue opposite the Houses of Parliament.

Westminster Bridge over the river Thames, appropriately opposite the British Houses of Parliament, and was much used by the British suffragettes in their campaign to secure votes for women. Both Zenobia and Boudica have therefore become powerful feminist icons.

Similarly, for today's Syrians, Zenobia is also a national hero. She has starred on Syrian television, and her head appears on many of the country's banknotes, as a symbol of that country's long search for national independence, first from the Ottoman Turkish empire, and then from control by France.

Zenobia was an object of knowing speculation and qualified admiration in classical and medieval times, and remains so today. She was the lead actor in a 'brief and violent ... extraordinary and unparalleled' episode in Roman history, says a contemporary historian.[4] The *Oxford Classical Dictionary* entry on Zenobia says that she was 'one of the most remarkable women of antiquity'. Another admirer says that she was 'one of the most remarkable figures in the entire history of the Roman and Byzantine Near East'.[5] A modern (female) Italian biographer of Zenobia characterises her as 'determined, proud, ambitious and combative'.[6] A recent author calls her 'a most infamous adversary' of Rome.[7]

This exotic Syrian queen is inseparable from the exotic city she ruled in the middle of the third century of our era. Palmyra sat astride a section of one of the world's great trade routes, the silk and spices road from China and Arabia to Rome and Europe. It was this trade that provided Palmyra, the City of Palms, more properly known to this day as Tadmor, with the wealth and architecture that has earned it the

A Syrian banknote with bust of Zenobia.

accolade of 'Venice of the Sands'.[8] Its ruins have fascinated generations of artists, writers, travellers and tourists. Trade may also have been one motive for Zenobia's bold but risky military adventure that brought her into conflict with Rome's legions. One key to Zenobia's career is to explain exactly how Palmyra came to occupy this pivotal position in the Roman empire's trans-border long-distance luxury trade when its only obvious asset was a salty spring feeding an oasis of palm trees in the dry steppe-lands of Syria.

Hosmer's life[9]

It is therefore easy to see how Zenobia came to hold such a powerful appeal to Harriet Hosmer. But how did it come about that a woman born in Watertown, Massachusetts, of diminutive physical stature, came to sculpt this and other larger-than-life marble statues at Rome, so far from home? That question sheds light on why Zenobia has been moulded and re-modelled so often by successive generation of writers, artists and historians – not always helpfully.

Harriet Goodhue Hosmer, called Hattie by her friends, was the daughter of a prosperous doctor. Both her mother and her sister died of tuberculosis and her father determined that Hattie should not suffer the same fate. So he brought her up virtually as a boy, emphasising physical activity and fitness. She became a skilled horsewoman, as was her subject Zenobia – perhaps an unacknowledged link between the two women. Hosmer was often referred to as 'petite' and pictures of her emphasise how tiny she looked compared to the colossal statues she often created, most notably her *Zenobia* and the monumental bronze statue of Senator Thomas Hart Benton now standing in Lafayette Square, St Louis, clad in a Roman toga and Roman sandals. In a photo of her at work on this colossus, she is standing high up on scaffolding and looks less than half

15

the height of the statue, as if almost to boast of the contrast. Perhaps her tall statues were the reciprocal of her own small figure.

To become a sculptor in the first place, Hosmer felt she needed to study anatomy. But the study of anatomy at that time was a male preserve in America. It was not considered proper for a woman to see unclothed or dismembered bodies. Sculpture itself was also considered a male preserve, since a woman surely could not wield the hefty hammer and chisel associated with sculpture, and it might involve gazing at nude models. Aesthetically, neo-classical sculpture and the nude were regarded as virtually synonymous. In fact, Hosmer never created a nude statue, and only rarely did statues of men. Her father supported her ambitions and managed to get her anatomy lessons. Then the problem arose of learning to sculpt. She decided to go to Rome, epicentre of the world of sculpture at that time and once the home of the most famous of all the neo-classical sculptors, Antonio Canova, whose sad and only partially successful task it had been to try to recover for Italy part of the vast haul of artistic loot that Napoleon had carried off from Italy during the Napoleonic occupation of that country.

Hosmer in Rome

Financed by her father, Hosmer arrived in Rome in 1852 and persuaded the English sculptor John Gibson to take her on as a pupil. Soon, a steady stream of neo-classical statues began to appear, and Hosmer joined the ranks of the 'literary sculptors' for whom the sculpture and the story it told were derived from Roman, Greek and biblical stories. Most of her work was done in the first 15 years or so of her career as a sculptor. Some malicious tongues suggested that her sculptures were really the work of Gibson, and he issued a rebuttal of that suggestion. That did not still Hosmer's critics, who then said that the quality of her statues was due, if not to Gibson, then to the skilled professional marble carvers and stone-cutters of whom there were plenty in Rome at the time. Hosmer sued and forced apologies to be printed. She even wrote a long article in the *Atlantic Monthly* in which she explained that the true creativity of the sculptor lay in the clay model that he or she created, but also in using plaster and wax for the final effect. The marble carvers, some 20 of whom are seen in one photo of her studio, were in effect artisan copiers who scaled up the model to the required size in marble, but without creative input, she said.

While this explained how a woman of small build could create marble statues well over life size, and is indeed the procedure followed by many sculptors then and now, it does not entirely rule out the possibility that these experienced marble carvers did bring something more to the finished product than just copying and enlarging. What is more, the availability of these carvers meant that multiple copies of any particular statue could be churned out if there was demand. It was common practice at that time (and remains so) to make more than one copy of a statue, and Hosmer was well aware of the financial possibilities that this opened up for repeat sales. When Hosmer's father fell on harder times she needed money, both for her team of carvers and for her horses. Records show that at least four copies of the full-size *Zenobia* were originally made and sold, as well as some half-size copies and indeed a bust. What happened to the rest of these versions is not known. Her 1855 statue *Puck on a Toadstool* was reproduced in 50 copies, selling first at $500, then at $1,000 apiece – almost a manufacturing production line. Distinguished visitors to Rome regularly visited her studio, which doubled up as a saleroom. Demand for her *Puck* and its rising price were due to its popularity with royalty. The Prince of Wales, the future King Edward VIII of Great Britain, bought one copy for his student rooms at Oxford, and Puck's plump legs caused the Crown Princess of Germany to exclaim:

> Oh Miss Hosmer, you have such talent for toes!

The visit by the Prince of Wales to her studio even warranted a cartoon in *Harper's Weekly* of 7 May 1859 in which Hosmer is shown standing next to her huge statue of Zenobia. With success like that Hosmer came to enjoy the company of the British aristocracy. At their invitation she travelled to England and wrote:

> I had a delightful visit at Raby, and then I came here to Lady Marian Alford, who is more darling than ever. On Monday I go to the Duchess of Buckingham for a few days, then Lady Ashburton claims me for a few more.

Less successful was the patent she took out for a new method of making artificial marble, and her experiments later in life with the problem of perpetual motion, using magnets.

The marmorean flock

The attraction of Rome to Hosmer was not just the sculpture and the stonecutters but also the freedom to adopt a life-style that contemporary America denied her. She was a prominent member of that group of expatriate American women whom the novelist Henry James famously dubbed 'the white marmorean flock'. Many of them sculpted and so used marble (marmorean), and they were with one exception white, the exception being Edmonia Lewis, whose father was Haitian of African descent and whose mother was of mixed American Indian and African descent. This group of women included some who were openly lesbian, notably the well-known actress and player of 'breeches roles' i.e. men's roles, Charlotte Cushman, whose house in Rome Hosmer shared. As Hosmer's fame grew, tourists came to visit her studio in Rome, not least to gaze at her mixture

17

of (in the eyes of the time) male and female clothing and her boyish short haircut. Hosmer herself never married, and said in a letter that for a woman artist marriage was 'a moral wrong' and that she herself was 'the only faithful worshipper of Celibacy'.

She had no children, but created a sort of substitute family, referring to her patron Wayman Crow, founder of the School of Medicine at Washington University, as 'The Pater' (father) and to her statues as her 'children'. Her most intense relationship may have been with that same Lady Louisa Ashburton whom she visited when in the UK, and in relation to whom, it is claimed, she used the term 'wedded wife'.[10] Hosmer became a close friend of Elizabeth and Robert Browning, the English poets living in Italy, who called her their 'great pet'; of Frederic (later Lord) Leighton, the English neo-classical painter who became president of London's Royal Academy, who called her 'the queerest, best-natured little chap possible'; and of the American novelist Nathaniel Hawthorne, who mentions Hosmer and her 'noble' statue of Zenobia in the Preface to his rather dull 1859 novel *The Marble Faun*. In 1858 Hosmer wrote

> I am busy now upon Zenobia, of a size with which I might be compared as a mouse to a camel. My mass of clay ... is stunning.

Hosmer's Zenobia became not only her best-known work but also one of the few that she undertook without a commission. So Zenobia must have spoken strongly to Hosmer, who sought out representations of her on Roman coins but rejected them as inadequate compared to her own vision of the Syrian queen. She also sought out Roman and later literary descriptions of Zenobia but rejected them whenever she found them inconsistent with her own evolving idealised conception of Zenobia. The initial inspiration for her Zenobia in fact came from another friend, Anna Jameson, who had included Zenobia in her book *Memoirs of Celebrated Female Sovereigns*, published in 1831, in which Zenobia appears alongside Cleopatra, Mary Queen of Scots, Queen Elizabeth of England, Catherine the Great of Russia and other powerful women. High society indeed. Hosmer and Jameson exchanged ideas about what the Zenobia statue should look like, in clothing and in bearing. But Jameson's judgements on the women in her book were in the end at odds with Hosmer's final judgement about Zenobia. Hosmer formed her own idiosyncratic picture of the Zenobia she wanted to embody in marble. How her vision of Zenobia chimed with or was at odds with other people's visions of the famous Syrian queen, and with what we can say today about the historical Zenobia in the light of the latest evidence, is the main theme of this book. Hosmer's infatuation with Zenobia illustrates how easily fact and fiction came together in the person of this Syrian queen.

1. Inventing Zenobias: pen, brush and chisel

Invention and discovery

The process of inventing and re-inventing Zenobia has gone on continuously from her own lifetime right up to the present time. The line between historical reality and historical fiction is, in the case of Zenobia, not just blurred, but almost non-existent. Zenobia

> represents a blaze of colour against the rather bleak background of the mid-third century. She has therefore suffered rather more than most historical figures in being shrouded in legend.[11]

She herself used legend – in particular the legends of Queen Cleopatra of Egypt; of Dido, Queen of Carthage; and of the great Seleucid dynasty that once ruled greater Syria after the death of Alexander the Great – as part of her political and ideological weaponry. Authors of her own time and soon after, as well as modern authors, reached for legend and invention in the inevitable attempt to explain what her ambitions were, and what exactly her personal magic was that brought her famous mailed cavalry into open military conflict with Rome's cavalry and legions. The legends about Zenobia and the aura of eastern romance surrounding her city are an integral part of her story, but also create a smoke-screen behind which it is difficult to discern the real Zenobia. That smokescreen obscures fictions as well as facts, dark qualities as well as heroic qualities. She both invented herself, and has been re-invented by others, from classical times right down to our own day. The industry of 'inventing Zenobia' is still in full swing, and it is precisely on her ability to be re-invented that Zenobia's attraction largely depends.

By Hosmer's time Zenobia had already enjoyed a long career in European art and literature stretching back as far as the fourteenth century. The early Renaissance Italian author and poet Giovanni Boccaccio included her in his *Lives of Famous Women* of 1374. This is the first known example in Western literature of a book devoted solely to women – all 106 of them, including Zenobia and Cleopatra. With Boccaccio as a source, Geoffrey Chaucer in his *Canterbury Tales*, written before 1400, devoted a large part of his *Monk's Tale* to Zenobia and Aurelian. Then the exotic ruins of Palmyra itself, situated where the Syrian steppe meets the Syrian desert, became the stuff of legend and romance after they were 'discovered' by Europeans in the late 1600s. They were made famous by the engravings in *The Ruins of Palmyra*, published in 1753 by explorers Robert Wood and James Dawkins.

Among painters, the Italian Giovanni Battista Tiepolo in 1720-30 devoted a series of fanciful but dramatic oil paintings to Aurelian and Zenobia. One, *Queen Zenobia Addressing her Soldiers*, is in the National Gallery of Art in Washington; another is in the Prado Museum in Madrid. Catherine the Great of Russia (empress 1762-96) was apt to liken herself

The ruins of Palmyra today.

to Zenobia, ignoring the difference in ideas of chastity between herself and the supposedly puritanical Syrian. (Zenobia is said, in what is surely an invention, to have slept with her husband only for the purposes of procreation.[12]) But it was Edward Gibbon in his great 1.5 million word history, *The Decline and Fall of the Roman Empire*, published between 1776 and 1788, who wrote, as if almost in love with his character, the most famous purple passage about Zenobia.

> Zenobia is perhaps the only female whose superior genius broke through the servile indolence imposed on her sex by the climate and manners of Asia. She claimed her descent from the Macedonian kings of Egypt, equalled in beauty her ancestor Cleopatra, and far surpassed that princess in chastity and valour. Zenobia was esteemed the most lovely as well as the most heroic of her sex. She was of dark complexion (for in speaking of a lady, these trifles become important). Her teeth were of a pearly whiteness, and her large black eyes sparkled with uncommon fire, tempered by the most attractive sweetness. Her voice was manly and harmonious. Her manly understanding was strengthened and adorned by study. She had inured her constitution to fatigue [and] generally appeared on horseback in a military habit ... The success of Odenathus [her first husband] was in great measure ascribed to her incomparable prudence and fortitude. (Gibbon, *Decline and Fall*, ch. 11)

Even allowing for the rhetoric of Gibbon's style and the gender prejudices of Gibbon's own time, not many women emerge like that from the pages of Roman history. They lived in a male-dominated society, and the authors of the time upon whom we rely for what we know about Zenobia were all men, often with marked disdain for anything that suggested subordination of male to female.

> Now all shame is exhausted, for in the weakened state of the commonwealth even women ruled most excellently, even a foreigner, Zenobia by name

sniffed one classical author about Zenobia's rule.[13] The Italian composer Gioachino Rossini thought he could improve upon Chaucer and Gibbon, and upon real life. In 1813 he wrote an opera about Aurelian and Zenobia entitled *Aureliano in Palmira*. In it Zenobia is hovering politically between Rome and her greatest enemy, the Persian empire, just as I suspect happened in real life, but Aurelian, in a nice but complete invention by Rossini, declares his love for Zenobia, only to be rebuffed in favour of her Persian lover Arsace.

Living the legend

So powerful was Zenobia's legend at that time in the early nineteenth century that it led, in one notorious case, to life imitating art, in the eccentric form of Lady Hester Stanhope, aristocratic niece of Britain's two-time Prime Minister, William Pitt. Stanhope tried to live out a fiction. When she rode into Palmyra in full Arab gear in March of 1813 (the same year as Rossini's opera, not by coincidence) and escorted by a cast of thousands, she was greeted

> by pretty girls singing and throwing rose petals as if she were their ancient heroine, Queen Zenobia, returned.[14]

Stanhope was as much in search of the remains of Zenobia as of the remains of Palmyra. According to one biographer

> Even in the wilds of the desert Hester Stanhope worshipped before the altar of her colossal egotism. She saw herself reflected in Zenobia's fame.[15]

She was, like Zenobia (and Hosmer) a fine horsewoman, and having chosen to live in the Middle East she rejected the suggestion of returning to England by asking what she would do there: 'Knit or sew like an Englishwoman?' Zenobia, one may guess, would have sympathised, but not with Stanhope's abominable treatment of her Arab servants and African slaves, whom she beat frequently and kept on duty to serve her whims 24 hours a day, every day. Fifty years later, at the height of the nineteenth-century 'romantic sentimentality' towards ancient ruins, Lady Jane Digby wandered through Palmyra's remains by moonlight and honeymooned there after marrying her Arab guide, a local sheik. The legendary queen and her romantic city exercised a powerful hold on the imagination, and still do.

21

Hester Stanhope in her eastern gear.

Hollywood and the web

If today Zenobia – or Bat-Zabbai to use her Arab-Aramaic name – is not as well known as, say, Cleopatra, it is thanks largely to her comparative (and surprising) neglect by the Hollywood film industry. In fiction there have been at least five more or less fanciful novels written about Zenobia in modern times, all in the United States.[16] But there is just one obscure and totally fictitious 1950s Hollywood sword and sandal epic, *The Sign of the Gladiator*, absurdly starring the blonde and busty Scandinavian actress Anita Ekberg as the dark-eyed Arab queen. This neglect by Hollywood is surprising because the stories told about Zenobia's life, true or invented, are full of memorable filmic scenes that lend themselves to big-screen treatment – caravans of rich merchants crossing the Syrian steppe carrying spices from Arabia and silk from China, oases and palm trees, cavalry charges, flight across the desert on camel-back, romantic ruins, the parading of the captive Zenobia in a gaudy triumphal procession at Rome, and much else. Zenobia does however enjoy a vigorous contemporary after-life on the web, with many websites at least partially devoted to more or less accurate or more or less fanciful accounts of her life.[17] One site says enthusiastically that she was 'chock full of sheer raw devil-may-care attitude'.[18]

1. Inventing Zenobias: pen, brush and chisel

Zenobia's story as told to us perhaps lacks the sex and stage effects that made Cleopatra the recurring darling of playwrights, script writers and painters. Zenobia was not delivered inside a rolled-up carpet, did not (despite Rossini) have a love affair with Aurelian, and did not commit suicide. But if Zenobia is not as well known today as she used to be, that is not because Shakespeare never wrote a play about her or because we no longer respond to the 'romantic fallacy' of Victorian history sculpture and painting, but because we are no longer sure of who exactly Zenobia was, what her driving motives were, and what exactly she stood for. In short, since the days of both Gibbon and Hosmer, we have learnt to be sceptical about the evidence and ask how many of the stories about her are or may be invention or part-invention, and by what standards we should assess her career.

Alternative endings

The problems about assessing Zenobia are twofold. On the one hand, she has been subjected to so much invention. For example, there are at least three versions in our sources of how Zenobia met her end, and they cannot all be true. Some must be inventions. There is the version with her starring role in Aurelian's triumphal procession, in her golden chains, after which Zenobia was given as a reward for playing her part well a comfortable retirement villa in Tivoli. Tivoli is the salubrious suburb of Rome where the emperor Hadrian's huge and still substantially extant villa complex still attracts admiring visitors today, much as the evocative remains of Zenobia's former city of Palmyra still attract the tourist crowds and cameras.[19] On this version, once pensioned off at Tivoli, Zenobia married (or was married off) for the second time and had more children to replace the one (or ones) she had lost in Syria. The late Byzantine writer George Syncellus in his *Universal History* affirms that Aurelian 'treated her with great humanity'.[20]

So Zenobia's story had a happy ending. But did it? There is a rival tradition that she simply died on the way to Rome, so could never have starred in Aurelian's triumph at all, let alone have had a happy ending.[21] Yet another story is that she was indeed put on public display in chains, but on a platform at Antioch.[22] Yet another tradition is that Zenobia made it to Rome, but was put to death there, beheaded 'in the old manner' – a far from happy ending.[23] On top of that, the golden chains may be just a literary cliché. One modern author claims that

> the motif of the oriental queen who can barely carry the weight of her gemstones was a familiar topos in contemporary [Roman] novels and rhetoric.[24]

Just as there are different versions of her end, so there are several different interpretations of Zenobia's character. If some of the stories about her are true, then there is a dark side to her which sits ill with her claimed status as heroine, whether feminist or nationalist. The most serious charges against her are her murky and potentially treasonous connections with Rome's perennial enemy the Persian empire; the allegation that she was complicit in the assassination of her husband Odenathus; and her ratting on her friends and supporters when she came to trial.[25] The strange circumstances of the simultaneous deaths of her husband and her stepson have caused her to be cast as the archetypal wicked stepmother. Then when Aurelian's soldiers were clamouring for the death penalty after her defeat, she bargained for her life in a way that has been held as a reproach against her ever since. Zenobia blamed her closest advisers for her political and military ambitions. They were summarily put to death while she lived on, so earning for herself the charge (not least from those feminists who would otherwise be her natural admirers) that she degraded herself by betrayal, cowardice and scape-goating.[26]

No asp for Zenobia

The charge of cowardice goes further. On that day of Aurelian's official triumph, if she was there – and I believe, on balance, that she was, with golden chains – Zenobia would surely have known that, some three centuries before, the famous Cleopatra, Queen of Egypt and lover of Julius Caesar and Mark Antony, heroine of Shakespeare and Hollywood, from whom Zenobia claimed descent and whose country, Egypt, she had briefly ruled, had committed suicide by the bite of the asp (so it is said) rather than face the humiliating ordeal of being paraded as a captive through those self-same streets of Rome. Cleopatra had been well aware that the frequent fate of defeated but captured enemies of the Roman empire at the climax of this elaborate victory parade was to be ritually put to death, as an all-too-final demonstration of the invincible might of Rome and as a lesson to anyone else who chose to defy her. One of these 'celebrity executions'[27] was that of Simon, leader of the great Jewish Revolt against Rome in the first century, who after being paraded through the street of Rome was noosed, dragged along the ground while his guards beat him up, and then was finished off in the middle of the Forum on the spot reserved for execution of criminals. Rather than face that, Cleopatra had chosen suicide. Zenobia had not. Cleopatra is admired for her courage: Zenobia is not.

In defence of Zenobia, the emperor Aurelian is said to have taken the view that it was not worth his while, indeed demeaning to his honour as a man and as a general, to summarily execute a mere woman. Zosimus tell us that Aurelian 'thought that the conquest of a woman would not bring him glory in the eyes of future generations'.[28] Anyway, he needed her for his ceremonial triumph, as a prize exhibit and star turn. He gives every indication of having understood as well as any modern political leader the propaganda value of showmanship, especially at that uniquely threatening period of Rome's long history. His theatrical instincts, his inventiveness, are part of Zenobia's story. The triumph was a centuries-old traditional Roman day-long extravaganza to celebrate victory over Rome's enemies.[29] In Book 7 of *The Jewish War* Josephus gives a vivid account of the elaborate triumph celebrated by the emperor Vespasian and his son Titus in 71 after their suppression of the Jewish Revolt, and Aurelian no doubt knew of that precedent. In Aurelian's case, however, there were three victories to celebrate simultaneously, one over Zenobia's evolving empire in the east, one over a longer-lasting breakaway Gallic empire in the west, and one over waves of Germanic invaders from the north – all achieved in a short space of three years by this remarkable but puzzling man.

Aurelian had begun as a humble foot-soldier from the Balkans and his spectacular military career had seen him rise through the ranks to commander of the cavalry and then to the supreme pinnacle of absolute power in the Roman empire. So it had been Zenobia's misfortune to run head-on into one of the ablest generals that Rome had ever produced. In a short reign of five years Aurelian pulled the Roman empire back from the brink and put it back together again when it was threatened (by Zenobia among others) with dissolution. It had been a clash of two extraordinary personalities, a clash in which one, Aurelian, had proved to be the nemesis of the other, Zenobia. You can therefore read Zenobia's meteoric rise and catastrophic downfall, as many do, as an archetypal example of punishment for *hubris*, the overweening pride that goes before the fall, in her case leading to the near-destruction of her city of Palmyra. Similarly, Boudica's destruction of London during her revolt was a serious set-back to the development of that city. Neither city did well out of their heroines, and it is Zenobia who must take the main responsibility for the ruins we see today of her once beautiful city.

The millennium crisis

This was a time when Syrians and Syria had for several generations been playing a big part in the affairs of Rome. Zenobia was only one of a group of Syrian princesses who had already, by the time of Aurelian's unilateral proclamation as emperor in 270, put two emperors onto the throne of Rome, Elagabalus and his successor Severus Alexander. But it was also the time of the so-called 'third-century crisis', a description which some modern historians have tried to talk away as an invention but which stubbornly persists as a true designation of the state of the empire. Only a few years before, in April 248, the inhabitants of Rome had celebrated (under, be it noted, an Arab emperor, Philip) the one thousandth anniversary of the foundation of their city, whose humble beginnings tradition (or rather the Roman scholar Varro) had ascribed to the year 753 BC. There were three days and nights of celebrations, featuring gladiators, rare animals, and stage events.[30] Over those ten centuries Rome had established an empire that encompassed most of the then known world, stretching from Hadrian's Wall across the north of England to the cities of the upper Euphrates and Tigris rivers in what is now eastern Syria, eastern Turkey and northern Iraq, the area traditionally known as Mesopotamia, the land between the rivers. By its millennium the empire had existed for so many centuries that people living inside it (and many living outside it) took it for granted as the natural and eternal order of things. Yet it was exactly around its millennium that Rome's empire came perilously close to disintegration. Aurelian, more than any other single emperor, was instrumental in putting it together again.

But if her retirement story is true, Zenobia lived to see the final irony of her confrontation with Aurelian. For Aurelian did not live to complete his work, and his achievements might have died with him, had not other capable men followed him. Aurelian was brutally assassinated by some of the very men he most trusted, his senior military officers sharing his own ethnic background in the Balkans. The motives for Aurelian's assassination are obscure, and his assassins were hunted down and killed by no less than two succeeding emperors, suggesting a serious and deep-seated conspiracy.[31] Perhaps Aurelian, like Zenobia, paid the price for *hubris*. The symmetry is striking.

Deconstructing the evidence

Zenobia's misfortune, and ours, is that the surviving evidence for her life and times is of poor quality compared to, say, the much-mined period of Cicero, Julius Caesar, Mark Antony, Cleopatra and Octavian/Augustus. So interpreting events and people in the third century is often about using historical judgment to arrive at what may be the least worst interpretation of what we have, an interpretation that is at least consistent and plausible if not totally provable. The evidence that most challenges the historian and biographer is that of the notorious Latin document called the *Scriptores Historiae Augustae* (the *SHA*, or *Historians of the Roman Emperors*), now more usually referred to as the *Historia Augusta*, or *HA*. For centuries this was assumed to be a reliable document. It offers by far the most elaborate account we have of Zenobia, Aurelian and the other main *dramatis personae* of their era. It was the *HA*'s account that lay behind all the romantic, detailed and admiring representations of Zenobia from Boccaccio and Chaucer to Gibbon, Hosmer and Schmalz. Only since their time have the faults of the *HA* been realised.[32]

The *HA* is now believed to have been written by one man, despite its elaborate pretence to the contrary, about a century after the events it narrates. One recent author calls the *HA* 'the mother of all confusions'.[33] Another says it is 'a labyrinth of rhetoric and invention' in which literary precedents, most notably Juvenal's famous sixth satire on women and passages in the Roman historian Tacitus about a quite different Zenobia, rather than historical evidence, drive the narrative. Specifically about the biography of Zenobia in the *HA* we are warned that

> a large part of the data about the person of Zenobia are based on the author's invention ... Zenobia is a highly fictitious entity ... the myth of Zenobia greatly benefited from it.[34]

On the other hand, other Roman and Greek authors such as Aurelius Victor, Eutropius, Zosimus, Eusebius, Malalas, George Syncellus and even the twelfth-century Zonaras, write usefully if often briefly about Zenobia. For them, she was certainly not a fictitious entity. Sometimes they support what the *HA* says: sometimes they do not. Sometimes the *HA* offers plausible supportive evidence to the accounts of these other writers: sometimes it does not. The question is – when does the *HA*'s vivid and attractive detail, if uncorroborated, slip over into unwarranted fantasy and outrageous invention? But can we do without the *HA*? There are nuggets of real and supplementary information folded inside this strange document. But which are those nuggets? That is where we are forced back, not on evidence, but on historical judgment. As Latinists know, the Latin word *inventio* from which our word 'invention' derives does not in fact mean invention in the modern sense, i.e. fiction. Rather, it denotes the process of discovery of the facts and of devising an argument from them, perhaps in court. *Inventio*, not invention, is the process we have to follow. Another question is, how far does the apparently objective evidence of inscriptions discovered at Palmyra and papyrus fragments discovered in Egypt supplement this ragged literary record, and how far do the inscriptions and papyri rely for their interpretation upon our interpretation of the ragged literary record?

A golden story

What makes the attempt worth while is that in an epoch during which women were second-class citizens, when their lives went largely unrecorded and invisible, Zenobia stood up to be counted as a high-visibility and formidable player in imperial politics. She was plainly a resourceful and well-educated woman, trilingual (in Greek; in the local language Palmyrene which was a variant of Aramaic; and in Egyptian, as there seems no reason to deny[35]) and with some interest in philosophy and literature. More than that, her opponent Aurelian was also a formidable player in imperial politics, and both of them were driven to confrontation, almost as in a Greek tragedy, by the imperatives of the existential crisis then threatening the Roman empire.

Depending on how you look at it, their story can have many dimensions, of man versus woman, of ambition and fall, of woman versus her social confines, of cavalry versus foot-soldier, of cruelty versus forgiveness, of desert versus town, nomad versus settler, even West versus East, Roman versus Greek, Arab versus European, even multi-culturalism versus the centralised state. Such oppositions may be 'too easy in the Hegelian mind',[36] but it is a story of flawed heroes and the dark side of legends. It is also a story in which the line between fact and fiction, reality and imagination, evidence and supposition, is not and cannot be firm and fast. Invention and re-invention are part of the story. So is judgment, both the writer's and the reader's. Above all, it is a story. The Romans loved stories. You could find storytellers at almost any street corner or crossroads of their cities, attracting the crowds and earning their supper. 'Toss me a coin and I'll tell you a golden story', said Pliny to a correspondent in jest.[37] This then is her and his story, warts and all, as best we can piece it together, and a violent and enigmatic story it is.

2

Zenobia – 'a brigand, or more accurately, a woman'

How splendidly she lived! It can't be told
Her magnificent plate and gorgeous dresses.
She was entirely clad in gems and gold,
Nor, though she loved to hunt, would she neglect
To gain command of different languages
When she had leisure; for her great delight
Was studying in books, from whose learned pages
She taught herself to lead a virtuous life.[1]

Thus Chaucer on Zenobia. But freed of literary and marble representations, what sort of a woman was Zenobia? She is unusual, if not
unique, in being known both from literature and from inscriptions, and in
being known from Arab, Jewish and Manichean as well as Roman sources.
Given that, it is surprising how little we can really be sure about her as a
person – her origins, her family, even her appearance. It is that uncertainty that forms the breeding ground for the legends, misconceptions and
inventions about her life, abetted by her own habit of exploiting legend for
her own political advantage. About her general qualities, however, we can
be reasonably sure. That sober raconteur Zosimus tells us that she

had the boldness of a man and ... equalled her husband in her careful
administration.[2]

John of Antioch says that she had 'a man's courage'.[3] (I am sure these were
meant as compliments.) The verbose and enigmatic *Historia Augusta*
naturally has much more to say about her. It tell us that the Roman
emperor Aurelian sent a letter to the Roman Senate informing it that
Zenobia was

wise in counsels, steadfast in plans, firm towards her soldiers, generous
when necessary, stern when discipline demanded.

The letter adds that the military successes claimed against Rome's enemy
the Persians by her husband Odenathus were as much due to her as to
him.[4] How far can we believe the *HA*? The *HA* tells us a lot more besides,
and much of it is quite plausible. It says that she was a good horsewoman

– not unreasonable in a city like Palmyra that depended on horses and camels for much of its business and profit: that she could walk substantial distances – not unreasonable for a city that lay on the edge of the desert: that she could hold her drink – surely an art to be learnt in the wealthy household she undoubtedly grew up in: that she knew how to look after money – not unreasonable in a trading city whose leaders must have know how to keep as well as make money: and that she spoke Greek as well as Palmyrene, the local dialect of Aramaic – not unreasonable in a bi-lingual city whose inscriptions were in Palmyrene and Greek. Thus far, we may give the *HA* some benefit of the doubt, although the Roman emperor Aurelian would certainly have had a motive for playing up how formidable an opponent Zenobia was. It made his ultimate victory over her look even better.

The author Aurelius Victor, however, is much less flattering. He speaks of the Roman East falling 'under the dominion of brigands or more accurately a woman'.[5] Equally ambivalent about Zenobia's qualities are those who see the *HA*'s description of her as deriving from literary themes rather than historical sources, specifically from Juvenal's famous sixth satire, perhaps the most vitriolic diatribe against women ever written. Those themes are: man-like woman, chastity, beauty and voice, ancestry, language and culture, table manners, and female weakness in dealing with heavy loads (i.e. her chains in captivity). Thus the author of the *HA*

> may have followed themes from the sixth satire while changing its misogyny into a positive portrait of a successful warrior queen.[6]

That surely is the point. The *HA* is not just a re-write of Juvenal. Its author may, or may not, have used themes from Juvenal's satire as a frame of reference. But if he did, they have been flipped over from negative to positive. Nor does this invalidate assessments of Zenobia which are shared between the *HA* and other sources or which are supported by what we know about her life and actions. As ever, use of the *HA* has to be cautious and selective, based on historical judgement.

Zenobia's life

In making such judgements it is the detail of her life that we are unfortunately lacking. Even Zenobia's personal dates are mainly 'presumed' because they derive from events. She is presumed to have been born about 240-1, to have been married to her husband Odenathus at the age of 17 or 18 as his second wife, to have had a first son Septimius Vaballathus Athenodorus soon afterwwards, and to have been widowed by the time she was only 26 or 27 when Odenathus was assassinated in 267-8. She then had a spectacular rise and fall as ruler of most of the Roman eastern provinces for the next five years or so, only to be brought down in battle

Relief in Aleppo museum which tourists are told is Zenobia.

by the emperor Aurelian in 272, when she was about 32. She would have featured in his triumph and in her golden chains at Rome in 274 when she was 34 or so, and finally been married off to a respectable Roman about the age of 35 (assuming that story to be true), young enough to have had new children with her new husband and live out a comfortable life of retirement in the salubrious hills of Tivoli outside Rome. So during her life she produced at least three children, and possibly more, as well as being a

31

queen and encountering Rome in battle. To have packed so much into her life before she was 40, Zenobia must have been a remarkably able, active and ambitious woman, with a gift for survival. But that may not be the whole story.

What did she look like?

Despite the many modern verbal and pictorial representations of her, such as the Harriet Hosmer statue (cover) and the Herbert Schmalz painting (frontispiece), we do not really know what Zenobia looked like. We do not really know what Cleopatra looked like either. So the faces and figures of both women became a sort of blank canvas onto which following generations could impose their own ideas of the exotic female, their own 'inventions'. Most take their cue from the *HA*, which gives us a glowing description of her beauty as a woman of the east.

What is left of the last remaining statue in Palmyra's Grand Colonnade.

2. Zenobia – 'a brigand, or more accurately, a woman'

Her face was dark and of a swarthy hue, her eyes were black and powerful beyond the usual wont, her spirit divinely great and her beauty incredible. So white were her teeth that many thought that she had pearls in place of teeth. Her voice was clear and like that of a man.[7]

We have no statue or portrait bust or other reliable contemporary artistic representation of what she looked like to prove whether the *HA* is right or wrong in its description. The statue of Zenobia at Palmyra that once stood high up on a pillar next to a similar pillar that bore the statue of her husband Odenathus has long since disappeared, perhaps torn down in the immediate aftermath of her dramatic fall from grace at the hands of the emperor Aurelian. Only one statue is left of the many that once lined Palmyra's Grand Colonnade, and that is in very bad condition. The stone relief in the museum at Aleppo, often described to visitors as representing Zenobia, probably does not.

There is, however, one exception to this visual vacuum, and that is her image on the coins that she issued in her own name during her brief but spectacular public career.[8] These coins carry a side-view of her crowned head that comes as quite a let-down after the handsome and majestic images conjured up by verbally by the *HA* and Gibbon and pictorially by Hosmer, Poynter and Schmalz. The image on the coins is faded and fuzzy but she appears, to our eyes at least, as a rather prim and dowdy woman, with a thin face, pointy nose and sharp chin, hair short and set in waves close around her head with a plain tiara, not at all like a dashing dark-eyed Arab princess or a dignified marble monarch. But a strong face nevertheless.

Above: Zenobia coins.
Below: drawing of Zenobia coin.

On the theme of Zenobia's self-presentation, the *HA* also tells that at public events she wore a helmet and a purple head-band with gems hanging from its lower edge and fastened by a precious stone called a 'colchis'.[9] The *HA* also emphasises her regal bearing and love of pomp. It tells us that

> it was in the manner of the Persians that she received worship and in the manner of the Persian kings that she banqueted ... at her banquets she used vessels of gold and jewels.[10]

Behind the claim that she acted like a Persian monarch there may have lurked a hidden insult. Persia was Rome's inveterate enemy, and its obsequious manners at court were repugnant to right-thinking Romans, especially the habit of prostration in the presence of the emperor – the act of worship known by the Greek term *proskynesis*, a style of obeisance later adopted (or demanded) by Aurelian himself, to his ultimate detriment. Not much of the *HA*'s pomp and glitter is apparent on Zenobia's coin-face, which is also at odds with the glamorous and heavily ornamented women whose imperious and perhaps idealised features stare out at us from the funerary relief busts of Palmyra, each with an elaborate coiffure, embroidered and bejewelled head-dress, multiple necklaces and precious stones hanging from their ear lobes. Many fine examples of these funerary busts are in the Ny Carlsberg Glyptotek in Copenhagen, in the collection put together in the decades up to the First World War by the wealthy owner of the Carlsberg brewery.[11] Others are in the Louvre in Paris.

Still less does Zenobia's coin face answer to an Arab tradition that she had hair so long and abundant that it trailed on the ground behind her – and blue eyes.[12] Admittedly, the coins depicting Zenobia are often of poor quality, and the coin portrait has either been ignored or dismissed as a Romanised stereotype, so not even attempting to represent the 'real' Zenobia. Cleopatra's coins also show a sharp pointy face at odds with her glamorous reputation. But Zenobia's coins were after all issued by and for Zenobia herself, so the image was presumably approved by her, and Roman coins did on the whole attempt to give some impression of what the emperor who issued them actually looked like. There was a strong tradition of realism and 'verism' in Roman portraiture. Only later, from the time of Diocletian, did imperial portraiture take on a more fixed and abstract quality.[13] Why should Zenobia be any different from her time and period? Tactfully, Chaucer's monk remarks that

> I won't say that there was no woman fairer,
> But she'd a figure that you couldn't better.

Of course, the citizens of the eastern Roman empire may not have seen the coin image as dowdy. That may be our visual perception, not theirs, or

2. Zenobia – 'a brigand, or more accurately, a woman'

Relief of Habba, daughter of Oga of Palmyra, now in the Louvre.

Zenobia may have wished to emphasise her respectability and ordinariness in Roman eyes and so downplay Roman suspicions about 'Eastern menace'. But Zenobia's rather plain appearance on her coins acts as a warning against taking too literally the flowery descriptions of her beauty given in the *HA*, by Gibbon, on internet websites and in some feminist writing. Her alleged good looks may be not the least of the inventions about Zenobia, on a par with the statement in the *HA*, repeated by Chaucer, that she refused to have sex with her husband Odenathus except to get pregnant.[14] Zenobia is often compared to England's heroine Boudica, and Cassius Dio's comments on Boudica and her uprising two centuries before Zenobia's time, at the other end of the Roman empire, show the same interest in her probably exaggerated appearance as the *HA* shows in Zenobia's. Dio tells us that Boudica possessed greater intelligence than often belongs to a woman (again, I am sure, meant as a compliment) and that she

> was very tall, terrifying in appearance, fierce in the glance of her eye, her voice harsh: a great mass of tawny hair fell to her hips: around her neck was a large golden necklace … she grasped a spear.[15]

Male Roman writers saw female native leaders

35

not so much as an assortment of individuals as a recognisable type ... [which] broke the acceptable gender roles of Roman society.[16]

We must beware of Roman (male) conventions about what these threatening ladies looked like: and of our own conventions on the same question, whether in marble or paint, literature or film.

Arab or Saracen?

In describing Zenobia's appearance, is it right to refer to her, as most do, as an Arab? What was her ethnic identity? To call her an Arab adds to her apparent glamour and mystery in Western eyes. But she never called herself an Arab, nor did the inhabitants of Palmyra generally call them-

Pastiche statue of Zenobia in the lobby of a Palmyra hotel.

selves Arabs, nor did her near-contemporaries who wrote about her style her as an Arab. Indeed, the *HA* says that 'neither the Arabs nor the Saracens ever moved against her'. That is not strictly true but shows that its author distinguished between Arabs and Palmyrenes.[17] Also, Zenobia's son Vaballathus goes out of his way to proclaim victory over Arabs by using the title *Arabicus*, suggesting that for him Arabs were 'other' people. It may depend what you mean by 'Arab'. If 'Arab' means speaking Arabic – Zenobia did not. Arabic is part of the same semitic language family as Palmyrene, which she spoke, but Palmyrene is a local variant of Aramaic. If you define 'Arab' as meaning nomad bedouin – Zenobia was not. She lived in a settled community. If you define 'Arab' as meaning coming from Arabia, whether the Roman province of that name or the much broader area south of Syria from which Islam later sprang – Zenobia did not. On the other hand, it is a fair assumption that there were many genuine Arabs living at Palmyra or visiting there, even if they left no written record (elsewhere they left plentiful written records – illiterate the desert nomads of the time were not[18]). Semitic Zenobia certainly was, like the Arabs, and if she herself was not a nomad bedouin, her recent ancestors may well have been. So the term, if not pressed too hard, may suit.

Referring to her as a Saracen is however more dangerous. Malalas refers to her as 'Zenobia the Saracen', just as he refers to Odenathus as 'emperor of the Saracen barbarians'.[19] But Malalas lived some 300 years later, when Saracen had become synonymous with Arab. In Zenobia's day, 'Saracen' (*saraceni* in Latin) was practically synonymous with 'brigand'.[20] But of course many Romans thought of her in just that light, a female (and Syrian) disturber of the proper order of things, like Boudica, a political brigand and a Saracen barbarian.

Zenobia's family connections

In discussing Zenobia's ethnicity, it would help if we knew more about her family origins. But we do not even have a name for Zenobia's mother. The report that Zenobia spoke Egyptian as well as Palmyrene and Greek brings a plausible suggestion that her mother may have been Egyptian, or that Zenobia's family may have lived and worked in Egypt. Palmyra, as a trading city, had strong trading interests in Egypt. Inscriptions found both at Koptos, Egypt's equivalent to Palmyra as a 'caravan city', and at Berenice, show groups of Palmyrene merchants working there and even a Red Sea captain from Palmyra. One dedication at Berenice wishes good luck to Palmyra.[21] This commercial connection could help to explain Zenobia's later readiness to occupy Egypt, and the apparent readiness of certain Egyptians to call her and her military forces into their country to take their side in Egypt's internal troubles. Zenobia is also said to have composed a brief history of the city of Alexandria,[22] which may be witness to some sort of Egyptian family connection as well as to her personal literacy. But that is speculation, though not for that reason unreasonable.

What about her father? It is reasonable to suppose that she came from a leading and wealthy Palmyrene family, otherwise she would not have made such a good match with Odenathus, Palmyra's leading citizen of the time. Zenobia's name in the local language is Septimia Bat-Zabbai.[23] Zenobia is in effect the Greek equivalent of Bat-Zabbai, in the bilingual tradition of Palmyra's inscriptions. *Septimia* may be because her family gained its Roman citizenship under the Roman emperor Septimius Severus, although it may equally be because her husband Odenathus bestowed the name *Septimius/a* on people close to him. So we don't know for sure what her birth or childhood name was.

Bat-Zabbai can be taken to mean 'daughter of Zabbai'. Who was this Zabbai and was he her father? No one is quite sure. A Zabbai was one of her leading generals in her campaign to occupy most of the Roman Near East, and some think he was her father.[24] But the phrase in Palmyrene can also mean simply 'of the family of'.[25] What is more, one inscription refers to her confusingly as 'Septimia Bat-Zabbai, daughter of Antiochus'. Antiochus was a common name in Syria, though not so much in Palmyra, but we don't know who this individual was – if indeed it was anything more than a claim to descent from the former Greek-Macedonian kings of a huge empire encompassing Syria and the Middle East, successors of Alexander the Great. If so, then associating herself with Antiochus was for Zenobia a political, indeed ideological statement, rather than genealogical. If therefore an Antiochus can be eliminated on these grounds as her father (not everyone thinks he can[26]), then a plausible candidate for the job of Zenobia's father was for long considered to be a man who did exist, as proved by an inscription.

This was one Julius Aurelius Zenobios, also called Zabdilah (to quote the Greek version of the bilingual inscription dated to around 242-3).[27] The similarity of the name Zenobios to Zenobia immediately attracted attention, and he had other recommendations also. He was a *strategos* of Palmyra, a civic leader or *duumvir* in Latin, when the emperor Severus and detachments of the Roman army visited the city in around 230, and used his money to benefit the city. So he came from a rich and distinguished local family. His statue was also prominent in the Grand Colonnade of Palmyra. So he was about the right age, and certainly the right social class, to be Zenobia's father. But recently this idea has been dismissed for want of proof, and Zenobia was never (as far as we know) also called Julia Aurelia.[28] What is more, Zenobios/Zenobia was often used as the Greek equivalent to several Aramaic names such as Zabdilah, Zabda or Zabbai, no doubt because of the similarity of sound, so this is unstable evidence.[29]

But *someone* was Zenobia's father, and as we shall see, Zenobia enjoyed wide support among the upper echelons of Palmyra society in her dash for regional prominence and regional status, and that had to be rooted in more than mere nostalgia for her late husband Odenathus. It had to reflect a solid political ambition and consensus among the leading citizens of Palmyra, and this Zenobios could have provided the right upper-crust social background for Zenobia to take on the role she did. Moreover, what proof of the paternal connection could be provided? Do the critics expect a birth certificate, carved in stone? We have no papyrus records surviving from Palmyra, even if there ever were any. So while admitting the weaknesses of the case, this Zenobios seems to be the best candidate for the job of Zenobia's father.

Descendant of kings and queens?

If that is the case, then Zenobia's use of the name 'Antiochus' looks even more likely to be a political and even ideological statement about rights to empire, not genealogical. Zenobia as queen was after all keen to play up her alleged historical connections for propaganda purposes, as part of her self-invention. The *HA* tells us, plausibly, that

> she boasted herself to be of the family of the Cleopatras and the Ptolemies.[30]

It also tells us that she was arrayed in the robes of Dido.[31] Some people today have taken all this literally, perhaps too literally. For example, the Wikipedia online encyclopaedia entry on Zenobia tells us, fairly enough, that she claimed descent from Dido, Queen of Carthage; from the king of Emesa Sampsiceramus; and from Queen Cleopatra VII of Egypt. But by this route the Wikipedia entry then appears to accept a complicated ancestry for her that goes back to the famous Mark Antony, Cleopatra's lover, on the one hand, and on the other hand to the family of Hannibal, the famous general of Carthage who almost brought down the Roman empire centuries before Zenobia's time. Through him the alleged bloodline goes back to Dido, Queen of Cartage, made famous by Virgil's epic poem, the *Aeneid*.[32] But there is no evidence for such an elaborate genealogy. Rather, Zenobia tried to exploit the PR value of claiming affinities to such famous names as Dido, Cleopatra, and the former Macedonian kings of her region. That is invention enough, without adding to it.

Zenobia's children

There is further confusion about how many children Zenobia herself had. This question has therefore aroused much controversy. There was certainly the Athenodorus Vaballathus for whom she acted as queen-regent after the assassination of her husband Odenathus. He was presumably her eldest child, not very old at the time of Odenathus' death, and is well attested on coins, in inscriptions and elsewhere.[33] Then another inscription refers to a son of Zenobia called Antiochus, who would therefore be a brother of Vaballathus.[34] This Antiochus possibly turns up again in Zenobia's story as heading, in name at least, a last abortive uprising against Rome after Zenobia's own defeat by the emperor Aurelian and the capture of both her and her first son Vaballathus.[35] It would have been logical of the Palmyrenes, however suicidally, to use another member of its most famous family to front its last stand against Rome. But that cannot be proved. A son called Hairan may also have existed, and there is even a reference to a younger Odenathus.[36]

But the *HA* also refers to two more alleged sons, Timolaus and Herennianus, in whose name (it says) Zenobia claimed to rule as regent. But the *HA* then backtracks and says that after all her regency was in the name of Vaballathus.[37] So its author seems unsure whether Timolaus and Herennianus really existed, and we may entertain the same doubt. Then after her downfall, Zenobia is said to have been married off to a Roman of senatorial rank,[38] and several say that she had descendants at Rome.[39] So she must have had children by this second marriage, and the report by Zonaras that she had several daughters, though garbled by an impossible idea that Aurelian married one of them, may reflect this new family that she created, having lost her first.[40]

So Zenobia may have been a fecund lady, able to have children up to a relatively late age by Roman standards. But how many children she had altogether can vary between one (Vaballathus) and as many as nine, depending on how you read the confusing evidence. I suspect, very cautiously indeed, that she had four children, that is, Vaballathus and Antiochus by Odenathus her first husband, and two by her second husband at Rome, whoever he was. In any case, it was Vaballathus as the eldest son who mattered politically, however many (or few) siblings he had.

Wicked step-mother?

There is however one son left out of this picture so far. That is Zenobia's step-son, probably called Haeranes or (in Greek) Herodianus, the son of Odenathus by his first wife.[41] About her we know nothing. But Haeranes was associated with Odenathus in his period of rule at Palmyra under the title 'exarch', and was assassinated along with his father in 267-8. We don't know the exact date, but of the assassination there is no doubt. But who was responsible for it? There are three versions of this part of the story, different but not mutually incompatible, so that all three could be part of the truth – or of the invention. One is that it was the direct result of a family quarrel. Another is that in the background the Roman emperor Gallienus, in power at Rome at the time, had a sinister hand in it. The third is that Zenobia, far from being the perfect lady, connived at the murders, perhaps anxious that her own son, not her step-son, should be the next ruler of Palmyra. In other words, a scheming and wicked step-mother.

This last allegation is often dismissed as unproven, even unthinkable, or just a stereotype of the jealous step-mother foisted onto Zenobia by hostile (anti-feminist?) propaganda, both ancient and modern – an invention. The *HA* is the only place where this allegation turns up, whereas the belief that Gallienus was somehow implicated is widespread among classical authors, and so is the suggestion that a cousin or family member was involved.[42] My own view is that for political reasons Gallienus probably did have a hand in the assassination of Odenathus, and if that is right, he had to act long-distance through others, such as members of the family, be that a cousin or a wife or both. Those were rough times and rough places. The picture of murky goings-on around the deaths of Odenathus and his son Haeranes seems clear enough, and Zenobia cannot be excluded from it. There appears to have been a smooth transition of power at Palmyra to Zenobia and her son Vaballathus, and this supports the notion that she was somehow complicit.

What is certain is that it was the assassination of Odenathus in 267/8 that thrust Zenobia into the harsh political limelight of the third century (or caused her to be thrust into it by her supporters) and handed on to her and to her advisers the military and political heritage of Odenathus. This in turn triggered the four to five year adventure that brought her into collision with Aurelian, who took office only in 270, two or three years after Zenobia and her son and supporters took over control of Palmyra. So the keys to understanding how Zenobia came into confrontation with Aurelian lie, first, in understanding the unique trading wealth and military power of the city she ruled; secondly, in understanding the vicious struggle then taking place between the Roman empire and the Persian empire; and thirdly, in understanding the power-base that her husband Odenathus had built up, and which she and their son inherited and exploited. Only with these three pieces of the political jigsaw in place can we return to an assessment of the real Zenobia and her career as queen.

3

Bride of the desert: deliberately
inventing Palmyra

How did Zenobia and her supporters get the resources to wage war? How did it come about that Palmyra, an oasis city on the fringe of the Roman domains, had the military and financial muscle to play a part in the armed struggle between the two warring empires of Rome and Persia that dominated the middle decades of the third century? If its city population was a mere 40,000-60,000, as some estimate, how did such a small and remote place manage to thrust its queen Zenobia, if only briefly, into world history and legend?[1] It all happened both despite and because of its unique location, and because of its unique ability to invent itself. Palmyra was a Syrian trading city, a 'port in the desert',[2] a caravan city built round a salty oasis at the interface between the steppe-land and the desert of the eastern Roman empire. Its Syrian name was and is Tadmor: Palmya was its Greek name – meaning city of palms. In part the importance and wealth of Palmyra reflected the importance and wealth of Syria itself.

> Syria remained at the heart of the Asiatic East – geographically central, rich, populous, by far the most urbanised of the legionary provinces, and location of the great city of Antioch.[3]

But Palmyra was a wealthy city in its own right. It was both a lucrative transit station for international trade and offered a flourishing internal market for goods and services. The immense Roman empire sucked in merchandise from outside. Appian tells us that the Palmyrenes

> being merchants, bring the products of India and Arabia from Persia and dispose of them in Roman territory.[4]

Strabo, while not mentioning Palmyra specifically, tells us that a fleet of 120 Roman merchant ships regularly plied between India and the Red Sea ports, and several inscriptions confirm that Palmyrenes also operated such ships from the head of the Persian Gulf to India.[5] The famous Palmyrene Tax Law, found in 1881 inscribed on slabs of stone and dating to 137, shows the extraordinarily wide range of goods traded at Palmyra itself, both mundane and exotic. It is bilingual in Greek and Palmyrene and lists all those items subject to local taxation. It gives a better idea than the dusty ruins visible today of what a sophisticated city Palmyra was,

Panoramic view of Palmyra: Grand Colonnade, Temple of Bel, oasis.

with its temples, Roman-style theatre and possibly an amphitheatre.[6] The items listed include slaves, dry goods, purple wool, perfumes and aromatic oils, olive oil, cattle, fats, salted goods, prostitutes, agricultural produce, salt, silk yarn, jade, muslin, spices, ebony, myrrh, ivory, pearls, precious stones, pottery, glass, jewellery materials and, not least, statues and bronzes – a predominantly but not exclusively luxury trade. Not surprisingly, there are water rates, and professional groups like cloth merchants are also taxed. The silk and jade must have come in from China and be largely for re-export (although silk has been found in use at Palmyra itself), whereas the statues, bronzes and pottery presumably were imports destined for local use as the city's wealth grew.[7] Clearly, there was money around at Palmyra.

The Russian historian Mikhail Rostovtzeff, in his 1932 book *Caravan Cities*, characterised Palmyra as a caravan city, along with three other cities of the Roman East, Petra and Gerasa (modern Jerash) in Jordan and Dura Europos on the Euphrates.[8] Of the four, it is Palmyra that most deserves that characterisation – perhaps the only one, although Little Petra was clearly an important caravanserai.[9] But the epithet 'caravan city', however romantic, needs careful interpretation. It is in its way a happy invention, conjuring up picture-postcard images of long lines of camels plodding across the desert carrying Palmyrene merchants and their exotic wares.

However, trade is of its nature a peaceful activity. Few if any cities in the Roman empire employed what was in effect a local militia or private

44

Little Petra: a very posh caravanserai.

army, but Palmyra did. The Roman imperial regime for obvious reasons looked with suspicion on any potential rival power centre, and eventually came to view Palmyra with just such suspicion, and under the emperor Aurelian, put a stop to it. But for a long time, perhaps two centuries or more, the Romans put up with Palmyra's military capacity, maybe even encouraged and nurtured it, until Palmyra over-reached itself and had to be stamped on.

City of Solomon?

Palmyra's origins, if obscure, certainly long predate its entry into Rome's imperial orbit. There are two references in the commonly used version of the Christian Bible to King Solomon founding 'Tadmor in the wilderness', in Chronicles and in Kings, and many have taken that to mean that Solomon founded Palmyra.[10] That would push its origin as far back as the second or third centuries BC. John Malalas certainly thought that Solomon built Palmyra, and says that it was the place where David fought Goliath in single combat, which is why Solomon made it a great city.[11] Flavius Josephus, writing about the year 100, also accepted the Bible's apparent confirmation that Solomon was Palmyra's founding father.[12] But this is almost certainly an invention based on a confusion of place names by the scribe or chronicler, since the place in question, as the Revised Standard Version of the Bible puts it, was 'Tamir in the wilderness, in the land of Judah'. That is, Solomon's city was somewhere else altogether, in Judaea. But Palmyra's natural advantages suggest that the site must have been in use from earliest times.

The Palmyra story

The extraordinary story of that city has been extensively debated and rehearsed elsewhere.[13] In the words of Professor Fergus Millar:

> What follows cannot pretend to do justice to the individuality of Palmyra, or to the innumerable questions it raises: for instance, the sedentarisation of nomads, the explicit syncretism of Greek and Semitic deities, the evolution of a very distinctive local art and architecture, the consistent bilingualism of its public and private monuments, the unique deployment of military force by a provincial city or the significance of long-distance trade.[14]

The real secret of Palmyra was water. As recently as 1926, the author Carl Raswan, the German-born British intelligence officer who for decades lived among the nomad bedouin, could write about the swarms of camels which during a drought came out of the arid waste every day to drink the 'sulphurous but wholesome' waters of Tadmor's oasis, with thousands of other camels perishing before they could get there. He tells us that water

Camels at Palmyra.

issues from the hills in a clear stream, which branches out into a hundred rivulets in the plain and the small gardens that surround the ancient city.[15]

Alas, there is little sign of those rivulets today. Wells have to be dug many metres underground to find water to provision all the tourists. But water seems to have been more plentiful in classical times. Josephus says that:

> The reason for founding the city so far from the inhabited parts of Syria was that further down there was no water anywhere in the land and that only in this place were springs and wells to be found.

Pliny remarks that Palmyra is famous for its situation (*nobilis situ*), for the richness of its soil and for its agreeable waters (*aquis amoenis*).[16] Thanks to water, Palmyra's hinterland included cultivated estates. The population of the whole area may have been about 250,000.[17] That is why it is wrong to think of Palmyra purely as an island in the desert. One recent author writes:

> Palmyra itself should not be characterised as a 'desert city', for its territory contained numerous small watering places and villages. These villages ... appear with the growth of Palmyra and disappear with its fall. Pack animals useful for transport and the caravan trade were probably raised there, as perhaps were war horses used by Palmyra's powerful militia.[18]

47

Strabo speaks of tent-dwellers who live in the area between Syria and Babylon, and refers to camel-drivers (*kamelitai* in Greek) who maintain halting-places which are sometimes well supplied with reservoirs, generally cisterns but sometimes using water piped in from elsewhere. Strabo also refers meaningfully to the camel-traders (*kamelemporoi* in Greek) who travel the desert in such numbers of both men and camels 'that they differ in no respect from an army'.[19] So Palmyra probably was an ancient settlement thanks to the camels and to the water supplies mentioned by these authors. Even that must however be treated with caution. The main Efqa spring and the oasis which it feeds may be the core of the original Palmyra, but the spring is too sulphuric for humans to drink and apart from the eponymous palm trees is good for little else but treating skin ailments and creating an export trade in salt – hardly enough to create Palmyra's later prosperity. Water had to be piped in from distances of up to seven kilometres.[20]

Between Rome and Persia?

Thanks to its natural assets, by the time it entered Roman history, Palmyra already bore its essential trading, military and political characteristics, as Roman authors make clear. In the earliest Roman reference to Palmyra, Appian tells us that in 44 BC Mark Antony sent his cavalry on a raid against Palmyra (then well outside the Roman empire) to plunder it. But the cavalry came away empty-handed because the Palmyrenes heard they were coming, retired to the other side of the river Euphrates with all their goods – no small distance away, at over 200 kilometres, showing how mobile they could be – and threatened to shoot down the Roman troops with their arrows if they tried to cross the river.[21] Appian observes that the Palmyrenes were expert bowmen.[22] So by that date Palmyra had archers numerous and skilled enough to scare off regular army units of Roman cavalry.

There are several other indicative points about Appian's story. One is that half a century before formal incorporation into the Roman empire Palmyra was already a well-established trade centre. Appian also makes two interesting political observations. One is that 'being on the frontier between the Romans and the Parthians, they had avoided taking sides'; the other is that the Parthians considered Antony's raid as an act of war, i.e. a raid into Parthian territory.[23] Years later, as the historian Herodian reminds us, in the time of the emperor Severus Alexander (emperor 222-235) the Persians, as successors to the Parthians, could remind a diplomatic delegation from Rome that Persia still laid claim to Syria and much of the Roman east as 'traditional possessions of the Persians'.[24] Pliny makes an often-discussed and often-derided comment on Palmyra's political position. He says that it is isolated from the world by nature having a destiny of its own between the two mighty empires of Rome and Parthia, and at the first moment of a quarrel between them always attracts the attention of both sides (*semper utrimque cura*).[25]

Thus Palmyra is pictured by Pliny as a sort of political football, at a time when the city may have been within Rome's sphere of influence for half a century. So some say that Pliny either did not know what he was talking about, or at best was quoting a very out-of-date source. But I am not so sure. Pliny may have been writing long before Zenobia's time, but I suspect he was voicing a perennial truism about Palmyra. In the light of the comments made by Appian and Herodian, Pliny should not be dismissed too quickly. Appian was after all writing much later than Pliny (in the middle of the second century), as was Herodian. So the perception of Palmyra as caught in the middle and as a bone of contention between the two great powers was consistently held by Roman writers over much of Palmyra's history. It is easy to see that Zenobia, like her husband Odenathus before her, may have had much the same political perception.

Cultural crossroads

Palmyra's very name or names betray the ambiguity and diversity of its cultural and political allegiances. Palmyra/Tadmor had its two names because its public life and public inscriptions were, uniquely for a Syrian city, expressed in these two different languages, Greek and Palmyrene, which is a local dialect of Aramaic and so related to Phoenician and to

Palmyra's Aramaic script.

Non-Greek modes of dress: funerary relief of Aqmat,
daughter of Hagagu, now in British Museum.

Arabic. Aramaic was a semitic language, the native language of Jesus and
the *lingua franca* of the Middle East until displaced by Arabic from the
seventh century onwards. Aramaic as a language is now considered an
endangered species. Like modern Arabic, the Palmyrene script was written
right to left, as opposed to the standard Graeco-Roman and modern Western
left-to-right, and its non-Roman alphabet had 22 letters but no vowels. Thus
Palmyra in Palmyrene was (as transliterated) TDMR or TDMWR – hence
Tadmor. So Palmyra is fairly described as a bilingual city.

This description should, however, be used with caution. It is reasonable to suppose that the wealthier classes there were indeed bilingual
in Greek and Palmyrene, for trade and diplomatic purposes if for no
other. But the main language of the people of the city and its area was
probably the Palmyrene version of Aramaic rather than Greek, and that
in itself raises probing questions about the city's cultural and therefore
political identity. It has been called 'a rendez-vous of two worlds'.[26] The
question is:

3. Bride of the desert: deliberately inventing Palmyra

Was the public use of a semitic language at Palmyra and non-Greek modes of dress there merely a veneer for an otherwise thoroughly Hellenised civic culture, or do these speak to us of a profound non-Greek consciousness?[27]

Admirers of Zenobia and Palmyra have sometimes seized on the evidence of strong Greek influence to show that she and they really were really civilised people in the best classical Greek and Western tradition and not just upstart semitic/Arab desert brigands, as some classical authors maintain.[28] But that may be wish-fulfilment – invention. More likely, there a colouring of Greek culture – which Zenobia certainly exploited for political ends – added to what began as and remained essentially a semitic/Arab city. Of the 3,000 or so inscriptions from Palmyra, only 200 or so are bilingual. Moreover, despite Palmyra being technically inside the Roman empire during its heyday, only a very few inscriptions found in the city are trilingual, that is, with Latin added as well. Given the city's location, it is also reasonable to suppose that many of its inhabitants also spoke Arabic, or an early form of it, but left no written trace, at least not at Palmyra. Elsewhere, some 30,000 Safaitic (i.e. proto-Arabic) graffiti or inscriptions have been found from all over the Syrian desert and dating to the first to fourth centuries AD.[29]

It must have been a matter of conscious choice, even conscious invention by the city's government to publicly exhibit Palmyra's identity in two languages, one looking westward, one eastward, even when it was in Roman terms part of the Roman empire, and so to proclaim its in-betweenness, facing both ways Janus-like, its difference from other cities. The very non-Greek style of dress maintained at Palmyra, as illustrated in its funerary busts, makes the same point. Zenobia herself was said to be tri-lingual, but in Greek, Palmyrene and Egyptian. Zenobia had little Latin, we are told – odd for the leader of a city within Rome's sphere.[30] The lack of Latin is all the odder since the city's greatest wealth, as evidenced today by its magnificent ruins, seems to have developed after its incorporation into the Roman empire, or at least into the empire's acknowledged sphere of influence, early in the first century AD with the visit there of Tiberius' nephew and adopted son Germanicus in around 18-19. That incorporation was later reinforced by the presence of a small Roman garrison of auxiliary troops.[31] Palmyra's ostentatious wealth seems to have reached its height under the Severan (and so largely Syrian) imperial dynasty of 193 to 235, that is, up to and after the likely time of the birth of Zenobia's husband Odenathus. Odenathus therefore knew personally how much his city stood to lose from the outbreak of endemic warfare between Rome and Persia from about 225 onwards, and so therefore did Zenobia.

Incorporation into the Roman empire probably brought to Palmyra a new level of prosperity by connecting it as never before to the internal trade routes of that huge empire, and opening up to its merchants a rich and sophisticated market with a high demand for foreign luxury products.

51

This market may have been Rome itself, and/or it may have been the empire's flourishing eastern provinces, including the great city of Athens. All the evocative buildings and ruins of Palmyra date from the Roman period, as do almost all the inscriptions on stone that have been found. On the other hand, construction of the great Temple of Bel, whose ruins are such a notable feature of Palmyra today, was begun around the time of Germanicus' visit or even before. This suggests that wealth was already there when he arrived. Moreover, the temple itself may have been at least one of the attractions that drew people to Palmyra and accounted for its expansion. Perhaps it was not just about trade or estates. Religious observance and pilgrimage may have played a part.

The irony is, however, that Palmyra's trade was exclusively trade passing between Parthian/Persian territory and Roman territory, and must always have passed through Parthian/Persian territory to get from the Persian Gulf to Palmyra. It is therefore hard to see how Palmyra could be anything but poised on a political seesaw between the two powers. The Parthian regime and its Persian successor could always have strangled this trade if it had chosen to do so. To avert that required diplomatic effort. Down the route of the Euphrates river itself to the point where it meets the Persian Gulf, and notably at Spasinou Charax, capital of the principality of Messene, but also at Babylon and Vologesias, there seems to have been a chain of Palmyrene representatives who oiled the wheels of trade, to enable the merchants to pass on their way up and down that vulnerable route.[32] Palmyra 'was a crucial mediator for the trade between the great powers of Rome and Iran'.[33] Where these 'trade representatives' (the word is too formal, but gives the flavour) were in the quasi-independent state of Messene at the mouth of the river, that is not problematic. But where they were on the higher reaches of the river, in Parthian or later Persian territory, and especially after Messene had lost its independence to Persia in about 150 AD, it raises interesting questions about the exact nature of the diplomatic relationship between Palmyra and the Parthians and Persians. It must have been complex. The Palmyrenes seem to have acted by permission of Rome's enemy as facilitators of a trade route through enemy territory. The Euphrates frontier shows how complex and delicate Palmyra's relationship with Parthia/Persia must have been, part mercantile, part military, part hostile, part co-operative.

Security services

However, the main creative contribution of the Palmyrenes was not along the river line itself, but in providing a secure route from the river and across the desert into settled Roman territory, unmolested by desert nomads, so that merchants could be persuaded to leave the course of the river and take a cross-country route they might not otherwise take. The most convincing and idiosyncratic theory to explain Palmyra's genesis is

Grinding stones in the precinct of the Temple of Bel at Palmyra.

that as a trading centre it was almost entirely an artificial construction, an invention of its inhabitants. They hit upon the idea that the best way to exploit the new trade opportunities offered by access to the rich markets of the still expanding Roman empire was to provide a secure trade route across which merchants could import into the empire luxury goods originating from India, China and Arabia. In other words, there was not a pre-existing trade route that the Palmyrenes exploited. Rather, they created the trade route by guaranteeing its security, and therein lay the origin and rationale of its military capacity – and the reason why it was tolerated by the Roman authorities for such a long time.[34] In other words, the Palmyrenes created, even invented, their own variant of the famous Silk Route.

Some, like the historian Rostovtzeff, have assumed that the trading barons honoured in Palmyra's much-discussed and unique stone inscriptions, the famous *synodiarchs*, were like the merchant princes of Italian trading cities such as Genoa and Venice or those of the powerful Hanseatic League trading cities of the thirteenth to sixteenth centuries in northern Europe, which, like Palmyra, provided military protection for their trading ventures. Perhaps, like them, Palmyra was 'a merchant republic' ruled by these 'merchant princes'? But that may be a misleading analogy, a 'romantic fallacy' attached to Palmyra. The role of the *synodiarchs* commemorated in those inscriptions had a much more specific – and military – connotation.[35]

One inscription refers specifically to a caravan being attacked by robbers in 144 AD.[36] Strabo tells us that the desert camel-drivers exacted lower tolls on transit trade than local chieftains exercising power along the line of the Euphrates river, which made it worthwhile for merchants to risk striking out across the desert.[37] So the wealthy *synodiarchs*[38] made famous by Palmyrene inscriptions probably performed two roles. They acted as bankers and financiers of each trading venture and as providers of the horses, camels and other logistical necessities. But they also themselves acted as leaders of the security forces – the caravan police – that ensured that each caravan of merchants got safely across the desert route from the Euphrates as far as Palmyra, and perhaps thence from Palmyra to the coastal ports and markets such as Antioch (though that part of the route is less certain).[39]

This would imply that these security providers – who could no doubt charge a good fee for their services – provided armed escort duties to ward off marauders, who would have to be other desert tribesmen and nomads, of similar ethic background to the Palmyrenes themselves. Thus the security corridor provided by the Palmyrenes was intrinsically bound up with the city's relation with the surrounding nomads from whom they themselves had probably originally sprung. Here then we find the origin and rationale of the military muscle of Palmyra, as 'caravan police' and escorts. The men who carried out these security duties in the field (or should one say, in the steppe) may have divided between permanent guards stationed on the Euphrates and at the watering holes or *caravanserais* (Strabo's cisterns) and those who travelled with the actual caravans.[40] In this way an unusual city created an unusual military expertise among its citizens and inhabitants, an expertise critical to Palmyra's trading success and valued by the Romans for use within their regular army.

The breakdown of mutual self-interest

Regular units of Palmyrene soldiers incorporated within the Roman army served the empire far and wide. One man turns up as far away as Hadrian's Wall in the north of England, about as far from Palmyra as you could get, some 4,000 kilometres. At South Shields, on the mouth of the river Tyne, Barates, a Palmyrene standard bearer or perhaps just a merchant selling military standards, put up an epitaph to his deceased (non-Palmyrene) wife Regina, with the text partly in Palmyrene. Palmyrene soldiers turn up in Dacia, Numidia, Egypt and of course Syria itself.[41] They were usually archers, probably on horseback (*sagittarii Palmyreni*), or camel-riders (*dromedarii*) on camels which were 'fast runners', the word 'dromedary' being based on the Greek word for runner. It was from the men of Palmyra that the emperor Trajan formed the first regular Roman army camel unit, the *Ala I Ulpia Dromedariorum Palmyrenorum*, and he was the first to recruit Palmyrene archers. The camel corps of Palmyra brings to mind the famous 'méhariste' camel cavalry deployed by the French army in North Africa between 1900 and 1960.

The French camel cavalry.

55

The experience of desert warfare and fast turn of speed of such special-ist units were useful to the Roman army as well, in African and eastern theatres of activity with deserts or steppes. It is also calculated that Syrian recruits formed about half of all the archers in the Roman army, so clearly use of the bow was a formidable local skill, as Appian says.[42] Veterans returning from service in the regular Roman army would have strength-ened Palmyra's military capacity. Procopius, writing much later under the emperor Justinian, gives us a fine description of the mounted archer.

> Today's archers go into battle with corselets and greaves fitted as far as the knee. Their arrows are slung on their right side and on the other their sword. In addition, some wear a spear and a short shield on the shoulders without a strap, capable of covering their face and neck. They are excellent horsemen, and they are able to draw the bow in either direction without difficulty, as the horse gallops, and to hit the enemy whether pursuing or fleeing ... giving the arrow such power that it kills whoever comes in its path.[43]

This of course was the famous 'Parthian shot', fired backwards when riding away in apparent or feigned retreat, and if Palmyra's archers had this skill, then it shows once again Palmyra's cultural indebtedness to its close neighbours, the Parthians. But the most famous regular unit of Palmyrene soldiers was the Twentieth Cohort of Palmyrenes (*Cohors XX Palmyrenorum*) stationed at Dura Europos, the great Roman fortress on the Euphrates, the empire's advance post against the Parthians and Persians. These were probably mounted archers, and soldiers of this type first appear at this stronghold in 164 when Dura was first incorporated into the Roman empire. As a unit of the regular Roman army, they are recorded there from 208 right up to Dura's final capture and destruction by the Persians in 256. It was probably much the same unit throughout.[44]

If, as many suppose, Dura was also a staging post for trade leaving the Euphrates and heading across the desert to Palmyra, then these expert soldiers were protecting *both* their own city's trading interests *and* the eastern frontier of the Roman empire. In short, for many years there was a shared and mutual self-interest between Rome and Palmyra, which is why Rome tolerated, even encouraged, Palmyra's military expertise. With the destruction of Dura, that mutual self-interest began to break down, with ultimately disastrous consequences for Palmyra.

4

Persia resurgent: the crisis of
the third century

What did the Roman world look like in the mid-third century when Zenobia's husband Odenathus and then Zenobia herself entered history? In 224 there had been a momentous regime change in Iran, with threatening consequences for Palmyra and for the Roman empire itself. The former Arsacid dynasty of Parthia was violently replaced by the Persian Sasanid dynasty, which immediately adopted a far more aggressive policy against Rome. In a series of vivid pictures cut into rock faces in the province of Fars, in southern Persia, modern Iran, the great Persian king Sapor boasts of his military humiliation of no less than three Roman emperors.[1] As commonly interpreted, one of them, at BiSapor, shows the Roman emperor Gordian prostrate under Sapor's horse, with the emperor Philip kneeling before him in supplication and a third emperor, Valerian, held by the wrist as the king's captive. In another, at Naqsh-i-Rustam, the most famous of these rock carvings shows Sapor on horseback with Philip kneeling in supplication before him and Valerian standing as prisoner, held by his cuffs. Gordian had been killed in mysterious circumstances in 244 while returning from a confrontation with Sapor and Philip had been forced to buy his way out of trouble in that same year of 244 by paying a huge ransom. But it had been the defeat and capture alive of Valerian in 260 that had sent both military and moral shock-waves throughout the Roman empire.[2]

This was the first time that a full Roman emperor had ever been captured alive in battle, and the humiliation of Rome was without precedent. It set off a train of events that almost split the Roman empire apart, and was the context for the rise to prominence of, first, Zenobia's husband Odenathus, and then of Zenobia herself. It simultaneously triggered both a 15-year breakaway Gallic empire comprising France, Britain and Spain, and the eastern 'splinter empire' of Palmyra – events which might easily have left the empire broken-backed for good, shattered into three (or more) pieces.

Sapor boasted of his achievements not only in pictures, but at great length in words. In the same area of Naqsh-i-Rustam is a trilingual Greek, Persian and Parthian inscription labelled (by moderns[3]) the *Res Gestae Divi Saporis*, the achievements of the divine Sapor, on the lines of the famous and still surviving *Res Gestae Divi Augusti*, put up by Rome's first

Sapor's horse tramples on one Roman emperor while he holds another captive by the wrist and receives the supplications of a third.

Sapor on horseback with Philip kneeling and Valerian held captive.

emperor, Augustus. In it Sapor tells us that in his second campaign against the Romans in about 253 he shattered a Roman army of 60,000 men at Barbalissos (an event not acknowledged in Roman sources), ravaged far and wide and then:

> in my third campaign [in 260] we set upon Carrhae and Edessa [in Mesopotamia] and ... Valerian Caesar came against us and with him was a force [later put at 70,000 men] from the province of the Goths and Germans ... and on the far side [west] of Carrhae and Edessa a great battle took place ... and we with our own hands took Valerian prisoner and the rest who were the commanders of his army, the Praetorian Prefect, and the senators, and the officers – all of these we took prisoner and we led them away into Persia. And we burned with fire, and we ravaged, and we took captive and we conquered the province of Syria and the province of Cilicia and the province of Cappadocia.[4]

In his long reign of 30 years (242-272) Sapor, following the example of his father Ardashir before him, sought in a series of campaigns to reverse the forcible encroachment of the Roman empire into what we now call the Middle East. In particular he sought to regain control of greater Armenia (as it then was) and Mesopotamia, the lands between the upper sections of the rivers Euphrates and Tigris which the Parthians and Persians after them regarded as their sphere of influence, their own political and military back-yard. In broader ideological terms, the Persians laid claim to all the ancestral lands of the old Persian empire destroyed by Alexander the Great centuries before, which would have meant Roman evacuation of all of Syria and Asia Minor.[5] Clearly, Rome was not going to do that.

Persia on the offensive

The precise sequence of events that followed is hard to pin down. But the period 226 to 260 saw almost continuous border conflict, and it is the scale and duration of this conflict that is the key to understanding the atmosphere of uncertainty and even fear that must have permeated the Roman east for decades. First, in 226-7, Ardashir attacked Hatra, in Mesopotamia, perhaps the most forward of all the Roman-held cities. In 230-2, he again attacked Roman-held territory. In 232-3 came a counter-attack by the Roman emperor Severus Alexander (a Syrian), but that did not prevent Ardashir capturing two other Roman-held border cities, Nisibis and Carrhae, in 235-6. In 240-1, the Persians finally captured Hatra.

Then between the years 251 and 260 Ardashir's son Sapor launched no less than three large-scale and more ambitious invasions into Roman-held territory, mainly territory which the Roman empire had acquired or absorbed only in the past 60 years or so, and therefore particularly contentious. Although the Roman army regained Nisibis and Carrhae in 243, Sapor was able to invade Armenia in 252, and in the following year

Cameo depicting the confrontation between Valerian and (*right*) Sapor, with Sapor once again grasping the wrist of Valerian, indicating taking him captive.

scored his great military success at Barbalissos. On the back of his military successes, he ravaged and looted Roman territory on a large scale, including at least once, perhaps even twice, the sacking of the greatest city of the Roman east, Antioch, with 'immense plunder' and 'a multitude of prisoners'.[6] In Sapor's second campaign, one arm of his invading force turned south from Antioch down the river Orontes and got as far as Emesa, but was checked there. But it was in the third and last of these invasions in 260 that Sapor confronted the Roman army advancing to meet him under the command of the emperor himself, Valerian, and destroyed it. Valerian was captured, along with many other distinguished Roman officers and officials and an unknown but large number of soldiers and ordinary citizens.[7]

The capture of Valerian was attributed by some not to defeat in battle, but to treachery perpetrated by Sapor during armistice negotiations.[8] One may suspect this to be Roman propaganda. Similarly, the famous stories about Valerian being badly mistreated during his captivity, in one version being used as a human mounting block for Sapor to mount his horse or carriage, and in another version after death being flayed, stuffed, dyed with vermilion and put on public display, also look like Roman propaganda; or if not that, then an invented story attributing just punishment for an emperor who persecuted the Christians. The second version is after all given by Lactantius in his work *On the Deaths of the Persecutors*.[9]

The rock reliefs give no hint of any such humiliation. Rather they show Valerian standing unharmed and unfettered, treated with greater respect than the other two Roman emperors.[10] After his victory Sapor returned slowly home with a massive amount of booty and a huge number of captives, both military and civilian. The evidence for this lies in the many building and other works carried out in Persia in the aftermath of 260 by Roman deportees, both soldiers and artisans, revitalising Persian urban centres, industries and agriculture. The scale of the losses to the Roman east, both military and material, must have been colossal.

Gallienus' bad press

Valerian's defeat and capture left his son Gallienus in a deeply unenviable position. Gallienus had become co-emperor with his father Valerian when the latter took control in Rome in 253, and they split the defence of the empire between them, Valerian taking the east, Gallienus the west, so foreshadowing the split responsibility that was to become characteristic of some later imperial regimes. But when Valerian met catastrophe in the east, Gallienus was immediately beset with problems that he strove to meet but which were probably beyond the capacity of one man to cope with – another lesson learnt by later emperors. Not only was he confronted by secessionist movements on two fronts, in Gaul (the so-called Gallic empire) and in Syria, but there were powerful raids by the Goths across the Danube and into the Balkans. If that were not enough, there was a succession of usurpers who sought to displace him. He himself was wounded by an arrow when confronting the secessionists in Gaul. Then there was a great plague. No wonder that Zosimus remarks:

> With the entire Roman Empire reeling in the direction of ultimate annihilation, a plague the likes of which had never throughout all time occurred broke out in the cities.[11]

This may have been the nadir of the much-discussed 'third-century crisis'. It is difficult to reconstruct the exact sequence of events in those seven or so years between the capture of Valerian by the Persians and the assassination of Gallienus himself by a cabal of his most senior generals. Gallienus has had a bad press, both from historians writing soon after his time and from some modern writers.[12] Aurelius Victor, for example, accuses him of shipwrecking the Roman state, and says that during Rome's misfortunes

> Gallienus frequented taverns and eating houses, kept up his friendships with pimps and drunkards and abandoned himself to his wife Salonina and to his shameful love-affair with the daughter of Attalus, a king of the Germans, whose name was Pipa.[13]

The *Historia Augusta* takes the same line, alleging that Gallienus was

> born for his belly and his pleasures, wasting his days and nights in wine and
> debauchery and caused the world to be laid waste by pretenders.[14]

Harsh that may be, but Gallienus was clearly far too preoccupied, either
by warfare or by Pipa, to be able to do much about the disastrous situation
in the eastern parts of his empire. In particular, he was preoccupied with
containing the secession of Gaul and the other western provinces, the
so-called Empire of the Gauls (see Chapter 7) which seemed a threat much
closer to home. The east would have to look after itself.

The squeeze on Palmyra

The resurgence of Persia left Palmyra in acute difficulties. The previous
Parthian regime had been relatively quiescent, and the principality of
Mesene at the head of the Persian Gulf which controlled the main transit
port to India at Spasinou Charax was either in independent hands or, as
some suggest, was actually a Roman client state. Palmyra's long-distance
trade from India and China continued without serious interruption. Negotiating a way through whatever diplomatic and political obstacles did arise
must have been what the groups of travelling merchants paid the
Palmyrene representatives and caravan captains for, in addition to ward-
ing off desert nomads and bandits.

However, with the advent of the new Persian dynasty matters changed
dramatically for the worse. First, probably in 235-6, that critical principality of Mesene was taken, or taken back, into Persian hands along with
other territory around the Persian Gulf, giving the Persian king control of
seafaring in the Gulf.[15] This must have adversely affected Palmyra's trade.
Then, perhaps more seriously still, the new Persian regime began its
series of great offensives up the Euphrates and/or through Mesopotamia
and these invasions must have seriously disrupted other trade routes on
which Palmyra depended. The loss to the Persians of the great trading city
of Hatra was only the first of the setbacks that directly affected Palmyra.
After changing hands several times during hostilities, the key military
base on the Euphrates at Dura Europos was finally taken and destroyed
by the Persians in 256. During that same period other Roman (or at least
Palmyrene) advance bases further down the Euphrates towards the sea,
at the island of Ana/Anatha and at Sura, were also taken by the Persians.

To what extent these places were actual transit-points for trade, as
opposed to Roman frontier posts, is hard to establish. Some say that Dura
in particular was a key trade transit station for Palmyra's merchants. It
was after all defended for many years by a unit of the Roman army
recruited from Palmyra, the Twentieth Cohort of Palmyrene Archers,
mounted bowmen suited to desert warfare. Others argue that the main

4. Persia resurgent: the crisis of the third century

The 'Palmyra Gate' at Dura Europos.

trade route towards Palmyra left the Euphrates much further down-stream, at a place called Hit, firmly in Parthian/Persian territory, even though the cross-desert part of that route was much longer. Perhaps there was no clear distinction at that time between a Palmyrene outpost protecting trade and a Roman outpost protecting Rome's frontier. But either way, the Persian depredations and the recurring warfare on the eastern front must have hit the Palmyrenes where it hurt the most, in their pocket (if, that is, their elegant robes had pockets). The latest proven Palmyrene caravan journey down the Euphrates attested by an inscription took place in 247. There were other attested but less specified caravan journeys as late as the 260s, so it seems that some trade persisted despite everything.[16] Not too much should be read into the hazards of survival of various bits of incised stone. But the political and military crisis along and across the Euphrates river must surely have meant that Palmyra's trade routes were severely disrupted. At least some of its trade destinations further into Roman territory, such as Antioch, had also been severely dislocated by the Persian attacks and sackings. One may suspect that in the wake of Persia's offensives the Palmyrene aristocracy and landowners faced ruin, so resorted to desperate and increasingly violent measures to try to shore up their position – hence the career of Odenathus and, after his assassination, the career of his wife Zenobia.

63

The warning of Hatra

The fate of Hatra (now in Iraq) may have been particularly vivid in their eyes. Hatra, like Palmyra, had been a caravan city based on an oasis and flourished at much the same time as Palmyra. It made its profits as a great transit point for caravan routes across central Mesopotamia and towards the upper Euphrates and its main river crossing point at Zeugma, the Roman city now submerged under today's artificial Lake Assad. Like Palmyra, Hatra was also a religious centre, a city of the sun-god, so received a stream of pilgrims. About 400 inscriptions have been found

US marine in remains of Hatra in 2008.

there, mainly in Aramaic, which attest to the semitic and Arabic character of a city that also exhibited Greek, Roman and Iranian features, much like Palmyra.[17] But mainly Hatra was also a fortress of great strategic importance. Herodian tells us that it stood

> at the very top of a precipitous ridge, encircled by enormous strong walls and teeming with archers.[18]

These walls were defended by about 90 large and 160 small towers. The lords of Hatra called themselves kings. At first the city was hostile to Rome, resisting two attempts by Roman emperors to capture it. Herodian says that on one occasion the defenders of Hatra fired clay canisters at the Roman soldiers filled with poisonous biting insects that got into the soldiers' eyes causing severe injuries – an early form of biological warfare. But some say that this story is an invention by Herodian. Then Hatra switched sides and became an ally of Rome and Roman troops were stationed there from about 222 onwards. In short, like Palmyra, it was balanced between the two great powers. Hatra was finally captured by the Persian army in 241, but only after a two-year siege. The Persians then destroyed the place and it never recovered. When Ammianus Marcellinus visited the site in 363, he found it deserted.[19] Today it is just an impressive ruin.

Hatra's chacteristics, as a multi-cultural caravan city with skilled archers and a temple, caught between Rome and Persia, are remarkably similar to those of Palmyra. For the Palmyrenes and its leaders, the destruction of Hatra must have been a moral tale and a military warning. The irony was that in striving to avoid the same fate, or perhaps to take advantage of it, Palmyra shared it.

Just another usurper? The political legacy of the first Mr Zenobia

What was Zenobia's political inheritance from her husband Odenathus? The career of Zenobia only makes sense in the light of the career of her husband during those critical years between 260 and his assassination eight years later, the period when the Roman empire was in a state of shock from its humiliation at the hands of the Persians. Conversely, misunderstandings and exaggerations about Odenathus have created the grounds for misunderstandings and exaggerations about Zenobia herself. The most entrenched misconception is that Odenathus was or became a loyal ally of Rome, was awarded a formal Roman position of command over much of the Roman East, and acted as a sturdy bulwark of the empire with the approval and delegated authority of the emperor at Rome. That misconception has had a misleading knock-on effect on estimates of Zenobia.

What did Odenathus do?

Odenathus was a remarkable man and chief citizen of a remarkable city. It is a pity that we do not know more about him. He steps firmly into history only at the moment of the Roman emperor Valerian's defeat and capture by the Persian king Sapor in 260.[1] Who was he? Well, about that there is much argument. We don't know his date of birth. It has been put anywhere between 200 and 220. We don't know what he looked like. There is no proven representation of him that has survived, but Yarhai (see next page) may give some clue. He may, on the analogy of Yarhai, have been bearded, to give him a very non-Roman appearance, and been dressed on more formal occasions in a heavily embroidered jacket and cloak, with jewellery around his neck – a decidedly non-Roman and eastern style of self-presentation.

His immediate ancestry was once the subject of much dispute. But the matter was (subject only to new discoveries) put to rest in a famous article by the distinguished archaeologist Michel Gawlikowski.[2] The main question was whether there were two men called Odenathus, one the forebear of the other, or only one. The answer was, only one. In 260 this man was certainly the chief citizen and military leader of Palmyra, a city which had been left untouched by the successive Persian invasions – one of the few

Not Odenathus, but Yarhai son of Elahbel, showing a
man of Palmyra in his best (and very non-Roman)
gear. Relief in the Louvre, Paris.

that were left unscathed, perhaps because of its remote location on the
margin between steppe and desert. In Sapor's previous campaign in 253,
one arm of his invading force had turned south from Antioch down the
river Orontes and got as far as Emesa, not too far west from Palmyra as
the camel goes, but had been checked there.

So in 260, Odenathus was able to rally what remaining Roman troops
he could find, add them to his own military force from Palmyra, and pursue
the returning and no doubt slow-moving Persian forces as they withdrew
down the Euphrates. He captured some of their booty and baggage train,
maybe even, it was claimed, parts of Sapor's harem.[3] Some say he even got
as far as Ctesiphon, the former Parthian capital. He may have regretted
pushing his luck that far. The *Historia Augusta* admits that his forces
suffered greatly when trying to besiege the place.[4] Nevertheless this was
claimed by some Roman writers to be a major victory over the Persians, a
sort of revenge for the humiliation of Valerian – 'The Empire Strikes Back'.

5. Just another usurper? The political legacy of the first Mr Zenobia

The writer Festus calls Odenathus 'the avenger of the Roman empire' and many have accepted Festus' view.[5] Indeed, it has become almost the accepted wisdom.

However, that is probably to over-rate Odenathus' campaign. Such Roman claims have a note of political propaganda about them, just as the capture of Valerian was attributed, not to defeat in battle, but to treachery perpetrated by Sapor during armistice negotiations.[6] Roman imperial pride was at stake. One modern historian has redefined Odenathus' raid down the Euphrates as 'a minor incident of uncertain date' and I agree with that modest verdict.[7] After his victory Sapor had probably spread out his army too thinly and was returning slowly with a massive amount of booty and a huge number of captives, both military and civilian. In the circumstances, it would not have been hard for Odenathus and his scratch but highly mobile force to catch up with parts of Sapor's army and regain at least some of the lost men and material. The claimed siege or even capture of Ctesiphon, though not impossible, seems unlikely for what must have been a fast-moving strike-force collected by Odenathus, not equipped with siege engines or heavy weaponry. Some say he also made a second military expedition down the Euphrates as far as Ctesiphon, but there is confusion about whether there were one or two such incursions into Persian territory.[8] It was of course in Odenathus' own political interest, as well as in Rome's political interest, to make exaggerated claims.

Odenathus' talent for the sort of propaganda available in his time may be shown in a mosaic discovered in 2003 north of Palmyra's Grand Colonnade. The mosaic has two panels, one showing a rider hunting a Persian tiger, the other showing a rider identifiable as the Greek mytho-logical hero Bellerophon riding his winged horse Pegasus and slaying that monster of fable, the Chimera. If that sounds familiar, it is the origin of the story of St George and the Dragon. But in this mosaic it is suggested that Bellerophon is a visual metaphor for Odenathus, and the Chimera is Persia.[9] The other panel, on this interpretation, would represent Ode-nathus' first son, Haeranes, in effect his co-ruler. This would confirm what Odenathus wanted people to believe about his exploits – attacking and slaying the Persians. The identification is attractive. On the other hand, one version of the Bellerophon legend has it that Bellerophon tried to fly to heaven on Pegasus, but as punishment for his presumption Zeus intercepted him with a gadfly that threw Bellerophon from his horse. Myth can redound on the mythologiser, and in the case of Odenathus, it eventually did.

In the following year, 261, Odenathus engineered the elimination of a Roman officer called Quietus, based at Emesa, who had declared himself to be a pretender to the Roman throne. Odenathus caused him to be murdered by the citizens of that city.[10] There is argument about why Odenathus did that. Some say that it was as a demonstration of loyalty to the official Roman emperor at the time, Gallienus, by eliminating a

The Bellerophon mosaic that may represent Odenathus.

potential rival. But Emesa was, in Syrian terms, just down the road from Odenathus' home city of Palmyra, so it is equally likely that Odenathus simply did not want an alternative power-centre developing right on his own door-step. Of course, for diplomatic reasons, he could then pretend he was doing it as a loyal ally of Gallienus.

St George and the Dragon: fresco in the wall of St George Greek
Orthodox Church at Madaba, Jordan.

In the same spirit of clearing out his own back yard, and finding himself
now in command of the only coherent military force left in the Roman
eastern frontier zone, Odenathus is then said to have regained for Rome
the Mesopotamian cities of Nisibis and Carrhae, captured by Sapor. Since
Sapor, despite his political ideology, showed no sign in practice of wanting
to gain territory as opposed to war booty, one must wonder what forces he
left behind in those two places: and therefore, what opposition Odenathus
was up against in regaining them. The *HA* says that he captured the

71

satraps left in those cities by Sapor, and sent them to Rome in order to keep in well with the emperor Gallienus – a political move if ever there was one, and an indicative note of caution from the *HA*'s author.[11] Zonaras says that he then razed Nisibis to the ground in retaliation for favouring the Persian cause, which suggests that its inhabitants were at best divided about where their loyalties lay at this juncture – to Rome or to Persia.[12] Or was Nisibis a rival trading centre, to be put out of action? Ironically, a rebuilt Nisibis later became a huge trans-shipment centre for goods after the fall of Palmyra.

In the same violent manner, Odenathus in the period 259-263 may have attacked and destroyed the important Jewish settlement of Nehardea on the Middle Euphrates, along with its famous academy. This depends on identifying the Papa ben Natzer named in Rabbinic sources as the perpetrator with Odenathus – an identification not without challenge.[13] But perhaps, given the history of rebellion and repression of the Jews under Roman rule, the Jewish population felt safer under Persian protection than under some quasi-Roman, and paid the penalty. Odenathus' activities in the East look odd if you try to view him as a loyal ally, let alone appointed official, of Rome. He seems to have gone round destroying places. One must wonder why. These were hardly the acts of a formally appointed Roman governor.

His far-reaching military sorties may however have made him some sort of local hero. The citizens of Tyre honoured him at some unknown date.[14] But his authority was still limited. It is noticeable that the provinces of Arabia and Egypt, which had not been attacked by the Persians, later offered resistance to Zenobia, so presumably had not accepted Odenathus either. There is indeed evidence for normal Roman rule in operation in the 260s both in Arabia and at Antioch, where Roman coins continued to be minted.[15] So Odenathus' expanding sphere of influence must have been circumscribed and not uncontested. At some point he turned northwards to help fight off an attack on Asia Minor by marauding Goths from the Black Sea area.[16] Then, sometime in late 267 or early 268, he was assassinated at Emesa, which (some speculate) he may have made his operational headquarters for his seven years in the historical limelight.

A god from the machine?

What was Odenathus doing before the momentous year of 260? Surely, some say, in 260 Odenathus did not just spring out of the Syrian steppe overnight like some ready-armed *deus ex machina* – some God from the Machine? You do not just suddenly confront the great king Sapor, even during a slow withdrawal back to base, and grab some of his spoils. An inscription found in Palmyra's Grand Colonnade shows that Odenathus was indeed a prominent local citizen and city official by the year 252, an *exarch*, so he did have a basis for his operations. But some have supposed that Odenathus must have been much more than that, must have been some sort of Roman military commander before 260, maybe even leading a contingent of Valerian's army, or that he had been Roman provincial governor of Syria.[17] He enjoyed the Roman title of *consularis* and this might indicate that he had held a job as a governor. Another suggestion is that Odenathus must have been involved in the defence of Dura Europos against the Persians in 253 and 256.

By way of contrast, yet another suggestion is that Odenathus may have been just a robber-king or former captain of desert bandits. The trouble is that, apart from that local job of *exarch*, there is no evidence to support any of these supposed pre-260 activities, and some powerful objections. Malalas is the only Roman-era author to suggest that Odenathus was active before 260, but his narrative at this point is confused and implausible. Malalas has 'Enathos' waylaying Sapor as he crossed the *limes*, the frontier zone, and killing him: and says that later Gallienus attacked 'Enathos' and killed him. Both alleged killings must be untrue.[18]

After 260: the loyalty card

Nevertheless, it remains obvious that between 260 and his assassination in 267/8 Odenathus was on a roll. Even if his achievements have been excessively played up by historians both ancient and modern, they are nevertheless remarkable. So it is hardly surprising that there has been much speculation, and even more invention, on the question of Odenathus' status and authority in the Roman military and administrative system post-260 and up to his murder. Was he acting as a Roman official under orders from Rome and with a remit from the then Roman emperor Gallienus – or something else? The dominant trend has been to see Odenathus (as some Roman writers also seem to claim) as a faithful ally of Rome acting to uphold Roman rule and authority with formal recognition from the Roman emperor and a whole raft of impressive titles to prove it. One historian talks of Odenathus being given

> the authority belonging to a formal, legitimate individual in power and carrying out tasks in the interest of security in the area, under the superior authority of the Augustus in Rome, as representative of the emperor in that area.[19]

Another refers to Odenathus 'acting as the representative and enforcer of legitimate Roman government' and as 'a functionary of Roman government … a loyal adherent of Gallienus'.[20] In the same vein we find this:

> To Gallienus, Odenathus looked like the defender of Syria … all in all, a loyal defender of the interests of the empire.[21]

Emperor Gallienus.

Yet another says that the emperor Gallienus gave Odenathus

> almost unlimited power [with] *imperium maius* over the Eastern Roman provinces from the Pontic coast all the way to Palestine.[22]

If true, these evaluations would make Odenathus a very important man indeed. The weight of opinion in favour of such an assessment of Odenathus is formidable. But it espouses a particular political picture of these years, and what is striking is that only one classical author actually says in exactly those terms that Odenathus was a loyal ally of Rome. Yet that has become the accepted wisdom. That one author is Zonaras, who simply says that Odenathus was 'loyal to the Romans'.[23] Zonaras lived in the twelfth century, many hundreds of years after the events he is describing. He was trying to explain events almost as distant to him as they are to us. It is not, in itself, a very reliable statement. Other Roman authors describe the deeds of Odenathus but leave open the question of his attitudes and motives. Even the *HA*, despite its many statements about Odenathus' power, stops short of ever using the words 'loyal' or 'ally'.

74

5. *Just another usurper? The political legacy of the first Mr Zenobia*

The titles debate: a pyramid built on sand?

On examination, the theory of Odenathus as a loyal son of Rome with resounding official titles to prove his legitimacy looks wobbly. It is based almost entirely on the job descriptions that Odenathus is supposed to have enjoyed during his lifetime. Appendix A looks in detail at the battery of titles rightly or wrongly attributed to Odenathus. Interpretation of them is complex because of the different languages and language equivalents used at Palmyra – in other words, Greek titles, Palmyrene titles, Roman (i.e. Latin) titles, and titles that were, or are claimed to be, the equivalents in one language of titles whose formal use and meaning originate in another.[24]

In summary, some historians assert that Odenathus was a formally appointed *Dux Romanorum* (commander of the Romans) or *Dux Orientis* (commander of the East) with authorised *imperium* (formal powers), so that his title of *strategos* (general) can be taken to equate with his being in a meaningful sense *corrector* or *restitutor* (restorer) of this most important segment of the Roman empire. The question is whether he enjoyed these titles during his lifetime – or they were attributed to him only after his death, which would be quite a different matter. The only titles that are well attested for Odenathus during his lifetime are comparatively modest local ones, such as *exarch* and *decurio* and *strategos* (a sort of mayor/commandant figure) of the city of Palmyra, an important man in the neighbourhood whose high status was confirmed by his honorary or inherited senatorial and consular rank within the Roman nomenclature and by his activities as a patron of local trade guilds. His were not formal Roman job titles. The title 'King of Kings' sounds grander but again was not a Roman title, and may only have been claimed for him after his assassination. The rest of the titles sometimes associated with Odenathus were similarly attributed to him after his death and, insofar as they are not just vacuous titles, they look more like retrospective political propaganda to boost the apparent status of his son Vaballathus and therefore of Zenobia herself. The *imperium* that Roman-era authors concede to Odenathus was not a formal grant of authority by the emperor in Rome but, in a looser sense of that Latin word, a simple recognition that by his own efforts he gained great power in the Roman east. In short, the battery of titles attributed to Odenathus is a pyramid of false assumptions built on sand, in this case, the sands of Syria. Those who remain uncertain may settle for Professor Fergus Millar's verdict, that

> Detailed examination of titles will not in reality help us, for they were being made up in an unprecedented and fluid situation.[25]

One may agree with the modest verdict of the Greek writer Agathias, who remarked that

> Odenathus was at first unknown and obscure, but won great fame as a result of the disasters he inflicted on Sapor.[26]

The wariness of the *Historia Augusta*

The fashionable but erroneous picture of Odenathus as a loyal ally of Rome masks the persistent clues and suggestions throughout our evidence that Odenathus was in fact playing a double game with Rome, a game of pretence and bluff. It was a game in which the Roman emperor Gallienus for a time connived, whether out of self-interest or because he had no alternative. But the emperor then took action to bring down an increasingly dangerous usurper, with only partial success. What these clues and suggestions show is that in dangerous times, in a dangerous area, Odenathus was both testing out the limits of independent action and trying to keep his lines open to both sides, Rome and Persia. Only by understanding this background do the subsequent actions of Zenobia make some sense and become at least explicable as opposed to purely foolhardy. This was more a game of political charades than a game of happy Roman families.

Once the idea is jettisoned of Odenathus being a loyal servant of Rome with titles to match, it is easier to pick up these signs of at least an ambivalent attitude towards him at Rome – and of his ambivalent attitude towards Rome. The *HA*, for all its fragility as evidence, drops heavy hints. Most obviously, it firmly places Odenathus (and Zenobia) among the ranks of the *tyranni*, the pretenders. More specifically, it remarks that while Valerian was held captive by Sapor 'Odenathus was threatening war'.[27] The context implies war against Rome. Why was he threatening war? We don't know, but this hardly sounds like an ally. Then when Odenathus ousted the Persians from the Mesopotamian cities of Nisibis and Carrhae in the same period, the *HA* tells us that he sent the captured Persian satraps (i.e. governors) to Gallienus, perhaps out of respect for the latter but more likely for the purpose of insulting him and displaying his own prowess.[28] Loyal allies, let alone subordinates, do not insult you like that. Later, the *HA* remarks that Gallienus 'made peace with Odenathus'.[29] Why did he need to make peace? Presumably because relations were strained, with Odenathus threatening war. It is striking that the *HA* displays such wariness about him. Behind the public show, to the Roman view Odenathus must have looked like just another usurper.

The roll-call of usurpers

During Gallienus' unhappy reign, he was harassed by a throng of usurpers. Odenathus was just another one on the list – and geographically a lot further from Rome than most of them. The *HA* lists in all 32 people it chooses to call *tyranni* (not 30 as the title of this section of the *HA* suggests), generally translated not as 'tyrants' but as 'pretenders', but better translated as 'usurpers' or 'rebels'. The list, characteristically of the *HA*, is a mixed bag. Some names are almost certainly fictional, some are there purely because they are the sons (real or imagined) of a usurper/rebel. All of these are probably there just to swell the number to 30, the number of the famous Thirty Tyrants of Athens – in other words, a literary device by the *HA* author. But again characteristically of the *HA*, over 20 of the 32 are genuine in the sense that they are also attested elsewhere, if only briefly. If women as well as under-age boys are excluded, plus those who were usurper/rebels under other emperors like Decius, Claudius and Aurelian, the number still comes down to about a dozen during Gallienus' reign.

It is plain that Gallienus was dealing, on average, with more than one usurper for every year he held office. His was a constant fight for survival. It was open season for challenges to Gallienus' authority and hegemony, and if no one pretender/usurper/rebel was exactly the same as another, they all had in common this menace to his position as Roman emperor. The most dangerous of these menaces were the leader of the break-away movement in Gaul, Postumus, who commanded real Roman legions and several whole provinces of the empire (see Chapter 7), and Aureolus, who as cavalry commander of the Roman army held a senior military position that not long after produced two full Roman emperors, Claudius and Aurelian. Viewed from Rome, Odenathus was also a menace but far less so, and so he had more latitude to test out his regional sphere of influence.

Gallienus strikes out

The *HA* seems keen to write off Gallienus as incompetent, probably in order to further glorify his immediate successor Claudius, the alleged ancestor of the emperor Constantine, in whose time the *HA* was probably written. This supposed blood connection was almost certainly an invention by Constantine to help legitimise his claim to supreme power, but the *HA* author was hardly going to deny it. By playing up Odenathus' abilities and achievements, the *HA* author was able, by contrast, to emphasise Gallienus' alleged deficiencies and sloth. The truth is, however, that for a long time Gallienus was far too preoccupied by wars on several fronts, by Gothic invasions and by the succession of usurpers, some at least of whom were very dangerous, to be able to do much about the situation in the eastern parts of his empire. In particular, he was preoccupied with containing the break-away in 260 of Gaul and the other western provinces, which was a much closer and more imminent threat to Rome than events in Syria. Gallienus repeatedly took action to combat Postumus in Gaul, but in vain. But the fact that he tried shows where his priorities lay. In relation to Odenathus, Gallienus seems at first to have acted from a position of weakness and played for time. At best he sought to use Odenathus' successes against the Persians as local propaganda and as an excuse for a personal triumph held at Rome in an effort to boost his popularity.[30]

But Gallienus' later actions speak of anything but amity towards Odenathus. Rather, they are symptomatic of extreme tension and deadly intent. The story told by Malalas that Gallienus actually attacked and killed Odenathus is part of a very garbled account of that period, but may be symptomatic of the tradition found among other classical authors of open hostility between the two men.[31] There are two main examples of that hostility.

One is the possible involvement of Gallienus in the assassination of Odenathus in 267/8. Gallienus would have been getting increasingly suspicious of Odenathus' rising independent power in the east of the empire, and so resorted to trickery to deal with it – successfully. The belief that Gallienus was implicated in Odenathus' assassination is repeated by several sources.[32]

The second example is the direct military strike at Palmyra initiated by Gallienus, as recorded in the *HA*. The *HA* story is that Gallienus sent one of his most senior military commanders, Heraclianus, on an expedition ostensibly against Persia but actually against Palmyra. The Palmyrenes understood this, and roundly defeated Heraclianus' force.[33] There is some debate about the exact date of this abortive attempt to bring Palmyra to heel. Heraclianus was deeply involved in the successful plot to assassinate Gallienus, an event that took place not long after Odenathus' own assassination. Clearly, the assassin's dagger was a fashionable item in that year. So Heraclianus must have been in Italy at that time. Perhaps it was Claudius, after he had taken over as emperor, who actually sent Heraclianus, but the expedition was already in advanced preparation when Gallienus met his fate.

Whatever its exact date, this failed military strike shows the suspicion felt about Odenathus and Palmyra in the imperial centre. It also shows, incidentally, that Palmyra was a military force to be reckoned with. It would also have warned Zenobia in her capacity as successor to Odenathus and as regent for her son Vaballathus that the new regime in Rome was no longer prepared to tolerate the freelance position of power built up over eight years or so by Odenathus. So sooner or later the regime would be back again to try to put a stop to it. Unless, that is, she could build it up still further, and quickly, to the point where the new Roman regime would be forced to negotiate some sort of political settlement with her. Only on that basis can her subsequent behaviour be rationally explained.

Double-dealing with Persia

Zenobia also inherited from her late husband a complex diplomatic relationship with Persia. There are several instances of Odenathus' double-dealing with Persia, even if they amount to strong indications rather than proof. On the one hand there was Odenathus' pursuit of the Persian king Sapor's army and the capture of some of his booty – hardly a friendly act. On the other hand there is the story told by Peter the Patrician, the Greek diplomat who worked under the great Byzantine emperor Justinian and who therefore probably knew what he was talking about. He records that Odenathus sent a diplomatic delegation to Sapor loaded with gifts carried on the back of camels and with letters asking for a peace agreement, protesting that he had done nothing against the Persians.

> Sapor however instructed the slaves who received the gifts to throw them into the river and tore up and crushed the letters. 'Who is he', he declared, 'and how has he dared to write to his master? If then he wants to obtain a lighter punishment, let him prostrate himself again with his hands in chains.'[34]

This embassy cannot be dated with accuracy. Peter gives no date. But Odenathus' protestation that he had done nothing to harm Persia suggest that he was anxious to downplay his part in pursuing the withdrawing Persian forces after their defeat of Valerian, and that would date it to the period soon after 260, by which time Odenathus was in practice already acting as a free agent. Peter's story suggests that having re-captured some of Sapor's booty, and having pushed his pursuit as far as the Persian regional capital Ctesiphon itself, Odenathus got cold feet when he met stiff resistance and realised how exposed he now was to Persian retaliation and so tried to make it up – perhaps with more long-term success than Peter's story admits. But the reference to 'a lighter punishment' seems appropriate to a time after Odenathus had earned Sapor's wrath by harassing the latter's journey back to base. If this was not the occasion for this peace mission, then what was Sapor's threatened punishment, punishment for?

Whatever its date and occasion, this delegation amounted not just to an act of insubordination but to an open act of treason against Rome by Odenathus. That is true even if he was just an important local office holder. Of course it would be even more true if he held a larger formal appointment in the Roman administrative system as some (wrongly) have believed. Therefore this diplomatic delegation is important politically as evidence for the wary double-dealing which was going on at this troubled and poorly documented period, on both sides.

There is further if more speculative evidence of Odenathus' double-dealing between Rome and Persia in the *Res Gestae Divi Saporis*. In it Sapor claims that among those of his contemporaries 'who are under my authority' is a certain Vorod, whom he calls 'the agoranome' but gives no other details. It has been suggested that this man is none other than the well-known Septimius Vorodes who figures in a raft of inscriptions found around Palmyra, one of which gives one of his offices as 'agoranome', that is, public notary.[35] Was he perhaps acting for Odenathus, as the latter's peacemaker at the Persian court? Vorod is after all honoured in the inscriptions for his part in piloting trade caravans successfully through Persian territory back to Palmyra, so he must have had useful diplomatic contacts with the Persian authorities. Alternatively, was he, as some have suggested, the leader of an actual rival peace party at Palmyra, opposed to Odenathus' military adventures? There is however little other evidence of such a peace party.

It is the political context of the time that makes plausible the identification of this Vorod as the Vorodes of Palmyra and as the ambassador of Odenathus. Either or both of these diplomatic contacts can be taken as evidence of Odenathus trying to shore up his relations with Persia at a time of great political uncertainty in the Roman empire: and of his willingness to risk being accused of treason by the central Roman authorities, even if dealing with Persia through a proxy. It is worth remembering also that Zenobia was later to claim that Persian reinforcements were on their way to help her resistance to the oncoming emperor Aurelian, reinforcements that Aurelian prevented from reaching her, and that she herself as a last resort tried to escape to Persia – gestures which have been dismissed as futile or implausible but which actually help to show the political connections, however fragile, that had developed between Persia and Palmyra as Odenathus sought, Janus-like, to face both ways at the same time.[36]

Local warlord

The basic decision to be made about Odenathus has been defined as

> to know whether we should see Odenathus' actions in response to Valerian's capture as those of a Roman governor with regular forces on the one hand, or of a local notable with local forces on the other.[37]

Which was he? With the collapse of Roman authority across much of the eastern empire in the wake of Valerian's humiliation in 260 and the widespread devastation caused by the Persian invaders, there was a clear vacant space into which a local warlord – for that surely is what Odenathus was – could move in order to magnify his own power and prestige. With the only well-armed and organised force left in action over large parts of the Roman East and with much of Syria and Roman Mesopotamia left in ruins or in chaos by the Persians, there was a clear temptation to consolidate power while he could and to play games with Gallienus in order to keep the Roman emperor guessing or keep him sweet. That is why he assumed – if he did – an eastern title such as King of Kings, not (as some have supposed) as a challenge to the Persian monarch – that would have been absurd – but to flaunt his new status without directly challenging Rome by using a Roman title.

So the answer to the question seems clear. Odenathus was a local notable with local forces. Sartre sums it up well by saying that Odenathus 'behaved more like an autonomous dynast than a subject of the emperor'.[38] Odenathus was engaged in the same political experiment as his counterpart in the so-called Empire of the Gauls – how far was it possible for well-equipped local leaderships to operate at arm's length from Rome in order to protect its cities and territories without precipitating the great Roman steamroller? Odenathus had seen the destruction of Hatra and Dura by the Persians and the elimination of Palmyrene garrisons at various points on the Euphrates river which was the key artery for Palmyra's trade and so the source of its wealth. Without that artery, the whole point of Palmyra might disappear – indeed, it eventually did. It is here that we come closest to Odenathus' driving motive. That motive was the very survival of Palmyra itself. At his death, Zenobia's problem was how to pursue that same objective, but in the altered circumstance that the regime in Rome was once again flexing its muscles.

6

Arms and the woman: Zenobia goes to war

What did Zenobia do with her political inheritance from her husband Odenathus? Zenobia now enters the pages of history in her own right, not just as the consort of Odenathus. Generally, Syrians were treated with some disdain by classical authors. Herodian remarks that

> Syrians, being characteristically erratic people, are always ready to upset the established order.[1]

But the *Historia Augusta* tells us that Odenathus' success was as much due to her as to him. Perhaps for that reason the succession at Palmyra seems to have taken place smoothly – we have no evidence to the contrary – and with the support of Odenathus' friends and supporters his widow took her place as queen-regent in the name of their under-age son Vaballathus. The political landscape around her was changing. The Roman emperor Gallienus with whom Odenathus had been dealing was himself assassinated within months of the death of Odenathus. Odenathus was removed from the scene at some date between August 267 and August 268; Gallienus in the early autumn of 268. So Zenobia's succession at Palmyra would have taken place only shortly before the murder of Gallienus, and her reign at Palmyra was to span no less than three successive Roman emperors, first Gallienus, then Claudius who lasted only two years in office (268-270), and then Aurelian who took over in late 270 and was to prove her ultimate opponent. This instability at the centre of the Roman empire must have been an important factor in the political and military decision-making of her new regime.

Another factor would have been that by Zenobia's time Syrians had for over half a century been playing a big part in Roman politics. One half-Syrian emperor (the hated Caracalla, emperor 211-216) and two full Syrian emperors (the much sneered-at Elagabalus, emperor 217-222, and the more respected Alexander Severus, emperor 222-235) plus one emperor from the nearby Roman province of Arabia (Philip, called 'the Arab', emperor 244-249, who may or may not have been an ethnic Arab) had held office. At least two Syrian women had risen to positions of power and influence. One was Julia Domna from Emesa, who married the emperor Septimius Severus in 187 and became the mother of Caracalla. Under his rule she enjoyed the title 'mother of the Senate and of the fatherland'. Another was her sister Julia Maesa, two of whose grandsons became emperors (Elagabalus and Alexander Severus). So there were precedents for able and ambitious Syrian women active at the centre of Roman power – but also precedents for paying the penalty for that involvement. Not only were all three Syrian emperors assassinated, but Julia Domna herself committed suicide after her son's assassination. So the message was mixed. But it did mean that Syria was not, in Roman terms, just a lunatic fringe of the empire.

The argument

There has been fierce argument about what Zenobia made of her political inheritance, just as there has been argument about what exactly that inheritance was. If you believe that Odenathus was in broad terms a loyal ally of Rome with official titles to match, then you may incline to think in the same terms about Zenobia and her son. If, however, you believe that Odenathus was a local war-lord testing out the potential for independent action and with at best brittle relations with Rome, then that suggests a quite different interpretation of Zenobia's extraordinary career of territorial conquest once she became Queen of Palmyra. In this programme of aggression, did Zenobia and her supporters break with the policy of Odenathus – or continue it by other means? Did Zenobia hold her high office with the approval or at least the toleration of the three successive Roman emperors with whom she overlapped, so that Roman administrative officials were able to shift allegiance easily between Rome and Palmyra? Hartmann for example argues that Zenobia 'was recognised by the government of the Roman emperor. Her rule was tolerated by Gallienus, Claudius and Aurelian.'[2] Others take the same view. But is that an ingenious invention plainly contradicted by her successive acts of military aggression – and by Rome's aggression towards Palmyra? More broadly, are we to see Zenobia in her traditional role as a heroine-rebel against oppression by the Evil Empire of Rome? Or as a local dynast over-reacting foolishly and fatally to events beyond her control or competence?

Set us free from Zenobia

By the time of Zenobia's accession, and however much the emperor Gallienus had been playing for time, the attitude of the central Roman regime towards Palmyra had hardened and become much less inclined to compromise. Gallienus may indeed have been implicated in Odenathus' murder.[3] Gallienus also authorised an attempted military strike headed by his general Heraclianus, ostensibly against Persia but actually against Palmyra, which the Palmyrenes fought off. Whether this abortive strike actually took place under Gallienus, as the *HA* asserts,[4] or in the early part of Claudius' reign, is immaterial to the main thrust of events.[5] Palmyra was coming under threat, and with it that degree of independence that

Odenathus had established. In other words, Zenobia was not starting from an inherited position of recognition or tolerance by Rome, and had no reason to expect such a position. On the contrary, by the time that Claudius took over as emperor, Zenobia and her supporters had clear evidence that the day of reckoning with Rome would come, sooner or later. 'Toleration' and 'recognition' were not on the agenda.

Attitudes at Rome were openly hostile to Palmyra. The story goes that when Claudius was declared emperor, the senators at Rome donned their togas, went to the Temple of Apollo on the Palatine Hill, and there (in Claudius' absence) chanted in unison the following acclamations:

'Claudius Augustus, may the gods preserve you!' – repeated 60 times
'Claudius Augustus, you or such as you we have ever desired for our emperor' – repeated 40 times.
'Claudius Augustus, the state was in need of you!' – repeated 40 times.
'Claudius Augustus, you are brother, father, friend, righteous senator, and true prince!' – repeated 80 times.
'Claudius Augustus, deliver us from Aureolus!' – repeated 5 times.
'Claudius Augustus, deliver us from the men of Palmyra!' – repeated 5 times.
'Claudius Augustus, set us free from Zenobia and from Victoria!' – repeated 7 times.
'Claudius Augustus, nothing has Tetricus accomplished!' – repeated 7 times.[6]

(Aureolus was Gallienus' cavalry commander, who had come out in revolt at Milan; Victoria was reputedly a wealthy Gallic aristocrat who supported the break-away regime in Gaul that paralleled Palmyra's venture).

In this lengthy series of senatorial acclamations, the kick was in the tail. The last 19 of the 244 chantings were the business end, asking Claudius to deal with the two secessionist movements then in full spate, in the west in Gaul, and in the east in Palmyra. This story about senators chanting in unison is usually neglected as inherently absurd, or as just another of those silly stories in the *HA*. The *HA's* whole account of Claudius is dismissed by one translator as an 'hysterical panegyric'.[7] But acclamations were a routine part of Roman political life and a routine method of formally saluting the emperor or members of his family.[8]

> They were not, as in the modern sense of the word, spontaneous outbursts of enthusiasm and approval, but took the form of a rhythmical ritual chant, often shouted out in unison and to a set and familiar formula, at formal state occasions.[9]

The *HA* itself records acclamations in honour of succeeding emperors such as Tacitus and Probus, as well as Claudius.[10] So this acclamation to

Claudius may well have happened, even if not in 224 parts. Its menacing tone towards Zenobia is unmistakable. There is only one piece of contrary evidence in the *HA* that can be cited to show that Claudius chose to 'tolerate' Zenobia's regime. That is when Aurelian as emperor is reported there to have said retrospectively:

> Claudius allowed her to keep power while he was busy with the Gothic invasions – or so they say – and did so deliberately and wisely so that with her looking after the eastern frontier he could finish off what he had started.[11]

This sentiment is expressed in a letter allegedly sent to the Roman senate by Aurelian, and the *HA's* letters are a particularly suspicious part of its narrative. But we can accept a degree of truth inside it. Claudius had his hands full coping with massive sea-borne Gothic invasions into the Balkan heartlands of the empire that culminated in the great battle at Naissus in 269. Zosimus says that 50,000 'barbarians' were killed at Naissus from an original invasion force of 320,000 with 6,000 boats – suspect numbers, but a massive invasion nevertheless.[12] After the failure of Gallienus' military strike against Palmyra, he probably knew that he stood no hope of taking on Palmyra again, or not just yet. He was being realistic in admitting that, temporarily, he had to put up with Palmyra. This does not mean that he, or the Senate, liked the situation. Aurelian does add the caveat 'so they say'.

Road sign near Palmyra.

6. Arms and the woman: Zenobia goes to war

All quiet on the eastern front?

From the Palmyrene point of view, after the failed strike against Palmyra by Heraclianus, it must have seemed highly likely that Rome would strike again, this time better equipped. But when? A dangerous break-away Gallic regime was in power in the west of the empire and Claudius was busy with the Goths. He might indeed go down to defeat before the Goths. Without the ultimate protection of the Roman empire and its army, what could Palmyra do to improve its chances of survival? Zenobia and her supporters had a window of opportunity to consolidate Palmyra's position before the Roman steamroller was once again set in motion, and took it. They embarked upon an expansionist policy which not so much reversed the policy of Odenathus, as some suggest, as pushed it to its logical conclusion.

The pointed reference in several Roman historians to her friends and supporters,[13] and the later prominence given to Zenobia's two leading generals, Septimius Zabdas, commander in chief of her army, and Septimus Zabbai, military commander at Palmyra itself, particularly the former, confirm the impression that Zenobia may have been one of a ruling clique rather than an autocratic queen, even perhaps a useful front-person or public face for a dominant faction among Palmyra's leading citizens.[14] It was Zabdas and Zabbai who put up the two famous but now long lost statues of Odenathus and Zenobia in the Grand Colonnade at Palmyra, known from the surviving inscriptions on the face of the columns. This faction would presumably have been supporters of Odenathus, perhaps put into high office by him. These are the people who now, literally, took the offensive, striking southwards against Roman bases. It is, however, idle to suppose a precise long-term master plan at Palmyra at this time. Zenobia and her supporters, like everyone else in that period, were feeling their way in uncertain, unsettled and threatening times. The provocative campaign of territorial expansion embarked upon by Zenobia, managed and perhaps driven by her generals Zabdas and Zabbai, appears to have been triggered not so much by a master plan as by a series of outside events that were as fortuitous as everything else that happened in this chaotic period.

As well as territory, there may have been a trade motive, to seize for Palmyra control of the trade routes that passed through Egypt to substitute for her own trade routes lost or damaged by the successive Persian wars.

It is not a coincidence that, when queen Zenobia of Palmyra became independent from Rome, she annexed Egypt and Arabia to her kingdom, to better control the Eastern trade.[15]

The destruction of Hatra and then of Dura Europos could well have turned Palmyra's eyes towards alternative trade routes from which to derive its income. But trade was perhaps a background motive: the opportunities to do something about it were fortuitous.

> Trade motives are likely to have figured in the thinking of Zenobia and her court [but] trade motives and political motives certainly do not have to be seen as mutually exclusive.[16]

There are differences of opinion about the exact chronology of the events that followed, and about when Zenobia actually set off on her career of conquest. Zosimus gives us the most sober and reliable account we have of what followed, and he places Zenobia's first expansionist move firmly *after* Claudius' big battle of Naissus against the Goths and *before* a series of subsequent mopping up battles and before many of the Goths, and many Roman soldiers, and Claudius himself, succumbed to the plague.[17] There is no good reason to overturn Zosimus' chronology. Events were on the move before Aurelian came to power.

First move: Arabia

The first strike of the new regime at Palmyra was against the Roman province of Arabia. There is good evidence for this both from literary sources and from an inscription. The inscription is on the lintel over the entrance to the Temple of Juppiter Ammon at Bostra, in Arabia. It refers to the temple as having been 'destroyed by the Palmyrene enemies' and later rebuilt.[18] It is undated. But Malalas, admittedly in a rather confused account, says that Zenobia took over Arabia and killed the Roman commander there, Trassus, along with his soldiers, and confirms that this event happened during the reign of Claudius.[19] At this point (I speculate) Zenobia may well have muttered to herself, as Julius Caesar famously is said to have done when crossing the Rubicon, '*Jacta alea est*' (the die is cast). But of course she did not speak Latin.

It is anyway logical to suppose that this attack took place as the Palmyrene army advanced from Palmyra towards Egypt, its main goal. Arabia stood in between, on the way, and surely no sensible Palmyrene general intent on a hostile take-over of Egypt would have left his rear exposed by leaving a Roman garrison in place to harass his supply lines and his return trip. It has been suggested that after their defeat by Zenobia's army, the regular Roman forces in Arabia then changed sides and went over to Zenobia.[20] While, if true, this might explain Zenobia's later reported reference to Roman soldiers having died in her cause,[21] there is no other evidence for this alleged side-switching, and it appears highly unlikely unless you espouse the view, discussed below, that somehow (and extraordinarily) Zenobia was still operating within or in collusion with the official Roman structure of government.

The (somewhat reconstructed) Roman theatre at Bostra.

Second move: Egypt

The next target was Egypt. The immediate trigger for Zenobia's invasion was simply that a certain Timagenes was creating trouble in Egypt, and invited the Palmyrenes in to help. So she took the opportunity offered to her. We know practically nothing about this Timagenes. Some have suggested that he was a Palmyrene himself and so perhaps acting at the instigation of Palmyra. But there is no proof of that.[22] What Zosimus tells us is that

> Zenobia, meanwhile, desirous of bigger things, sent Zabdas into Egypt, where a certain Timagenes was seeking the dominion over his country for Palmyra.[23]

So Timagenes was in some sense leading a revolt in Egypt in an effort to ally that country with Palmyra and needed outside help. In this period leading Egyptians must have been as worried as the leading citizens of Palmyra about the future of their country in an apparently disintegrating empire. Moreover, as we shall see, there were pro-Palmyra factions in other cities of the Roman east as well as in Egypt. But in Egypt there was a problem, in the shape of the Roman governor of Egypt, a man called Probus or Probatus, with a military force at his disposal.[24] He was however away from Egypt at the time, trying to clear the eastern Mediterranean of those elements of the Gothic invasion force that had taken to the sea as sea-borne pirates. So events came together, perhaps fortuitously, to offer Egypt to Zenobia on a plate. The Palmyrene army marched into Egypt more or less unopposed – at first. According to Zosimus, it was a large Palmyrene army of 70,000 men (a suspicious number which seems to mean basically 'a lot') commanded by Zabdas and Timagenes, and it seized control of Egypt. When his army departed, Zabdas left behind Timagenes and a Palmyrene garrison of 5,000 men to hold the province.

Nevertheless, it quickly developed into a hotly contested take-over by the Palmyrenes. Probus hurried back to Egypt when he heard the bad news and with his own troops augmented by Egyptians opposed to Timagenes twice got the better of the Palmyrene garrison, which he drove out of Egypt. He then occupied a strategic site near Babylon, a major Roman fortress in the Nile delta which barred the route to and from Syria. But Timagenes returned and took advantage of his knowledge of the local geography to turn the tables and defeat Probus. Probus was captured and committed suicide, presumably rather than face the ignominy of defeat by a 'band of rustics'.[25]

Seizing Egypt by force was about the most provocative thing that Zenobia and her advisers could have done, whatever their mixed motives. Egypt was a province directly administered by the emperor, and had been since the far-off days of the first emperor Augustus. It was a vital source of Rome's food supply, with its annual fleet of corn ships, and of course of tax revenues and (not insignificantly) of the papyrus out of which Roman 'paper' was made. No Roman regime could tolerate for long the loss of control of such a key province. The contested but successful military take-over of Egypt by Palmyra itself casts severe doubt on the idea that first Odenathus and then Zenobia were in some way acting within the imperial administrative structure, or with its approval or even tolerance.

Third move: towards the Black Sea

Zosimus records the next moves. After the Arabian and Egyptian seizures, Zenobia and her men moved on to Asia Minor and took control of a number of cities up to and including the modern Ankara (then Ancyra) in the middle of what is now Turkey, then the Roman province of Galatia, and her troops may even have got as far as the coast of Bithynia on the Black Sea, at Chalcedon.[26] This was probably in 271, after Aurelian had taken over from Claudius and while he was still struggling with the Gothic and other invasions across the Danube and into Italy itself. Sometime in this period Zenobia also caused to be built a new city-fortress on the banks of the Euphrates, which she naturally called 'Zenobia', perhaps to replace the now destroyed fortress of Dura Europos.[27] This has been identified with the modern twin sites of Halebiyeh and Zalebiyeh, roughly facing each other on opposite sides of the river, the ruins of the former much visited by today's tourists, the latter in too dangerous a state to visit. Palmyra now controlled the larger part of the Roman east, a rich and strategic area.

Ruins of Halebiyeh, once Zenobia, looking over the Euphrates.

The pro-Palmyra factions

Palmyra seems to have enjoyed widespread support in its take-over of much of the Roman east. Zenobia's was not just a fool's errand. Egypt clearly had a robust pro-Palmyra faction. The cities of Asia Minor must also have had pro-Palmyra factions since her army was certainly not large enough or well enough equipped to take them over by force or by storm. Negative evidence of this is that these cities quickly sided back with Aurelian when he finally advanced into Asia Minor in 272. In Syria, one of the cities that Zenobia took control of was the great metropolis of Antioch, and it is clear that in Antioch, as in Egypt, there was a strong pro-Palmyra faction that supported the ambitions of Palmyra. When Aurelian finally got to Antioch in his counter-offensive, a large group of its citizens left the city in a panic, fearing revenge, and had to be persuaded back by promises of clemency.[28] At Chalcedon too there was a pro-Palmyra faction.[29] The city of Tyana actually shut its gates against Aurelian, which suggests serious opposition to him. It gave rise to the famous story in the *HA* that Aurelian promised not to leave a dog alive in Tyana, and when the soldiers clamoured to be allowed to sack the place, he told them they could only kill the dogs – fortunately, the soldiers saw the joke.[30]

While Claudius was heavily preoccupied elsewhere, and when Aurelian had only recently taken over at Rome, Palmyra may still have seemed the best bet for survival for these men of Egypt, Antioch, Tyana and Chalcedon. Antioch had after all been sacked not once but twice by the Persians, and must have suffered badly. No Roman army had been there, or anywhere near it as far as we know, since 260, a gap of over ten years, and Antioch's citizens, like many in Egypt, would have had understandable worries about who, in the future, would defend their interests – except Palmyra.

New titles for Vaballathus

Among Zenobia's provocative acts was the steadily rising crescendo of grand titles claimed by her or by her regime for her son Vaballathus, as evidenced by milestones and coins. This crescendo of titles may have gone in three stages. The exact dating is far from clear but the trend is clear enough (see Appendix A for extended discussion of all these titles). At first, in the early period 268-270, Vaballathus is given the titles of 'illustrious king of kings' and *epanorthotes*, the Greek equivalent of the Latin *corrector* or *restitutor* (restorer). These titles were either (as some claim) used by Odenathus and inherited by Vaballathus, or (much more likely) attributed to Odenathus retrospectively in about 271 by the Palmyrenes for current propaganda purposes.[31]

Then in stage two, in early 272, the titles used for Vaballathus expand beyond anything used by or even claimed for his father. He becomes *vir clarissimus, rex, consul, imperator, dux romanorum* (senator, king, consul, general, Roman military commander).[32] Odenathus never claimed to be *dux romanorum* (whatever weight we give to that term). He also never claimed the title *augustus*. But in stage three, by the spring of 272 at the latest, when battle against Aurelian's advancing Roman army was about to be joined (but some say earlier) Vaballathus is promoted still further to claim on coins and milestones the imperial title of *augustus* along with *imperator* or *imperator Caesar* (all meaning roughly 'emperor').[33] This is surely an absurd concatenation of titles to claim for an under-age Syrian boy with no imperial ancestry to call upon. So there has been much discussion about how to interpret the political ambitions lying behind these assumed and surely propaganda titles. They can hardly amount, as some suggest, to a formal claim to the throne of the Roman empire itself. But they can and do form the basis for supposing that Palmyra's ambition was to force acceptance by Rome of a 'co-regency' formula for rule of the Roman east in which Aurelian and Vaballathus (or Zenobia in his name) would agree on some type of joint suzerainty or power-sharing in the region. That is guesswork, but offers a plausible – perhaps the only plausible – explanation of what Zenobia's longer-term strategy may have been.

A straightforward tale of war and re-conquest?

It has also been suggested that Zenobia and Aurelian got further than propaganda and were actually experimenting with some form of co-regency in the east. Despite her use of military force to conquer Egypt, on this interpretation Zenobia ruled Egypt for the brief period she did in some sort of coalition or fluid arrangement with Rome, with Roman officials moving seamlessly between the two camps, a period in which Aurelian and Vaballathus (and so in effect Zenobia) were acknowledged as co-rulers of Egypt. If correct, this would have been a remarkable political arrangement, coming as it did in the wake of open warfare. The most important and complex evidence for it is equally remarkable (discussed in detail in Appendix B). This is one slim strip of papyrus probably from Naucratis, the oldest of the Greek towns in pre-Roman Egypt. The original papyrus was torn down the middle, and only the left-hand half survives. The surviving strip has written on it 46 part-lines of the text of a petition presented to a governor of Egypt by a man who is objecting to being obliged, as part of his municipal duties, to perform and/or pay for liturgies, that is, some form of religious ceremony. The evidence for the co-regency/ coalition theory is not the surviving half of this papyrus, but what might have been written on the lost half.

The issue for a historian is whether the missing half of this mutilated strip of papyrus, as restored by experts, proves that a certain Statilius Ammianus was the governor of Egypt *both* under Zenobia *and* (without a gap) under Aurelian after Aurelian's reassertion of Roman control of Egypt. Such a picture would indicate that Zenobia was somehow operating within or by arrangement with the formal Roman imperial administrative structure and so with the approval of the emperor in Rome. Three other Roman officials are said to have performed the same balancing act. If so, it would colour the whole picture of what Zenobia was up to, not only in Egypt but in all her activities, and might also support retrospectively the interpretation of Odenathus' career as a rather chummy political relationship between Palmyra and Rome. Perhaps there was an actual or at least pretended experiment in coalition under way until Aurelian rudely ripped it up. Equini Schneider argues that when he became emperor Aurelian at first recognised Zenobia's conquests and that there was no open breach with Rome until quite late, in 272, the year that Aurelian actually marched his legions against Palmyra. The coins issued by Zenobia on which her son Vaballathus and Aurelian are given equal billing simply masked the real seizure of power that had taken place in the east.[34] J-P. Rey-Coquais agrees that at first 'Aurelian tolerated the autonomy of Palmyra'.[35] So perhaps Zenobia's story was not just a straightforward tale of war and re-conquest.[36]

The crucial bit of evidence is that half-papyrus, known in the trade as P.Wisc. 1.2. The elaborate process by which this torn papyrus, taken with another papyrus fragment known as P.Mich 5478a, has been extensively reconstructed so as to become the proposed proof that Ammianus was in office both under Zenobia and under Aurelian is set out in Appendix B, as is the evidence for the other three men. As this Appendix makes clear, two of these men can be explained differently and do nothing to substantiate the coalition theory, the third is a genuine puzzle, while Statilius Ammianus as prefect of Egypt presents the trickiest problem.

The question is, does the notion of high-ranking Roman officials switching and sliding between the two camps makes any sense at a time when Zenobia had taken violent military action against Roman Arabia and

Egypt, causing the death of an incumbent Roman governor in the process? To my mind, it does not make any political or military sense at all. It may therefore be respectfully suggested that the proposed reconstruction of the missing text of the two papyri. P. Wisc. 1.2 and P. Mich. 5478a, while clearly sound in terms of papyrology, is based on a problematic preconception of what was actually happening on the ground. At best, to base a particular historical reconstruction of events upon words that do not, after all, even exist, is surely an invention too far, especially when it flies in the face of the literary evidence for a rather different historical situation.

Of course, that does not mean that Zenobia and her supporters were not trying to force Rome to agree to some sort of broad political accommodation. Indeed, and to repeat, an ambition to achieve such an agreement is the only plausible explanation of what Palmyra's longer-term plan may have been in the highly risky venture upon which it had embarked under Zenobia. At her post-defeat interrogation by Aurelian, Zenobia is said to have acknowledged that her ambition was a territorial one, to gain a share of power 'if distribution of territory allowed it'.[37]

That is according to the *HA*, but it has a ring of plausibility about it. Perhaps it really was, after all, 'a straightforward tale of war and re-conquest'. Whatever had been going on, in late 271 Aurelian moved to Byzantium and prepared for war in the east. Then in the spring of 272 he moved into Asia Minor for the final reckoning with Zenobia and her forces. If the galaxy of titles claimed for Zenobia and her son did contain a hint of the political co-regency arrangement that the Palmyrenes hoped to achieve, Aurelian (if he had ever entertained the idea) now decided to spurn it. Zenobia and her supporters must have wondered what sort of a man and what sort of a general they were now up against, and how to defend themselves against the Roman steamroller. Could they at least hold him to a draw in the military contest that was about to begin, and so perhaps force him to the negotiating table and hammer out a deal for 'distribution of territory'? The leaders of the Gallic secession, notably Tetricus, its last 'emperor', must have been equally interested in the outcome. If Aurelian could master Palmyra, he would surely come after Gaul next. The situation in Gaul may therefore shed further light on what Palmyra was out to achieve, and why.

7

The French connection: guardians
of the Rhine

For all of its brief history, the separatist movement begun by Odenathus and expanded by Zenobia in the eastern Roman empire had a mirror-image in the western Roman empire, the so-called Gallic empire. Can this Gallic empire, created at the same time and for similar reasons and better viewed as a secession rather than an empire, shed light on what Palmyra was up to?[1]

There is no evidence of any direct contact between the two separatist movements, east and west, no direct messages or messengers that we know of between Odenathus and Zenobia in the east and their opposite numbers in the west. But even though news travelled slowly in that era compared to today's near-instant communications, news and people did travel, and over the dozen or so years that both secession movements co-existed, it is inconceivable that they did not know about each other, perhaps a lot about each other. At her post-defeat interrogation by Aurelian, Zenobia is said to have likened herself directly to Victoria, mother of one of the later Gallic emperors Victorinus and patron of the last one, Tetricus, in her ambition to gain a share of power 'if distribution of territory allowed it'.[2]

That story comes from the *Historia Augusta*, so is not to be taken too literally. Maybe indeed Victoria never existed at all, but was a neat invention by the inventive author of the *HA* as a counterpart to Zenobia – troublesome women on all sides. On the other hand, maybe the story hides a political insight about a possible redistribution of power that never actually came about but might have done. Unfortunately, the common feature of both the Gallic and Palmyrene secessions is that the bulkiest account we have of both of them is to be found in the *HA*, with all the problems that creates of separating truth from invention. The existence and duration of the Gallic secession is however not in doubt. It is attested, if only briefly, by the usual clutch of Roman era authors on whom we rely for this period, although they differ in detail, making exact reconstruction difficult, even with the support of archaeological and coin evidence.[3] The extensive coin hoards found in France dating from this time might be expected to provide harder evidence than literary sources, but in practice they do not help much.[4]

Emperors of the West?

Like the Palmyrene empire, the break-away Gallic empire sprang into being in the wake of the disastrous defeat and capture of the Roman emperor Valerian by the Persian king Sapor in 260. That disaster created a military and political vacuum which both separatist movements sought to fill, one in the east and one in the west, and thereafter the fate of the Gallic secession was inextricably linked with that of the Palmyrene secession. From its beginnings in 260, the Gallic empire at its height consisted of Gaul, Spain and Britain. In other words, it was extensive and formidable. The experiment of the Gallic secession lasted in all about 14 years. The founder of it was one Marcus Cassianius Latinius Postumus – the Odenathus figure of the west – and Orosius tells us that

> Postumus took control of Gaul, to the greater good of the republic because, showing great courage and moderation over a period of ten years, he chased out enemies who had asserted power and restored lost provinces to their previous state: but was killed in a military mutiny.[5]

Eutropius says that

> while Gallienus was abandoning the state, the Roman empire was saved in the west by Postumus and in the east by Odenathus.[6]

When Valerian suffered his great defeat, there were momentous repercussions. 'Barbarian' (in Roman terms) war bands took the opportunity to pour across the northern frontiers and penetrate far and wide. Having crossed the Rhine, Franks attacked what is now Tour; some got into Spain, where they ruined what is now Tarragona: some even got as far as Africa. The Alamanni broke through the important frontier defences known as the *Agri Decumates* between the headwaters of the Rhine and Danube and penetrated the central Swiss plateau. Some invaded what is now the Auvergne, and some got into Italy itself, only to be turned back by the emperor Gallienus near Milan. The *Agri Decumates* were an important strategic asset to Rome because they shortened its long northern frontier line, but one result was that this key area was finally lost to the Alamanni and never recovered. It was the first and ominous sign of retraction of an empire that had for centuries been expanding. It became a structural fault in the Roman empire. For ever after its loss, this area formed a sort of enemy salient into Roman territory through which 'barbarian' tribes could penetrate Roman territory. In a further and larger contraction, the abandonment of the trans-Danube province of Dacia (roughly, modern Romania) was also begun under Gallienus and (probably) completed later by Aurelian when he needed troops for his final confrontation with Palmyra.

Gallienus had left his son Saloninus in charge of the Rhine frontier, but after a quarrel Saloninus was killed and Postumus entered into open revolt. Who was Postumus? We don't know exactly, but he was apparently a man from a poor background who rose to an important military position, perhaps in charge of the frontier region of the lower Rhine.[7] His rule lasted ten years, until his assassination.[8] Postumus filled the military vacuum on the Rhine and before long assumed the title previously assumed by Gallienus – 'Restorer of the Gauls'. The coins issued by Postumus show him helmeted and armed, lifting up a kneeling Gaul, represented as a woman extending her hand to the Gallic 'emperor'. In other cases, Postumus has his foot on a prostrate enemy.[9] Spain and Britain went over to Postumus. Spain had after all suffered that nasty invasion from beyond the Rhine, and Britain always did have close ties with Gaul. By winning over Spain and Britain, Postumus had at least protected his own flanks. Britain indeed stayed part of the Gallic empire from its beginning to its end.[10] But Postumus was murdered by his own troops in 269 because he refused to allow them to plunder the city of Mainz which had supported a rival challenger to his position. After Gaul's own troubled 'Year of Four Emperors', Postumus' job finally devolved upon Tetricus, whose two- or three-year term in office was abruptly ended by the emperor Aurelian in 273/4.

No road to Rome

Postumus' ten-year supremacy in Gaul and his ascendancy over Spain and Britain made him potentially a much more dangerous contender for supreme power in the Roman empire than ever Odenathus or Zenobia could have been. Not only did he have real and experienced Roman legions at his command, but he was also geographically much nearer to Rome, with ready access to Rome across the Alpine passes that he controlled. The most remarkable thing about Postumus therefore is what he did *not* do. Untypically for a usurper or pretender, he did not immediately (or ever) march directly on Rome and attempt to seize supreme power in the empire. Furthermore, he consistently refused to rise to attempts by the central emperor Gallienus to provoke a showdown. Postumus conspicuously stayed within his chosen bailiwick. Some say this was out of a sense of duty or loyalty to Rome or personal conscience. More likely, he knew his strengths and weaknesses as Gaul's chosen champion. The most graphic proof of this is that when Gallienus' cavalry general Aureolus revolted at his headquarters in Milan and offered his allegiance to Postumus, thus opening a clear road to Rome, Postumus conspicuously failed to come to his aid and left him to his fate.[11] If Postumus left Gaul for Rome, his frontier would once again be exposed. Postumus had achieved considerable success in holding off the invaders from across the Rhine. The *HA* says that he built or rebuilt numerous forts on the far side of the Rhine which had been evacuated by Gallienus. That however is disputed.[12] Perhaps surprisingly, there seems to have been little effort to build new or improved fortifications along the line of the river at this period.[13] If that is the case, it was all the more important to Postumus to stay where he was, on hand. Self-interest rather than idealism kept him away from Rome. If that applies to Postumus, then perhaps it applies the more so to Odenathus and to Zenobia, champions of local interests in a more distant area of the empire with less military firepower than Gaul.

So despite the name conventionally given to it, it is wrong to see the Gallic secession as an empire at all; it was more of a medium-term fix for a local crisis when no other fix was available. The Palmyrene empire may be seen in much the same light, and the actions of Odenathus and Zenobia judged accordingly. Only one of the Roman-era authors who describe the Gallic secession actually refers to it in terms of a full-scale Gallic empire, a *Galliarum Imperium*, and that is Eutropius.[14] So we must be careful about whether authors living much nearer the time actually saw events in Gaul as constituting a *Galliarum Imperium*. Perhaps it too is an invention or exaggeration by moderns.

> This phrase, strongly reminiscent of Tacitus' *Imperium Galliarum* of the first century, is the only hint of a recognition of the Gallic Empire of the third century as a distinct historical phenomenon to be found in any of our sources. On the other hand, it could simply be a rhetorical flourish, signifying that Eutropius saw Gaul as the place where a set of usurpers happened to hold sway for the time being.[15]

Perhaps the Palmyrene empire needs to be downgraded in a similar way – to be seen as a place where a set of usurpers happened to hold sway for the time being. It is notable that neither the Gallic empire nor the Palmyrene ever developed or attempted to develop fixed frontiers, as far as we know. They were fluid spheres of influence and activity rather than states with frontiers. For example, coins seem to have moved between Gallic and core empire areas, and the mint at Milan seems to have issued coins for both authorities, though at different times.[16] Indeed, the creation of mints in places other than Rome may have encouraged the rise of local pretenders and secessions, by creating local means to mint coins to pay soldiers. So the mint at Trier played a key role in the Gallic secession, and Zenobia's expansionist venture may be seen in part as her attempt to control the money supply from the Alexandria and Antioch mints, for the same purposes.

Routine usurpers?

Perhaps both Postumus, first and longest of the Gallic emperors, and Odenathus and Zenobia, are best seen therefore as vacuum-fillers. Both had limited objectives. In both east and west, on the Euphrates and on the Rhine, a local dynast proved more able to deal with insistent local military problems of invasion from across the river and regional security than the more distant figure of the emperor in Rome. The role assumed by the Gallic 'emperor' as a quasi-independent local defender of the Rhine frontier and of Gallic interests in default of the central Roman emperor offering anything better, applies equally to the rulers of Palmyra.

On the other hand, it would be wrong to dismiss Postumus and his successors, or Odenathus and Zenobia, as just routine usurpers from the same mould as all the other long line of usurpers in the third century. There were, according to one recent tabulation that subsumes the 30 Pretenders listed by the *HA*, no less than 55 such usurpers between 218 and 300.[17] Of these, 15 were under Gallienus, a record for one emperor's reign and a sign of just how troubled his time was and how beset he was. Interestingly, 14 of the grand total of 55 were associated with Syria, a sign perhaps of both the importance and the restiveness of that province and its leading figures, such as Zenobia. In that troubled period both secessions, Gallic and Palmyrene, showed staying power well beyond that of most usurpers (except for those usurpers who became emperors, of course – eight of them – but some of those did not last long either) and showed staying power beyond the assassinations of both their founders, Postumus and Odenathus. This shows that there was much more than mere personal ambition driving both of them. Both secession movements answered to some real social and economic forces.

Regional self-confidence

It appears that during the half-century or so preceding these events, the Gallic provinces had reached a level of prosperity that they probably never reached again.[18] They had strong economic interests to defend, and when the invasions by Franks and Alamanni across the Rhine began in earnest, they urgently needed an effective on-the-spot protector and had the financial muscle to support and pay for that protection. In other words, the Gallic empire was in part a symptom of growing regional self-confidence. Similarly, Palmyra had experienced rising financial prosperity based on its command of a lucrative trade route and had strong economic interests to defend and needed an effective on-the-spot protector, which its citizens found in the persons of Odenathus and then Zenobia and her generals.

On the cultural front the three provinces into which Gaul was divided during this period of prosperity retained and to a degree revived elements of their pre-Roman culture, just as Palmyra retained and displayed – much more obviously – strong elements of her semitic and non-Greek origins, despite being incorporated into the Roman empire. In both cases, there was thus a degree of local nationalism at work, even though in neither case should this component be blown up into a pure nationalist rebellion, as some have been tempted to do.[19] Nor should these secessions be seen as early prototypes for the later Frankish/French state of later centuries or of the independent Syrian state that only came into being in the mid-twentieth century – tempting as that is. Growing wealth had certainly brought increasing regional self-confidence, and the grant of citizenship to all free men of the empire by the emperor Caracalla in 213, had widened the scope for career ambitions among formerly subject nations and among soldiers who previously had been confined to the non-citizen auxiliary units. The regions benefited.

Asset or threat?

So were the two separatist movements, while they lasted, more of an asset than a threat to the empire, (perhaps paradoxically) helping to prevent rather than precipitate its disintegration at this time of crisis? Were they part of the problem, or part of the solution? On the basis of positive judgments like that of Eutropius, both the Gallic secession and the Palmyrene secession are often characterised as creating effective defensive bulwarks of the empire against its dire external threats. By holding on to territory that might have otherwise been lost, some argue, they made it easier to put the empire back together again.[20] The secessionist leaders are characterised as able and wise men (and a woman) who did Rome's job for it and were in effect saviours of the empire.[21] This characterisation must however be treated with caution. Perhaps it is an invention. One reason is that the *HA* in its praise of the separatist leaders is patently using this argument as a way of discrediting the legitimate central emperor, Gallienus, who (according to the *HA*) was not up to the job. Such a verdict is unfair. Gallienus had his hands full on all fronts. Far from being an asset, the situation in Gaul as viewed from Rome must have looked increasing unpredictable and menacing as time went on, and Gallienus did try to put a stop to it. In 265 he attempted to displace Postumus and twice came near to defeating him in battle, only to be twice frustrated, once almost certainly by double-dealing by Aureolus and once because he was wounded by an arrow and had to retire. His hostility towards the Gallic secession was continued by his successors. From Rome's point of view, 'what had started as a helpful reaction against a threat to Roman rule had become a threat to that very rule itself'.[22]

The next emperor, Claudius, while himself occupied elsewhere, moved against Gaul in 269, sending in one of his senior commanders, Julius Placidianus, to occupy parts of southern Gaul, notably Grenoble but perhaps including some Alpine passes, at a time when Spain also seems to have reverted to direct rule from Rome. Whether or not this was a limited effort at containment rather than a full-scale offensive against the Gallic empire, it was hardly taking a passive or permissive attitude.[23] Claudius failed to come to the aid of the city of Autun when it tried to revert to Roman rule, but this is evidence more of the incipient disintegration of the Gallic secession than of Claudius' intentions. The Aedui of

7. The French connection: guardians of the Rhine

Autun jumped the gun and paid a terrible price for it when the angry Gallic legions sacked their city. In short, it is not the case that the emperors in Rome simply sat back and allowed the Gallic secession to get on with the job of defending the Rhine frontier with their tacit approval. They did not see it like that at all. When and as they could, they tried to stop it. It was left to the emperor who took over after Claudius died of the plague, Aurelian, to push this policy to its logical conclusion and finish off both secessions.

When he became emperor, Aurelian chose to confront Zenobia and her supporters in the east first, and some have interpreted this as a decision by Aurelian that Zenobia and her territorial gains were the greater threat of the two, and so had to be eliminated first. On the contrary, it is more likely that he expected Zenobia to be the easier to eliminate, so decided to tackle her first as he built up his support and his military resources for the final confrontation with the danger nearest home, the Gallic secession. He surely knew that the fight with the professional Gallic legions would be the toughest, and so it was to prove.

The two separatist movements, in the east and in the west, had common characteristics – something more than common usurpers, something less than full-scale empires; something more than personal ambition, something less than a claim to the Roman imperial throne; something more than temporary, something less than permanent; something more than a military escapade, something less than a nationalistic uprising. Both began as a positive response to external threats to the empire, both developed into an internal threat to the empire. Neither went down easily when the central Roman war machine finally attacked. That said, neither movement had any long-term future. They were or became too unstable, and were to prove no match for the core provinces of the empire which, at that period of Roman history, produced most of its generals and soldiers. In hindsight, one can see that either both secession movements would succeed or neither. Symbolic of this east-west symbiosis was the presence in the emperor Aurelian's victory parade held in Rome in 274 of both the last emperor of the Gauls, Tetricus, and of Zenobia herself, last ruler of Palmyra. Who was this man who finally brought both secessions to heel?

8

Warrior and showman: the 'puzzling' emperor Aurelian

What sort of man was the Roman emperor who in 271/2 finally set off to confront Zenobia for a show-down on her own ground? With justice the *Cambridge Ancient History* calls Aurelian 'the most puzzling of the emperors of the period', and another author comments that 'few would leave a legacy more deeply contested'.[1] Orosius, who lived over a century after Aurelian's time, tells us in his *History against the Pagans* that Aurelian 'excelled in the art of war', and Eutropius at about the same time agrees that he was 'an effective man at war'.[2] Malalas calls him 'the warrior'.[3] On the other hand, the main weight of comment from most Roman-era commentators concerns his alleged cruelty, his *severitas*. Eutropius says that he had 'an unrestrained temper and was excessively inclined to cruelty'.[4] Lactantius says he was 'fierce and headstrong and prone to cruel acts'.[5] The *Historia Augusta* keeps coming back to this theme of cruelty. Aurelian, it says, 'was a stern, savage and blood-thirsty prince'[6] characterised by 'excessive ferocity'[7] and lacking that supreme gift of emperors, *clementia*, the quality of mercy.[8] The *Epitome of the Caesars* accuses him of 'extreme cruelty' in suppressing the so-called mint workers' revolt at Rome in his first year of office.[9]

The near unanimity of our sources is striking, especially as it appears to be backed up by Aurelian's imperial peer group – if the *HA* is to be believed. Already in the middle of Aurelian's military career, well before he aspired to the highest office, the ill-fated emperor Valerian is reported there to have referred in a letter to Aurelian's 'excessive severity ... not suited to our times'.[10] Aurelian's distinguished but hardly squeamish successor the emperor Diocletian is reported by the same source to have said that Aurelian should have stuck to being a general rather than an emperor.[11] Eutropius sums up Aurelian by saying that he was 'a necessary emperor rather than a kind one'[12] and in very similar terms the *HA* sums up Aurelian as a 'necessary rather than a good emperor'.[13] That might be called damning with faint praise. Malalas in his *Chronicle*, written in the sixth century, appears to buck the trend when he praises Aurelian for his magnanimity, but then seems to contradict himself by reporting that he severely punished the mint workers of Antioch when they also, like their equivalents at Rome, rioted.[14] The Roman historian Ammianus Marcellinus tells us that after the state treasury had been left empty by the end of Gallienus' reign, Aurelian 'fell upon the rich like a torrent'.[15]

Any judgment of Aurelian must allow for the hostility of Christian writers towards an emperor who intended, had he lived long enough, to renew the persecution of Christians. It must also allow for the hostility of the senatorial class, to which classical writers tended to belong, towards an emperor who ignored their traditional privileged status and put to death members of their class who opposed him. More puzzlingly, these allegations of excessive cruelty appear to be flatly contradicted by the evidence in favour of Malalas' 'magnanimity', notably the clemency that Aurelian was to show towards the inhabitants of cities that had gone over to Zenobia, and initially towards Palmyra itself – and Zenobia herself. So is Aurelian the victim of class prejudice, the hostility of the Roman upper and senatorial class towards an upstart foot-soldier? Or of the common presumption among Christian writers that anyone who even proposed to persecute the true church was intrinsically evil?[16]

Balkan origins

Aurelian's family probably lived somewhere near the city of Sirmium in the Roman province of Pannonia, now Sremska Mitrovica in modern Serbia, not far from Belgrade.[17] His father is said to have been a *colonus* (something like a tenant farmer) on an estate owned by the Roman senator and aristocrat Aurelius – hence Aurelian's full Latin name of Lucius Domitius Aurelianus.[18] Other authors place his birth more vaguely in the Roman provinces just south of the Danube river. In Roman terms, he was an Illyrian, and unlike Zenobia he would have spoken Latin as his main or only language. The Danubian provinces, and farmer's sons, had been the main recruiting grounds for the Roman legions for generations. It was no longer, strictly speaking, a Roman or even Italian army, as it had been during Rome's greatest period of imperial expansion. The Illyrians were in effect both geographically and militarily the core of the empire, and by Aurelian's time they also ran it.

Aurelian was born in September of 214 or 215 – we don't know exactly which. His mother is said by the *HA* to have been a local priestess of the Sun cult, but that could be an invention based on Aurelian's later interest in that cult.[19] Aurelian would have joined the Roman army at around the age of 20, in about 235. According to the *HA*, he was tall, good-looking and famous for his strength, if a bit prone to eat and drink too much. Malalas says that in later life he was 'tall, slender, slightly bald, with small eyes and completely grey beard'.[20] He also quickly earned a reputation for being quick on the draw – with a sword, of course. Among his fellow soldiers he got the nickname *manu ad ferrum* (which we may translate as 'hand on hilt'), a foretaste perhaps of his later displays of quick anger and resort to violence. That is according to the *HA*, which goes on to report the most absurd feats of arms allegedly performed by Aurelian in battle.

Among his *egregia facinora*, says the *HA*, his 'remarkable exploits', was the slaying of 48 Sarmatians in a single day, and a grand total of 950 of them in just a few days, so that little boys made up songs and jingles about his derring-do.[21] There is a story in the *HA* about his being adopted in mid-career by one Ulpius Crinitus, in an elaborate ceremony held at Byzantium in the presence of the emperor Valerian.[22] This reads like pure fiction, but it does underline how Aurelian too could be the stuff of legends and invention. His insistence on stern discipline in the army units he commanded also became legendary, and much more plausibly so. The *HA* has a story that a soldier under his command was caught in adultery, so his legs were tied to two separate bent-over saplings so that once the saplings were released the wretched man was torn in two.[23] True or false? Some say fanciful, some say only too likely to be true.

Sirmium and the soldier emperors

By the time Aurelian joined the army, a seismic change had taken place in the governance of the Roman empire. In broad terms, however much skullduggery had been going on – and there was a lot of it – from the time of Augustus emperors had been chosen from the aristocracy and the senatorial class, preferably in some kind of dynastic succession, and were subject to at least the nominal approval of the formally assembled Senate at Rome. But at almost exactly the time Aurelian joined the army, the emperor Alexander Severus, the last of the quartet of emperors that formed the Severan dynasty, was assassinated in 235, and there set in the era of the so-called 'soldier emperors', senior generals who one after another were proclaimed emperor by the army, or by a powerful section of it, without any pretence of dynastic, aristocratic or senatorial legitimacy. It began with Maximinus the Thracian, who, says Eutropius, 'was the first to come to power solely as the choice of the soldiers, since the authority of the Senate had played no role and he himself was not a senator'.[24] He was also, like Aurelian after him, a 'ranker', having signed on as an ordinary foot-soldier. This was the atmosphere in which Aurelian's entire career was formed, and from which he was to benefit when he too rose from bottom to top by the same escalator of military promotion. It was a system that made Aurelian emperor – and then destroyed him.

What is more, the soldier emperors that ruled Rome from 235 onwards came in the main (though not entirely – Philip the Arab was a notable exception) from those self-same provinces on the Danube that we may today call the Balkans. Among them, the men of Sirmium played a strikingly prominent role. Indeed, the Roman empire seems to have been ruled for much of the century by a cabal of soldier-emperors and would-be emperors who came from not just the Balkans, but from the Sirmium area in particular, so in many cases may be presumed to have known each other, served with or under each other and shared a very similar military and political outlook. Decius (emperor 249-251) was the first of this group of Sirmian emperors, and by his time Aurelian had already been in the army for 15 years. Aurelian's immediate predecessor Claudius (268-270) and Claudius' brother Quintillus (very briefly in office in 270) came from the same Danube area. Then came Aurelian himself, followed by Aurelian's colleague and successor-but-one Probus (276-282).

Other emperors came from a very similar part of the empire, such as Maximinus the Thracian and most famously Diocletian, emperor from 284 until – *mirabile dictu* – he retired from office in 305 to live and die naturally of old age in his immense palace complex which still stands at the heart of the modern tourist resort of Split on the coast of Croatia. But even he chose as his first back-up co-emperor Maximinianus, who came from near Sirmium. Indeed, for over a century, starting with Claudius, there would be only one emperor who did not come from a Balkan family.[25] If these men lacked the dynastic blood-line legitimacy of previous generations of emperors and the sanction of senatorial approval, neither were they just a haphazard collection of upstart, boorish and ignorant foot soldiers, as they are often portrayed. There was, in effect, an Illyrian dynasty and within that a Sirmian dynasty almost as tight as any bloodline or class connection, and this should give pause to those who see this period as one of endemic instability and chaos – an 'age of anarchy'.[26] Between them, the Illyrians saved the empire.

In Roman times, Sirmium became one of the most important cities in the empire; it had been an important military base since the time of the emperor Marcus Aurelius. It was a provincial capital, had a fleet operating on the Danube, a mint for striking coins, and an arms factory. Later, under the Tetrarchy set up by Diocletian not many years after the death of Aurelian (the Tetrarchy was an experiment in devolved government whereby the empire was divided into four parts for administrative and military purposes, each with its own co-ruler), Sirmium became one of the decentralised capitals of the empire, along with such cities as Trier, Milan, and Nicomedia. None of them, be it noted, was Rome itself. Rome continued to have great political and psychological importance. But it was no longer Rome's empire, and it is an interesting and much debated question as to whose empire it now was. Did the army exist to protect the empire and its people, or did the empire exist to justify and pay for the massive and expensive military machine?

Today Sirmium has largely disappeared from sight. After being abandoned to 'barbarian' occupants when the Roman empire contracted in the fifth century, the city was decisively sacked by raiding Avars in 582, and that was its end. It is said that the modern town is the site of the largest unexcavated Roman racecourse arena anywhere in the empire. Unfortunately, unlike some former Roman racecourses such as that in modern Libya outside Leptis

Magna, it lies squarely under the modern town centre, and an offer some years ago to relocate inhabitants to a new town so that excavations could take place was turned down by the local authorities.

The cavalry commander – *capax imperii*

Nothing much is known about Aurelian's early career. He comes into clear view quite late, when he was already in his fifties, and it is as a cavalry commander – a crucial fact about him when it came to his two decisive military encounters with Zenobia, both of which were primarily cavalry battles. Aurelian was probably already one of the senior military officers on the staff of the emperor Gallienus when Gallienus moved to meet the massive Gothic invasions into Asia Minor and the Balkans in the year 267 and then hurried back to Italy to confront a revolt by his new cavalry commander Aureolus, based in Milan. Gallienus had reorganised the cavalry of the Roman army to make it the centre of Rome's new mobile strike force. Traditionally Rome had relied for its defense on its infantry, its famous legions stationed at fixed point round the empire's perimeter. Now the cavalry was moving towards the pivotal role that it came to occupy in the following century as the elite arm of Rome's rapid response force. During the third century the ratio of cavalry units to infantry units increased from 1:10 to 1:3.[27] Aureolus was the cavalry's first overall commander, and the first but not the last to realise the potential of this key military appointment as a springboard to supreme power. The commander of the cavalry was *capax imperii* – capable of being emperor.

When Aureolus came out in revolt and was killed, Gallienus promoted Claudius, more or less a contemporary of Aurelian, to replace him as cavalry commander, little knowing that both these men were part of a group of senior officers from Illyria that was plotting his assassination. After the assassination Claudius took Gallienus' place as emperor and he promoted Aurelian to be commander of the famous Dalmatian cavalry units and thereafter to his own old position as commander-in-chief of the entire cavalry, *dux equitum*.[28] Aurelian was to

Roman light cavalry depicted on Trajan's column in Rome.

107

take full advantage of this key position when his turn unexpectedly came for a shot at the top job.

The Gothic invasions and the making of Aurelian

As cavalry commander Aurelian was in the thick of the intense fighting that took place all along the northern Rhine-Danube borders of the empire as successive invaders, chiefly the formidable Goths, sought to plunder if not actually occupy prime Roman territory. In judging Aurelian's career, it is important to understand this gathering threat to the ancestral Italian heartland of the empire. Hostilities with the Goths went back twenty years or more. Hardly had the emperor Philip the Arab finished his elaborate celebrations of Rome's 1000th anniversary as a city in 248 than the first of many invasions by the Goths, other Germanic peoples and some non-Germanic forces began to break into the frontiers of the empire in search of plunder and booty. Rome's millennium was also almost its Armageddon. The exact dates, sequence and frequency of these invasions are far from clear, but their seriousness is absolutely clear. The Goths invaded the Balkans in 249-250 and again in 253. Over the years 262-267 the Goths ravaged parts of what is now Turkey, and in 268, while Gallienus was still emperor, stormed Athens itself, cultural capital of the Greek east.[29] On the Rhine frontier a tribal coalition called the Franks invaded Gaul in 260 and even penetrated as far as Spain[30] – their first entry into history as the eventual founders of modern France – the same year as the Alamanni and Juthungi first attacked Italy itself. Then in early 269, in his new capacity as cavalry commander, Aurelian would certainly have played a big part in the defeat that the new emperor Claudius inflicted on the invading Alemanni (about whom the writer Ammianus tells us that they 'had long hair, dyed red, and liked strong drink'[31]) and their allies the Juthungi near Lake Garda in northern Italy.

Later in 269 there came another huge Gothic invasion, this time seaborne. Aurelian was once again at the eye of the storm with his Dalmatian cavalry which was also to feature prominently in his confrontation with Zenobia.[32] Zosimus tells us that a confederacy of tribes headed by Goths (whom he calls 'Scythians') mustered at the mouth of the river Dniester with 6,000 boats and 320,000 men; they apparently (an ominous sign) had siege engines with them as well, because after failing to take several Black Sea towns and losing ships and men in bad weather, they laid siege to the important Greek coastal city of Thessalonica and almost took it, using these siege engines. They then started plundering the countryside, but this was when Aurelian and his cavalry rode to the rescue and checked them, and when Claudius with the main Roman army arrived the Goths suffered their heavy defeat at Naissus, allegedly losing some 50,000 warriors in the battle.[33] So by the time he became emperor, Aurelian was not just an experienced warrior, but in particular a highly experienced and successful cavalry commander fully aware of the potential of his military office, and also fully aware of the fragility of the empire.

Aurelian the conspirator

How Aurelian got to be emperor, shows a different and less heroic aspect of his character. Going back to 268, while Aurelian's predecessor as cavalry commander Aureolus was still under siege in Milan after his abortive revolt, the Illyrian generals around the emperor Gallienus plotted to assassinate him, perhaps because of dissatisfaction with his handling of the appalling crisis then afflicting the empire, or perhaps for other reasons too.

> Gallienus displayed a lack of comprehension for the intellectual currents of his time. People no longer showed much understanding for androgynous beings and his cultural activities were regarded as useless pastimes, unsuitable for an emperor. Some of his more extreme expressions of self-deification probably even aroused resentment in his entourage.[34]

The conspirators included Claudius, Gallienus' new cavalry commander, and Heraclianus, the general who according to one source was the chief conspirator but with Claudius in on the plot.[35] According to another source it may have been Aurelian himself who was the principal plotter.[36] Aurelian must at least have been party to the conspiracy. Gallienus was given a false alarm about a faked enemy attack, rushed out at night without his bodyguard and was run through with a spear. Later his brother, his widow, and their only surviving son were also dispatched. It was a ruthless coup d'état, one among many in that bloody century. Ironically, but perhaps as a familiar copycat ruse, Aurelian in his turn was to be assassinated at the peak of his powers by means of a similar deception. He who lives by the sword, shall it seems die by the sword.

With Gallienus thus removed, Claudius was quickly proclaimed emperor in his stead. When two years later in 270 the plague swept away Claudius, the gate to power was suddenly open again, and there were two men who were deemed *capax imperii* – Claudius' brother Quintillus and, of course, the master of horse Aurelian. The outcome showed once again Aurelian's ruthless drive for the top. Quintillus was said to be 'a man of singular moderation and grace', and as the next of kin to the deceased emperor was the natural and theoretically legitimate successor. Indeed, some of the army thought so too. Quintillus was in Rome, and we may suppose that it was the Praetorian Guard stationed there that favoured him. The Senate promptly ratified his claim, thus enhancing his legitimacy. But what did the Senate matter in that period? Aurelian clearly thought little of it, and when his front-line troops in the Balkans proclaimed him emperor, he does not seem to have been bashful about accepting. Quintillus realised that he stood no chance against Aurelian's legions, his military supporters deserted him, and he either committed suicide by having his veins cut open by a physician and so bled to death, or was killed by his own previous supporters, after a mere 17 days in office.[37] So perished a man who might have been a good emperor.

It was, once again, a ruthless coup d'état, though one in which the main beneficiary as well as chief plotter was Aurelian himself. But it stored up trouble, both for him and for some of the senators who had favoured Quintillus, and Aurelian's subsequent treatment of those senators played a key part in those later accusations against him of excessive cruelty. It also meant that Aurelian was a usurper just like all the others, and left questions, relevant to our understanding of Zenobia's political ambitions, about the legitimacy of his claim to the throne. It is interesting that Aurelian, in an effort to ward off this charge of being a usurper, dated his reign from the day of Claudius' death, so implying that it was Quintillus, not himself, who was the usurper. In this way, late in the year 270, Aurelian became emperor at about the age of 56, with a track record of swift military promotion, harsh severity verging on cruelty, intense and successful cavalry engagements, and conspiracy to murder. Not an attractive record. But perhaps the times called forth the man.

Aurelian's first year: the showman

Aurelian would have become emperor around September/October 270, and by September of the following year he was setting out from Rome for the east to confront Zenobia. The year in between was a year of frenetic activity, and shows one of Aurelian's main and most impressive qualities – his raw energy. No wonder Malalas calls him 'quick moving'.[38] The exact chronology and detail of what happened are disputed. But the main lines of events are clear enough. With some of the Goths still marauding around the Balkans, Aurelian was immediately confronted with two or possibly three new incursions into Roman territory, one by Vandals across the upper Danube, and one or perhaps two into Italy itself by the Juthungi, who had already been in conflict with Rome before. Alongside all that, Aurelian had to get to Rome to consolidate his imperial position in the empire's symbolic capital.

The Vandal attack was repulsed by Aurelian and a peace agreement negotiated.[39] The main debate concerns whether there were two incursions into Italy by the Juthungi on either side of the Vandal attack, or only one after it.[40] But the sheer amount of riding and marching to and fro by Aurelian that would be entailed by supposing one Vandal and two Juthungian invasions within such a short space of time surely means that there can only have been one. More interesting for an analysis of Aurelian's character are the question of who and what these Juthungian invaders were, and the significance of the famous river-bank meeting

110

which Aurelian held with their envoys when they bargained for a laissez-passer to get back home. These tell us a lot about another, more unexpected talent that Aurelian now began to display – a talent for showmanship, or what one modern author calls 'the power of display'.[41] He was to show that talent for showmanship in Rome itself in 274, with Zenobia playing a star part in the show.

Some say that the invasion by the Juthungi was a massive incursion involving many thousands of Germanic horsemen in an onslaught of the *terror germanicus* (German terror) that threatened the empire's Italian heartland on a scale not seen since the time of Hannibal over 400 years before and a foretaste of what was to come in the final break-up of the western empire in the fifth century. If that was the case, Rome was in grave peril of a terrible sack. But was it? What appears to have happened is that after dealing with the Vandals Aurelian suffered a serious setback when he first encountered the Juthungi in northern Italy, and so they continued on their way southwards following the Via Aemilia down into modern Umbria and continued down the east coast to what is now Fano, deep into Italian territory, with Aurelian in pursuit. They then appeared to turn inland along the Via Flaminia (which began at Fano) in the direction of Rome itself, where panic set in, since the city was largely defenceless. But on the river Metaurus near Fano Aurelian caught up with them again and inflicted a severe defeat. As a result of that they sent envoys to negotiate a safe passage home.

This meeting is recorded by the Greek writer Dexippus in his work *Scythica*, some substantial fragments of which survive.[42] Dexippus, incidentally, had organised resistance to the Goths when they attacked Athens, so he knew something about warfare. In their presentation to Aurelian during the cease-fire talks, the Juthungi boasted that they had at their disposal 40,000 experienced warriors on horseback. This claim lies at the heart of the supposition that, even allowing for exaggeration of numbers, this was a massive Germanic invasion army that came hard on the heels of the great Gothic invasion of the east and came near to destroying Rome itself, and with it perhaps the Roman empire. Was this the absolute nadir of the 'third-century crisis'?

On the other hand, this is perhaps a gross exaggeration. Perhaps Aurelian was dealing with nothing worse than roving bands of marauding horsemen who, however much a nuisance, were too small to be able to threaten the might of the Roman empire.[43] It all depends on that one phrase that the Juthungian envoys are reported by Dexippus to have used, the phrase or boast that may be translated as 'we can put into the field' 40,000 horsemen.[44] The point is that the envoys do not necessarily say that they have actually put that many horsemen into action: just that they could do so, true or not. The force that penetrated Italy could have been much smaller, not migrating tribesmen but bands of young warriors maybe 500-600 strong exploiting current Roman weaknesses to win fame and glory.[45]

River-bank theatricals

Aurelian at any rate does not seem to have been too bothered by the Juthungi, judging by the grand reception he laid on for their negotiators – a classic set-piece of imperial bluff. Dexippus' vivid account is as colourful as anything in the *HA*:

> When Aurelian heard that delegates of the Juthungi were coming to sue for peace, he ordered his troops to be drawn up in full battle formation. Then he ascended high up onto a lofty platform, clothed in purple, and had the whole army formed up in a moon-shape around him. His officers present were all on horseback. Behind the emperor were the standards of the army clustered together. There were golden eagles, portraits of emperors, and lists written in golden letters of the army units, carried on silver-covered spears. Then he ordered the Juthungi to be brought in. They were stupefied, and at first did not know what to say.

It must have been an intimidating scene. In the event, Aurelian refused their request for peace and chased them out of Italy, with heavy losses to their ranks. Few seriously doubt that this scene actually took place as described by Dexippus. The question is, where did it take place? Dexippus seems to imply that it took place on the banks of the river Danube. But that makes little sense. If the Juthungi were virtually home already, why negotiate for a safe passage home? The scene only makes sense if it took place when the Juthungi were furthest away from home and knew their luck had run out. So it is better located on the river Metaurus, just after their first defeat by Aurelian, outside Fano. Aurelian's evident talent for showmanship was to find further and more grandiose outlets as his reign consolidated.

The wall as theatre

Aurelian's most visible response to the invasion of the Juthungi was to build a defensive wall around central Rome. His great wall still to this day encircles the inner section of modern Rome. Yet not many tourists who queue alongside a part of it to get into the Vatican Museums, and not many motorists who drive through its gateways to and from down-town Rome, know exactly when or why he put the wall there. When he put it there, is a comparatively easy question to answer. Why, is however controversial. Aurelian's Wall was later much extended, mainly upwards, for purposes quite different to those he intended, by Roman emperors and claimants to the imperial throne, by Byzantine generals, by medieval popes and monarchs, and was the scene of Garibaldi's last stand against the foreign enemies of the City of Rome's brief experiment as a republic in the mid nineteenth century. In short, it is a wall saturated with almost two millennia of history, despite its rather plain and architecturally undistinguished appearance, a wall much in use until modern gunpowder, iron

Aurelian's wall: the Porta San Sebastiano.

cannons and shot made brick and cement walls fatally vulnerable and so obsolete. But the basic structure of the wall is Aurelian's.

On arrival at Rome after dealing with the Vandals and the Juthungi Aurelian personally oversaw the start of work on the wall, which is nearly 19 kilometres in length and encloses some 2,500 hectares.[46] The wall is basically made of Roman-style concrete, faced with brick or tile, and is just over 6 metres high and over 3.5 metres thick. A rampart walk ran along the top, raising the total height to 8 metres, and the wall is dotted with over 380 towers built to enable the use of Roman *ballistae* (catapults) to engage an enemy, but with 18 main gateways and many smaller ones left in the wall. To get the wall built quickly, Aurelian pressed into service the trade guilds of the city, since he had no soldiers to spare except perhaps some military engineers for supervision work, and the guilds were given the honorary title 'Aureliani' in recognition of their services. Even so, the wall was only finished under Aurelian's successor Probus,[47] and it was left to a later pretender Maxentius in the next century to raise the wall to its present height of 15 to 20 metres.

Criticisms have been made of Aurelian's wall. One is that it was not high enough and had too many gateways in it to repel any sizeable professional army. Another is that to defend the walls would have needed

113

some 700 *ballistae* and at least twice that number of men trained to use them – a quite unrealistic requirement. Only with the massive improvements of Mexantius, especially his provision of high-level archery slits all round, did the wall become a serious defensive wall. Up to then, say the critics, it was not much better than the studio scenery walls that figure in so many Hollywood sandal-and-toga epics – in other words, gesture politics or PR invention. In summary, 'His Roman walls were imposing but in military terms superfluous and flawed.'[48]

But a prolonged siege is not what Aurelian's wall was originally intended for. If indeed the Juthungi constituted, or could again constitute, a huge Germanic invasion force menacing Rome itself, armed with siege engines like the Goths at Thessalonica, then perhaps the wall could be dismissed as token theatre or political bluff designed to buy time and reassure the city's inhabitants, in the hope that the bluff would never be called. But if these were really bands of roving mounted marauders large enough to be a nuisance but not large enough to bring Rome, the city or the empire, to its knees, then the wall was fit for its limited purpose, which was to prevent those marauders from riding unhindered into the city and inflict a sort of smash-and-grab raid on its treasures. Aurelian's wall, with gates that could be closed, was good enough for that. Of course it had a domestic political purpose as well.

Trouble on the home front

While at Rome, Aurelian faced a serious internal challenge to his authority. He was attempting to reform the much debased currency issued at Rome, whose silver content had shrunk alarmingly over preceding decades. Aurelius Victor tells us that at the instigation of the treasurer of the mint, one Felicissimus, there followed a revolt by the mint workers when Aurelian discovered that they had been tampering with the coinage by extracting silver for their private profit. The fighting to put down the revolt was so intense, says Victor, that 7,000 of Aurelian's soldiers were killed.[49] It is impossible that civilian mint workers on their own could have put up such a stiff fight. So something else must have been going on as well. It looks more like civil war. Zosimus tells us that

> the situation round Rome was in turmoil as certain senators were brought to trial on the grounds of plotting together against the emperor and were sentenced to death ... and there came under suspicion of revolutionary activity Septimius and Urbanus and Domitianus [military officers] and they were immediately apprehended and punished.[50]

How all these events were connected, if at all, we can't know. It is interesting that the mint workers at Antioch were also tampering with the currency, and were also punished by Aurelian,[51] so this type of corruption

En route for Palmyra.

may have been rife, and one cannot fault Aurelian for cracking down on it, just as he cracked down on various provincial officials accused of extortion and embezzlement.[52] The senators on the other hand may have been members of that faction that favoured Quintillus as emperor, and saw in the mint workers' revolt a chance to reassert themselves. They may also have been protesting against the still recent decision by the emperor Gallienus to bar senators from senior army commands, which tradition-ally had been a senatorial prerogative and one source of their power.[53] The military officers on the other hand may have been chancing their arm as usurpers, like so many before them, and their elimination may have marked the end of that group of officers that had risen to prominence under Gallienus and served under Claudius. Aurelian had come out top of the heap and intended to stay there.

More than anything else, it was this period of early political unrest and challenge, and how he dealt with it, that earned Aurelian his reputation for cruelty. There is no record of his having pardoned any of his internal enemies. So it is all the more remarkable that, as the next two years were to show, there is solid evidence of his pardoning some though not all of his external enemies – including Zenobia herself. Aurelian may indeed be a puzzle, but in all his actions cold calculation was his most obvious hallmark.

This then is the man who marched east to confront Palmyra. Zenobia was up against a hardened professional soldier, experienced in the use of cavalry, noted for his energy, ruthless in disposing of enemies, and with an unexpected talent for imperial theatre. All of these qualities would be displayed in his confrontation with Zenobia.

115

Showdown: Aurelian *versus* Zenobia's cooking-pot men

But with her honey Fortune mingles gall:
No longer may she rule, this mighty queen;
She lost her throne, for Fortune made her fall
Into the pit of misery and ruin.
                    Geoffrey Chaucer, 'The Monk's Tale' (Zenobia)

Was Zenobia in any position to withstand or repel the advancing Roman juggernaut? On display in the National Museum of Damascus is a complete set of horse armour found at Tower 19 in the perimeter wall of Dura Europos, the tower through which the Persian king Sapor's army forced its entry into that great Roman frontier fortress on the River Euphrates in 256 and reduced it to the dusty and evocative ruins across which tourists and archaeologist trudge today. We do not know whether it was Roman or Persian horse armour, or whether it was actually used, or whether it was just war booty. Does it offer some clue to Zenobia's military resources and so help to answer the key question of whether she was in any position, militarily, to mount a challenge to or even for the Roman empire, or for a significant part of it? If she was, then that suggests one interpretation of her ambitions. If she was not, then that suggests another, much more modest ambition.

As Aurelian marched eastwards from Rome to Byzantium and then across Anatolia to confront Zenobia in Syria, he must have asked himself much the same question. When the *Historia Augusta* quotes Aurelian as saying that Zenobia 'fears like a woman but fights as if fearing punishment', that would be no bad verdict on what happened – if one could believe the *HA*.[1] It is a neat aphorism more likely to be a literary invention than the *bon mot* of a rough soldier – but who know? The only detailed glimpse we get of what Zenobia's military resources really looked like on the ground is given to us by the writer Zosimus, who describes at some length the two main battles fought between Aurelian and Zenobia.[2] Why he was so much more interested than others in this bout of rather unusual warfare, is not clear. But at least his account can be taken as reliable, even if it is irritatingly vague on some points, like the exact location of each battle. It is also presents a further opportunity to evaluate the *HA*, which for all its blatant faults supports and supplements Zosimus at various junctures.

Zosimus' account raises interesting issues about Zenobia's and Palmyra's strengths and weaknesses. One is the leadership of the Palmyrene forces exercised by Zenobia's general Zabdas rather than by Zenobia herself. Whereas the ever-inventive *HA* portrays her as every inch the fierce warrior queen (she fights), Zosimus represents her as essentially reliant on Zabdas and other military and political advisers. She may therefore have been a politically convenient figurehead for the real controllers of Palmyra. But we have no insider view of that. Secondly, there are clear indications of armed support for Palmyra, actual and potential, from Rome's arch enemy, Persia, which echo the effort made by Odenathus, her assassinated husband, to strike up an understanding with Persia some years before (see Chapter 5). This reinforces the picture of Palmyra and its leaders as double-dealing between Rome and Persia, rather than as loyal or at least cooperative allies of Rome. Pliny's often derided statement about Palmyra being on a political seesaw between Rome and Persia looks close to the truth.

Bring on the cavalry

Then there is the military question of what troops Zenobia could deploy against her advancing opponent. As we have seen, some classical authors were contemptuous of the military force put together by Palmyra. Orosius refers to it as a bunch of peasants (*agresti manu*), and Festus, Jerome and Jordanes take a similarly scornful view.[3] But in the event Zenobia's relied almost solely on her heavy cavalry, the mailed horsemen known as *clibanarii* or 'cooking-pot men', who may or may not have used the horse armour on display in Damascus. The Latin word *clibanarius* is based on the Greek word *kribanon* meaning a cooking-pot or baking oven, and refers to the solid metal helmet that the rider wore with only an eye slit to see through. Zosimus simply tells us that Zabdas and Zenobia used horsemen with heavy equipment, especially breastplates made of iron and bronze. It is Festus who actually terms them *clibanarii*.[4] Why did Zenobia rely on these exotic horsemen, and who were they? How Aurelian, with a more conventional Roman army at his command, coped with these 'cooking-pot men' became the decisive factor in the ensuing engagements.

These mailed horsemen, known also as cataphracts, originated in and were strongly associated with the nations of the Middle East, the Parthians, the Sarmatians and the Persians. Their use went far back into Near and Middle Eastern warfare. King Antiochus III had 3,000 cataphracts at his battle against the Romans at Magnesia in Asia Minor in 190 BC (he lost). But Parthian cataphracts 'blazing in helmets and breastplates ... their horses clad in plates of bronze and steel' played a big part in Crassus' terrible defeat at Carrhae in 53 BC.[5] Similarly, the soldier-historian Ammianus Marcellinus, writing in the century after Aurelian and Zenobia, says of the *clibanarii* that

118

you might suppose them statues polished by the hand of Praxiteles [the legendary Greek sculptor].[6]

The emperor Hadrian was the first to incorporate units of cataphracts into the Roman army, where they were not always successful. In 357 at Strasburg the Roman heavy cavalry broke ranks and fled when confronting the Alamanni.[7] It is not clear what, if any, the difference was between the *clibanarius* and the *cataphractarius*. Both were heavy cavalrymen, and it was of course the latter term which came into general use later on to denote the heavily armoured knights of the Middle Ages. The term cataphract conjures up, for British readers anyway, a vision of the French cavalry clad in gleaming metal charging the British archers at the battle of Agincourt on St Crispin's Day 1415.

Some think that the *clibanarius* had horse armour as well as personal armour, whereas the *cataphractarius* did not. Some say that the former term refers only to the Parthian and Persian armoured horsemen, whereas the latter means any such mailed trooper. The *HA* has the emperor Alexander Severus tell the Senate in Rome that what the Romans call cataphracts, they (the Persians) call *clibanarii*.[8] Some say it is a difference of weaponry – the former had bow and lance, the latter lance and shield. Whichever way, the main offensive weapon carried by these mailed horsemen was a very heavy and very long spear or lance or pike, the *contus*, some 3 to 5 metres in length. The most famous representation of a *clibanarius* in full gear is neither a fresco nor a mosaic nor a stone relief, but a crude graffito found at Dura Europos, probably of a Persian trooper, with horse armour just like the set in the Damascus Museum.

The most famous written description of a Persian mailed trooper is not

Graffito of a cooking-pot man found at Dura Europos.

from a work of history, but from that extraordinary Greek novel entitled *Ethiopian Story*, by Heliodorus. Heliodorus lived at Emesa, proxy capital of Zenobia's mini-empire and site of her second battle with Aurelian, was of semitic origin like the Palmyrenes, and may have lived there only a few decades before Zenobia's time. So he would have known what he was talking about.

> Their fighting equipment is furnished in this way: a picked man, chosen for his bodily strength, is capped with a helmet which has been compacted and forged in one piece and skilfully fashioned like a mask into the exact shape of a man's face; this protects him entirely from the top of the head to the neck, except where eye-holes allow him to see through it. His right hand is armed with a pike of greater length than a spear, while his left is at liberty to hold the reins. He has a sabre slung at his side, and his corselet extends, not merely over his breast, but also over all the rest of his body. His corselet is constructed thus: plates of bronze and of iron are forged into a square shape measuring a span each way, and are fitted one to another at the edges on each side, so that the plate above overlaps the one below, and laterally one overlaps the next one to it, all forming a continuous surface; and they are held together by means of hooks and loops under the flaps ... It has sleeves and descends from neck to knee ... The greaves reach from above the flat of the foot to the knee ... The horse is protected by similar equipment ... His pike projects with its point thrust far ahead: it is supported by a loop attached to the horse's neck ... [The rider's] impetus transfixes anyone who comes in his way and may often impale two persons at a single stroke.[9]

So they were formidable horsemen, but had fatal weaknesses, as events in Syria were to show.

Round 1: the Battle of Immae

A narrative of what actually happened need not take long. Zosimus tells us that as Aurelian advanced across Anatolia in early 272, cities all across the region hurriedly shook off the Palmyrene faction and hastened to reaffirm loyalty to the emperor. This at least shows that Palmyra had met with some support in these cities, as it had in Egypt. Aurelian recovered Ancyra (Ankara), Tyana and all the other cities as far as Antioch, says Zosimus. The *HA* agrees that Aurelian recovered Bithynia without opposition, but disagrees about Tyana, in Cappadocia. It offers a very plausible variant to Zosimus. It says that Tyana shut its gates to Aurelian and had to be stormed by his troops, who wanted to plunder the place (a normal practice with a city that offers opposition) and were only with difficulty restrained by Aurelian, who wanted to create a reputation for clemency – a policy that was to pay dividends later.[10] But the incident once again shows that Zenobia enjoyed substantial support across the Roman east. Arriving in Syria, Aurelian found Zenobia's army waiting outside Antioch to block his advance. Orosius remarks that Aurelian then recovered Syria from Zenobia 'more by fear of battle than by battle itself'.[11] This odd remark may be a hint that Zenobia's 'peasants' were indeed frightened of engaging professional Roman soldiers. There is no mention in Zosimus of any Palmyrene infantry, either in this or in the subsequent major battle. Festus tells us that Zenobia in her eastern adventure relied upon 'many thousands of heavy cavalry and archers', rather than on her infantry.[12] This fits with what Zosimus tells us about the battle:

> noting that the Palmyrene cavalrymen boasted heavy defensive armour and had far more experience in horsemanship than did his own men, he [Aurelian] drew up his infantry apart, across the Orontes River. Then he passed along word to the Roman horsemen not to engage the cavalry of the Palmyrenes at the outset while it was fresh but, having awaited its attack, to appear to take flight, doing this until they should see the enemy riders and horses alike giving up the chase beneath the burning heat as well as the weight of their armour.[13]

Where did this first battle take place? Three Roman-era authors, Syncellus, Jordanes and Jerome, add the detail that it happened at Immae, which lies some miles east of Antioch. It seems clear that Aurelian deliberately chose to place his infantry out of harm's way, on the other side of the Orontes river.[14] The Palmyrene heavy cavalry charged the lighter Roman cavalry, but following Aurelian's orders the Roman cavalry deliberately gave ground. Then when the Palmyrene riders and horses were so exhausted from the heat, from the weight of their armour and from the effort of their charge that they could no longer move, the Roman cavalry counter-attacked and the Palmyrene horsemen just fell off their horses. They were then either trampled to death or cut down with swords. Aurelian's tactical skill won the day.

Aurelian, it will be remembered, had been Rome's top cavalry general, with much experience in fighting Gothic and other horse-borne warriors. Indeed, if the *HA* is right – and it could be – he had once had in his own command a force of 800 cataphracts.[15] So he knew how to deal with them. His tactic also kept his infantry intact for the inevitable second battle, which was just as well given how it turned out. The stragglers from the Palmyrene formation made it back to Antioch, where it was Zabdas who devised a ruse to convince the locals that he had actually captured Aurelian, as a cover for a swift nocturnal evacuation southwards of all his remaining men and of Zenobia herself. One gets the impression that Zabdas, about whom little is known, was a very resourceful man, perhaps the real *de facto* ruler of Palmyra at this time, a second Odenathus. When Aurelian started to implement the rest of his tactical plan, to catch the battered Palmyrenes in a scissor movement between his cavalry and his infantry, he found the bird had flown.

His first reaction was to issue proclamations of amnesty to those citizens of Antioch who had sided with Palmyra but had now fled the city

The hill at Daphne, as depicted in the seventeenth
century by Ortelius.

for fear of reprisals. This again shows how widespread was support for
Palmyra in those crisis years. Call it a gesture of mercy or a shrewd
diplomatic manoeuvre, first practised at Tyana – it worked, and the
self-exiled Antiochenes flocked back into the city, leaving Aurelian free to
deal with his next problem. Zabdas had left behind a rearguard to delay
Aurelian's pursuit, atop a hill above the suburb of Daphne and barring the
road south. This engagement at Daphne is also mentioned in the *HA*, but
as the only engagement outside Antioch.[16] Perhaps this was the only time
that Palmyrene infantry, rustic or not, was engaged. It showed how right
they were to be fearful. Aurelian's men formed the famous *testudo* (tor-
toise) formation, shields above their heads to form a solid canopy of
protection against missiles and stones, and stormed the hill. The defenders were routed, many falling to their death down the craggy hillside.

Round 2: the Battle of Emesa

Aurelian then went on his way, with more cities opening their gates to
him. They could hardly do otherwise. He learnt that the Palmyrene army
was now awaiting him for a second contest, in the plain outside Emesa
(modern Homs). What happened was almost a re-run of the first encoun-
ter, but not quite. Zosimus says that the Palmyrenes and their allies
numbered 70,000, but that number, like most numbers of that era, must
be taken with a pinch of salt. Nevertheless, Zosimus also says that this
time the Palmyrene cavalry far outnumbered the Roman cavalry, and it

seems clear that all along the main Palmyrene force was waiting to meet Aurelian outside Emesa, which had anyway been a sort of proxy capital for the Palmyrene secession. When the two sides met, it was again the Palmyrene heavy cavalry that charged and almost surrounded the weaker Roman force, which suffered heavy casualties. Even the Roman infantry gave ground, which indicates that this time it was engaged in the fight. Clearly, it was not going to be, and was not, an easy victory for Aurelian. The *HA* remarks with justice that Zenobia 'could scarcely be conquered by Aurelian'.[17]

Just possibly history might have turned out differently at this point for Zenobia. But then the Palmyrene cavalry made the classic mistake of breaking ranks and allowed its line-up to become badly disrupted. Then it was the Roman infantry that saved the day for Aurelian. It wheeled around and attacked the disrupted Palmyrene lines, but with a perhaps unlikely ally – a unit of Palestinians armed with clubs and cudgels with which they were able to literally knock the iron cooking-pots off the shelf, or rather the iron-clad men off their horses. The Palmyrene horsemen were apparently terrified of these crude but effective weapons and turned and fled back to Emesa, leaving corpses of men and horses scattered over the plain. This was, in effect, the end. The *HA* remarks that 'the whole issue of the war was decided near Emesa in a mighty battle', but with typical perversity and invention it then attributes that last-ditch rally of the exhausted Roman troops to some sort of divine intervention or vision. What makes this story particularly suspicious is that it is closely akin to the divine intervention that later, allegedly, brought victory to the would-be emperor Constantine in his battle at the Milvian Bridge to become master of Rome and patron of Christianity.

Inside Emesa, the senior Palmyrenes consulted – one more sign that Zenobia was part of a group leadership – and decided to retreat back to Palmyra, partly because the citizens of Emesa were understandably getting restless. The Palmyrenes had to abandon most of their money and assets, which Aurelian promptly seized when he occupied the city. He pursued Zenobia across a hundred miles of often arid steppe, perhaps more quickly than the Palmyrenes thought possible, but not without trouble. The *HA* adds the plausible detail that he was harassed en route by brigands and encountered many mishaps, so that he became exhausted and worn out.[18] The *HA* then records an alleged exchange of letters between Aurelian and Zenobia. Aurelian asks her to surrender Palmyra in return for guarantees about her life and the rights of Palmyra's citizens but without any guarantees about their cash and valuables. Zenobia haughtily refuses, claiming that she was imminently expecting reinforcements from Persia.[19] Whatever you think of the *HA*, such an exchange seems to me quite plausible in the light of Aurelian's policy of clemency at Tyana and at Antioch.

So rebuffed, arriving at Palmyra, Aurelian laid siege to it. Zosimus says that Palmyra had a defensible city wall, and there is much discussion about exactly what and where that wall was, and whether it could really have withstood a siege. The matter is complicated by the subsequent extensive building of defences there by both the emperor Diocletian and the emperor Justinian. Diocletian made Palmyra a garrison town on his elaborate eastern frontier defence line. Nevertheless, Zosimus clearly thought that there was a wall that could be defended. He says that the Palmyrenes hoped that Aurelian would have to give up the siege because of lack of food supplies to this remote place. The *HA* quotes Aurelian as saying that Palmyra was well stocked with defensive armaments, including flame-throwers.

Instead it was the Palmyrenes who ran short of food first and decided to take emergency action. Zosimus has been mocked for saying that at this point they hoped to win help from the Persians. If Palmyra had previously been fighting Persia, why would the Persians send them help? But Zosimus is a relatively reliable witness, and if Palmyra had all along been playing a double game, then a last desperate attempt to arouse the Persians made some sense. The *HA* does say that Aurelian actually cut off reinforcements sent by Persia, so whatever the political motives, the attempt failed.[20] It was probably Aurelian's luck that the Persian monarch Sapor died that same year of 272 so that Persia was in no position to send Palmyra more help than it did.

Zenobia herself then broke out of the city on a swift camel – a she-camel, says Zosimus meaningfully – in an attempt to get to and across the Euphrates river into Persian territory. Perhaps this was indeed a last-ditch attempt to get Persian help. Or perhaps it was just cowardice, trying to get away before she had to face Roman retribution. But Roman horsemen sent after her by Aurelian caught up with her just as she was boarding a boat to cross the river and arrested her. Given the large distance from Palmyra to the river, at least a hundred miles to whatever point she tried to cross it, it must have been a dramatic and drawn-out chase. When the Palmyrenes heard of Zenobia's failure to reach Persia, some wanted to make it a fight to the finish, others wanted to surrender, and it was Aurelian's offer of clemency (not unqualified as it turned out) that tipped the balance. It is possible that a certain Septimius Haddudan, head of the college of priests at the huge Temple of Bel in Palmyra, brokered a peace deal.[21] The city and its citizens surrendered, and that was the end, or almost the end, of the Palmyrene secession.

About the cooking-pot men[22]

Why did the awesome *clibanarii* fail? For all their frightening appearance, such mailed horsemen suffered from inherent weaknesses, as Zabdas and Zenobia discovered – and as the Romans themselves discovered in their own use of cataphracts. They quickly became exhausted because of the

The river that Zenobia failed to cross: the Euphrates at Dura.

weight they carried, especially under a hot sun. If they fell or were knocked off their horses they were almost helpless. Their horses' bellies were vulnerable to foot soldiers who got in between the troopers' ranks. As shock cavalry using shock tactics they might frighten and disorganise the enemy, but their horses would not charge right into a solid wall of disciplined infantrymen, perceiving them as just that – a solid wall. Hence the long pike, intended to enable the trooper to reach into the ranks of opposing infantry at a distance and so disrupt their formation. But the lack of stirrups, not brought into use until much later, must have been a particular disadvantage in achieving that aim. Upkeep was also expensive. For every trooper put into the field, there had to be a spare horse, a pack-horse and a groom.

It would be wrong, however, to dismiss these tanks of the ancient world as more formidable in appearance than in reality. The Roman army increasingly became a cavalry army from the third century onwards in a process apparently begun by the emperor Gallienus and for centuries retained such heavy troopers as part of its array of troop types. Aurelian certainly did not find Zabdas' and Zenobia's mailed troopers an easy push-over at Emesa. But what is striking about the Palmyrene shock attack is that, as far as we can tell from the surviving accounts, it was not properly backed up or supported by archers. Only Festus mentions archers in Palmyra's line-up. Even Heliodorus, mere novelist that he was, knew (see *Ethiopian Story* 9.14) that you should have mounted archers right behind your mailed horsemen, protected by them but able to shoot over their heads and perhaps break up the wall of infantry facing the oncoming troopers so that the horses would then charge right into them and the cataphracts could win the day. The odd thing is that whereas Syria generally and Palmyra in particular were famous for their mounted archers, there appear to have been none present or none actively used at either of the two show-down battles. That, rather than the *clibanarii* themselves, may have been the fatal weakness of the Palmyrene battle-plan. After Palmyra's demise, the Roman army seems to have devised other sources for its increasing reliance on mailed horse-archers.

On the other side, it was Aurelian's skilful and typically Roman use of battlefield tactics that won him the day on both occasions, using almost the same tactics as Constantine later used to defeat Maxentius' *clibanarii* near Turin in 312 in their struggle for control of Rome. Aurelian had lighter-armed Dalmatian and Moorish cavalry at the battle of Immae, which proved much more flexible in their use. These events more than anything else show that Palmyra's army, however competent on its own ground in desert or steppe-lands, could never have mounted a serious challenge on Zenobia's behalf to the professional Roman army.

Who were the cooking-pot men?

What is also odd about Zenobia's heavy cavalry is that at no time before these battles against Aurelian would she and her generals have had any use for such specialist heavy horsemen. Palmyra's successive military campaigns over a short period of time to gain control of Roman Arabia, Egypt and a series of cities in Asia Minor would have necessitated fast-moving mobile forces able to travel long distances. The same applies to Odenathus' earlier forays down the Euphrates as far as Ctesiphon. Our sources make no mention of heavy cavalry in these campaigns, and it would be surprising if there were any. So where did these Palmyrene *clibanarii*, these mounted ovens, suddenly spring from? Some have supposed that it was just the aristocratic youth of Palmyra putting on a show of bravado. But Palmyra was hardly big enough on its own to produce a corps of trained heavy cavalry large enough to face Roman regular horse-men and infantry. Selecting and fitting out these mailed horsemen was a skilled, time-consuming and costly business, with all the back-up they needed. You could not just whistle up these shock troops.

The only people near at hand with the ability to produce a large body of heavy mailed cavalry at short notice when news of Aurelian's imminent invasion reached Palmyra, were of course the Persians. None of our sources say that Palmyra's shock cavalry were actually Persians – except perhaps one. The *HA* says that Aurelian

> declared war on the Persians, whom he had already defeated at the time he conquered Zenobia.[23]

This is an odd statement to make. Even if you distrust the *HA*, it appears logical and inevitable that Palmyra's heavy cavalry must have been either

Persian mercenaries or units of Persian regulars – insofar as there was any clear distinction between the two. If Persia tried to send further reinforcements which were intercepted by Aurelian, and if Zenobia's last throw was to try to drum up last-ditch support from Persia, then it reinforces an insistent and consistent picture of Palmyra attempting to play off its two powerful neighbours one against the other, double-dealing between Rome and Persia, Janus-like looking both ways. This may be why Aurelian appears to have launched a punitive expedition against Persia, which can only have been in the wake of his victory over Zenobia, just to show that Persia could not interfere in Rome's sphere of influence without inviting retaliation.[24] He awarded himself the title *Persicus Maximus.*

Having captured Palmyra, its queen and her leading supporters, and having deflected Persian attempts to help, Aurelian then had to decide how to deal with them, and with the riches that had fallen into his hands. It was to be a test of his *severitas* and his *clementia,* and of his larger ambitions as emperor. It was also to be a test of Zenobia's character. How would she react to defeat, and how would he react to victory?

The end of the affair: golden chains and silver statue

Palmyra's streets and you
Forests of columns in the level desert
What are you now?
                    Friedrich Hölderlin (German lyric poet 1770-1843)
          in his poem *Lebensalter* (*Ages of Life*), tr. David Constantine

How does Zenobia emerge from her conflict with Aurelian? It is from the aftermath of her military defeat, rather than from the military defeat itself, that most of the awkward questions arise about Zenobia's character. Not only had she failed to get across the Euphrates successfully, whether to get Persian help or just to escape, but at her trial she blamed everything onto her closest advisers in order (so it can be alleged) to save her own skin. By so doing she sent them to their deaths, allowed herself to be humiliated by being paraded as a captive in Aurelian's triumph at Rome some months later, and generally can be held responsible, by her reckless behaviour, her *hubris*, for the destruction of the very city that she had championed. Such are the charges against her. Aurelian also stands charged with two accusations of alleged cruelty. One is that he destroyed the uniquely beautiful city of Palmyra, akin perhaps to the purposeless destruction of the beautiful German city of Dresden by Allied bombers in the Second World War. The other is that among the many men he took vengeance on in Palmyra or in cities that had sided with Palmyra was the most famous intellectual at Zenobia's court, Cassius Longinus, who was neither a Palmyrene nor a soldier. For other writer-intellectuals of the Roman empire, this was the worst crime of all.

Zosimus however makes it clear that in the first instance, and in keeping with his previous policy at Antioch and elsewhere, Aurelian pardoned the generality of Palmyra's citizens, accepted their peace offerings, and 'dismissed the citizens unhurt'. His motive was not just, or not so much, clemency as his need for cash and cash equivalent.

> He now became lord and master of the city, its movable and immovable wealth and votive offerings.[1]

Given the high status of the Temple of Bel, those votive offerings would have been very valuable. Probably, whatever else happened, that stripping of financial assets from Palmyra would have ended the city's career as a trading centre. But it did not amount to destruction. That came later, at a time when it could not be laid directly at Zenobia's door – but indirectly, it still could.

The purge of supporters

What cannot so easily be mitigated is her behaviour at her trial. Zosimus tells us that Aurelian returned from Palmyra to Emesa and there put on trial both Zenobia and her main accomplices. The Roman soldiers present at the trial, no doubt angry at the problems that Palmyra had created for them, clamoured for the death penalty.[2] In her defence Zenobia resorted to flattery of Aurelian. She is reported to have told him:

> You, I know, are an emperor, because you win victories ... the others I have never regarded as emperors.[3]

Worse, according to Zosimus, Zenobia claimed that she, a woman, had been led astray by her advisers, so playing the 'I am but a weak woman' card that sits ill with her claimed status as a warrior queen and feminist champion. Some are so outraged at this suggestion that they dismiss Zosimus' story as pure Roman propaganda. Zenobia 'was surely capable of assuming a noble dignity in the face of adversity'.[4]

But Zosimus is as good a witness to events as we have got, and anyway, there may have been enough truth in her self-defence to win her at least a stay of execution. If, as I have suggested, she was less of an absolute ruler and more of a front person for the dominant political faction at Palmyra (an interpretation that later events seem to confirm) then her plea of diminished responsibility may be accepted. Certainly Aurelian found it convenient to accept it, though perhaps for mixed motives. Executing a woman was beneath his dignity, and anyway, he wanted her for his great triumphal parade at Rome. Instead, Aurelian wrought vengeance on just those advisers and accomplices at whom Zenobia pointed the accusing finger. Zosimus does not specify all the names but remarks that, in addition to Longinus, 'others likewise whom Zenobia had denounced underwent punishments'. That meant execution, and presumably included her prominent generals Zabdas and Zabbai. John of Antioch adds the damning detail that her denunciations extended well beyond Palmyra itself to include people in all the cities that had sided with Palmyra. He says that

> Aurelian put to death many distinguished men in each city who were accused by Zenobia.[5]

In the case of the two generals, their fate may be regarded as the pitiless fortunes of war. But Zenobia does not come well out of this episode if it is true that she provided Aurelian with hit-lists of all the chief culprits in different cities, a list that included someone she must have been especially close to, Cassius Longinus. The episode it also shows that Aurelian's much advertised *clementia*, clemency, towards the citizen body of the cities he re-conquered was matched by displays of his equally advertised *crudelitas*, cruelty, towards Zenobia's leading supporters.

Cassius Longinus was not perhaps a top-notch intellectual. Eunapius said that he was more of a 'living library and a walking museum'[6] – a catty hint that he was learned rather than original. A Syrian perhaps born in Emesa, he taught in Athens for around 30 years until the attack on Athens in 267 by invaders from the Black Sea area displaced him and sent him back east. His literary works are largely lost, but he did at an unknown date write a speech in praise of Odenathus, perhaps a politically unwise thing to have done, and was invited to Palmyra to become, at least ostensibly, tutor in Greek to Zenobia and tutor to Zenobia's son Vaballathus.[7] Longinus became the central figure in what has been claimed to be the intellectual circle that Zenobia collected together to adorn her court, in imitation of the circle of savants created some decades before by Julia Domna, Syrian wife of the Roman emperor Septimius Severus. Another member of Zenobia's circle may have been Callinicus, a teacher of rhetoric from Petra who dedicated a ten-volume history of Alexandria to Zenobia, identifying her with Cleopatra. Given Cleopatra's history as a rebel against Rome and her notoriety in the Roman political psyche, this identification may not have done Zenobia much good in the eyes of Rome, even though she herself adopted it. Paul of Samosata, the heretical bishop of Antioch finally deposed by a church synod held in the city at about the time of the death of Odenathus, may have found shelter at Zenobia's court.[8] Other names have been associated with Zenobia's supposed 'cabinet of intellectuals'.

This in turn is used as evidence that Zenobia, in addition to all her other great qualities, was also herself a bit of an intellectual. The *Historia Augusta* says that she spoke Egyptian as well as Greek and Palmyrene and a bit of Latin, and that she was learned enough to compose a summary, an epitome, of the history of Alexandria and the Orient.[9] But this alleged circle of intellectuals is somewhat insubstantial, as is Zenobia's own pretention to be an intellectual, and it is Longinus who bears the odium of the accusation that he was the mastermind and ideologist behind Zenobia's war of secession, the brains behind the muscle. Aurelian presumably agreed with this view, and Zosimus says that Longinus went to his death with dignity, as befits a philosopher. The dignity of his death contrasts with Zenobia's special pleading. The *HA* says that

> it was regarded as a cruel thing that Longinus the philosopher should have been among those who were killed.[10]

But being personal tutor to a queen and to the son in whose name she reigned was inevitably a political as well as a literary position, as in the more famous case of Seneca and the emperor Nero, for example. So Longinus was in an exposed position, to say the least. Like Seneca, he paid the ultimate price.

The second revolt: Palmyra

Even with this blood-letting, Aurelian's problems in the east were not yet over. He installed a 600-man garrison at Palmyra and a regional governor to keep things in order. Then, having as he thought settled matters, he set off for Europe and his next task, confrontation with the break-away regime in Gaul. But no sooner was his back turned than trouble flared up again both at Palmyra and in Egypt – a sign perhaps that there remained widespread support for some alternative to Roman rule. In what seems in retrospect a doomed and foolish venture, the citizens of Palmyra came out in revolt again, massacred the garrison, and tried to persuade the governor, Marcellinus, to have a shot at supreme power – in short, to declare himself a usurper or pretender. Perhaps the Palmyrenes thought they might get a better deal from Marcellinus than from Aurelian. It is hard to know. A certain Antiochus was made front-person of the revolt at Palmyra. He may perhaps have even been Zenobia's other son, which would confirm the dynastic nature of politics at Palmyra. But Marcellinus would not play ball. Instead he warned Aurelian of what was going on.

Aurelian hurried back, surprised the citizens of Antioch at a horse-race (they seem to have spent a lot of time watching the races: the Persian troops of Sapor had surprised them in exactly the same way) and having terrified them with his show of force, just in case they were thinking of emulating or joining the Palmyrenes, he marched on to Palmyra for the second time. He took the city without a struggle, says Zosimus, and it was on this occasion that he razed it to the ground.[11] Some say that the grand ruins of Palmyra still standing prove that this is not correct, that he did not raze the city to the ground. After the extensive rebuilding and remodelling of the site that took place under later Roman emperors and modern archaeologist-administrators, and after the city suffered from later invasions by Arabs (in 634) and by Tamerlane (in 1401), it is impossible to be precise. But the grand ruins still standing may equally prove the opposite, that he did raze the city to the ground: hence the ruins. If he did, Palmyra had asked for it. He had let the city off lightly the first time by the standards of the era, and he wanted no further trouble. With the stripping out of its financial resources and the disbanding (presumably) of its caravan police and local militia, Palmyra's days as a great trading centre were over anyway. The city sank into relative obscurity, just one garrison town along the eastern defence line that Diocletian constructed a few years later to protect his frontier. It was an ignominious and catastrophic end to a secessionist venture that cannot be masked by Zenobia's subsequent glamour status as a warrior queen.

10. The end of the affair: golden chains and silver statue

Ruins of the entrance arch to the Grand Colonnade of Palmyra.

The second revolt: Egypt

Aurelian then marched on to Alexandria, where there had also been a fresh outbreak of resistance to Rome. The *HA* tells us that a certain Firmus was a petty thief (*latrunculus*) who was a friend and ally of Zenobia (*amicus ac socius*) and sought to make Egypt into a free state (*civitas libera*) with the purpose of defending what was left of the pro-Zenobia party (*partes quae supererant Zenobiae*). He succeeded in interrupting the grain supply from Egypt to Rome – a serious matter – but was defeated, tortured and killed by Aurelian.[12] He was, says the *HA*, just a *minusculus tyrannus* – a teeny-weeny pretender. But however vain and foolish it looks in hindsight, this last-ditch revolt in Egypt, like the one at Palmyra itself, is further evidence that there was a deep-seated desire for an alternative to Rome as ruler, and that Zenobia's brief dash for empire was not based just on desert sand, not just a foolhardy venture. It is possible that this bout of fighting around Alexandria was the occasion, or one of the occasions, when serious destruction was inflicted on the famous library of Alexandria. Zenobia's attempted political secession caused a lot of cultural collateral damage. Aurelian meanwhile issued coins from Antioch boasting that he was

Restitutor Orientis and *Pacator Orientis* – Restorer and Pacifier of the East.

But what about *Occidentis* – the West? Having with such difficulty brought the east back under central control, Aurelian now set off to deal with that other and much longer and more dangerous secession, the break-away 'Gallic empire'.

Dealing with Tetricus

Aurelian's opponent in Gaul, Zenobia's opposite number so to speak, was Tetricus, a man possibly from a Gallic family who had risen under the break-away regime to become governor of Aquitania. The soldiers proclaimed him emperor of the Gauls in about 270, at Bordeaux, when that job became vacant. In contrast to his short-lived predecessors, Tetricus rode the tiger successfully until Aurelian invaded Gaul in 273. In the event, and perhaps as a tribute to his diplomatic skills, he successfully rode the tiger even after that. Not one but two Roman authors tell us that Tetricus got fed up, maybe frightened, in coping with his unruly soldiers and their constant mutinies.[13] So he entered into secret and even treasonous correspondence with Aurelian in which he offered to hand victory to the Roman emperor, using a quotation from Virgil to make his point.

Eripe me his, invicte, malis.[14]

Freely translated, this means 'You are the winner. Get me out of this mess.' Fortunately Aurelian as well as Tetricus knew his Virgil, and when the two armies came face to face at Châlons-sur-Marne there was apparently a hard fight at first for appearances' sake but then Tetricus went over to Aurelian, his soldiers were left leaderless, and the so-called Gallic empire was at an end. Zosimus remarks that Aurelian, once again displaying his *severitas*, 'visited the rebels with suitable vengeance'. But Tetricus himself, no doubt as part of the secret deal, not only survived but prospered. What were left of the Gallic legions were incorporated back into the Roman army, where they later played a big part in defeating fresh invasions across the Rhine river frontier. However, as at Palmyra, this was not yet the end of the matter. In Gaul also there was a sort of valedictory footnote which proved that all these secessionist movements were more than about personal ambition and had a basis in deep-seated local or regional concerns for security even after the main actors in the secessions had been removed from the scene. Zonaras tells us that Aurelian in 275 had to quell some further outbreak of unrest in Gaul, just as he had done earlier in Palmyra and Egypt.[15] This is added evidence that there was a strong element of support for what the Gallic emperors and their Syrian counterparts, Odenathus and then Zenobia, were trying to do. But at the end of it all Aurelian had restored the unity of the Roman empire, after a period of fifteen years or so in which it might well have split apart into unstable successor kingdoms. The worst of the 'third-century crisis' of the empire was over. What then happened to Tetricus and Zenobia?

Zenobia's fate

At her trial Zenobia had saved her skin, if not her reputation. There are several versions of what happened next. Which one should we believe? Zosimus reports the most dismal of the possible endings for Zenobia. He says that Aurelian set off back towards Europe taking with him Zenobia and her son Vaballathus plus others who had taken part in Zenobia's rebellion (not of course those he had executed). But he then reports a version in which Zenobia died either of starvation or illness and the rest perished by drowning during the sea crossing from the Asian side of the Bosphorus to Byzantium. Only her son survived the crossing, says Zosimus, but after that we hear nothing more about Vaballathus from any source. He fades from history. Zosimus does qualify this part of his account with 'they say', so he was obviously not sure.[16] Zonaras also reports that Zenobia died on the journey, from grief at her failure, but gives the alternative version that she did get to Rome.[17] Malalas has a more dramatic if cruel ending. He says that Aurelian displayed Zenobia in chains for three days at Antioch then took her to Rome, where he paraded her in his grand military triumphal procession in 274, and then 'he beheaded her in the traditional manner'.[18]

So Zosimus apart, there is broad agreement that Zenobia did in fact make it to Rome, and did figure prominently in Aurelian's triumph. Malalas, Jerome, Jordanes, Festus and Eutropius all agree on that. So does the *HA*.[19] More arguable is what happened to her after that. Malalas is right to say that the traditional culmination for a defeated enemy being paraded through the streets of Rome was to be ritually slaughtered, either by beheading or by being thrown from the Tarpeian Rock so that the unfortunate victim was either fatally broken on impact with the ground beneath or was finished off by waiting solders. But George Syncellus reports that Aurelian

> treated Zenobia with great humanity and honoured her by marrying her to a man of senatorial rank.[20]

Jerome agrees that Zenobia lived on to enjoy an honourable old age at Rome, and Zosimus gives as an alternative version that Zenobia was married off at Rome to a man from the more distinguished classes of society. Several writers add the detail that she had descendants at Rome. The weight of evidence is therefore that she did survive the journey, did feature in Aurelian's triumph, and did live on in respectable and conventional retirement. The *HA* says that she was given a nice villa to live in at Tivoli. Little wonder that Chaucer in 'The Monks' Tale' remarks:

135

She who went helmeted to fight in furious wars
And stormed the stoutest citadels and towers
Must now wear on her head a woman's cap;
And she who bore a sceptre bound in flowers
Must carry a distaff and earn her keep.

Her golden chains; his trousers

But – and this is the crucial question for modern representations of Zenobia – does all that mean that we can accept the entire colourful and exotic description of Zenobia's part in Aurelian's grand triumph handed down to us by the ever fanciful *HA*? For it is on the *HA's* elaborate narrative of the event that Harriet Hosmer's statue *Zenobia in Chains*, Schmalz's painting *Queen Zenobia's Last Look upon Palmyra*, and many other accounts such as those of Chaucer and Gibbon are based. In short, it is to the *HA* that we owe this iconic picture of the great desert warrior queen, defeated but dignified, weighed down in captivity by her golden chains. Her golden chains are what has fired the romantic imagination. That she played a starring role in Aurelian's triumph, is beyond doubt. Festus says that she walked directly in front of Aurelian's chariot. Eutropius and Jerome both add the extra pictorial detail that both she and Tetricus, the defeated last emperor of the Gauls, walked in front of that chariot. Tetricus, a mere male, does not however figure in those modern representations. As a consolation, it is known from several sources that Tetricus not only survived his ordeal but went on to be restored to favour and hold a regional governor's post in Italy.[21] If Tetricus survived and prospered, it makes it all the more plausible that Zenobia did too. But now comes the difficult bit. In a famous purple passage the *HA* says:

> She was led in triumph with such magnificence that the Roman people had never seen a more splendid parade. For, in the first place, she was adorned with gems so huge that she laboured under the weight of her ornaments; for it is said that this woman, courageous though she was, halted very frequently saying that she could not endure the load of her gems. Furthermore, her feet were bound with shackles of gold and her hands with golden fetters, and even on her neck she wore a chain of gold, the weight of which was borne by a Persian buffoon.[22]

If true, this reference to a Persian 'buffoon' (in Latin, a *scurra*) is perhaps the sting in the tale – a reminder of the consequences of dealing with the Persians. Zenobia is also heavily burdened to the point of exhaustion by foot shackles and a neck chain, unlike those modern representations which show her only in lighter hand manacles and still unbowed. So is her ordeal softened for modern sensibilities and ideals. Also colourful but much shorter is the *HA's* description of Zenobia's walking companion.

136

10. The end of the affair: golden chains and silver statue

In the procession too was Tetricus, arrayed in a scarlet cloak, a yellow tunic and Gallic trousers.[23]

Trousers were for barbarians: true Romans wore togas. Tetricus too had to grovel as the price of later forgiveness. The humiliation of Zenobia and Tetricus was emphasised by Aurelian's magnificence. In his procession, says the *HA*,

> there were three royal chariots, of which the first, carefully wrought and adorned with silver and gold and jewels, had belonged to Odenathus; the second, also wrought with similar care, had been given to Aurelian by the king of the Persians; and the third Zenobia had made for herself, hoping in it to visit the city of Rome. And this hope was not unfulfilled, for she did indeed enter the city in it, but vanquished and led in triumph.[24]

Once again, the closing detail is the sting in the tale, as if mocking her ambition. She got her wish, but not in the way she intended. But note that the *HA* says only that she had intended to visit (or more in accord with the Latin, see) Rome in that chariot, not, as some have interpreted it, arrive there as a claimant to imperial power. The *HA* then adds a mass of extra detail about all the animals that bulked out the parade (elephants, tigers, giraffes etc.), and all the captives who marched in it, hands bound, including Goths, Vandals, Arabs and of course some men from Palmyra and some from Egypt.

What are we to make of all that? The story of Zenobia would be much the poorer without this garnish of exotic detail, larded onto a bedrock of acceptable truth. Some dismiss it all just because it is in the *HA*, or argue that it is a gross exaggeration. In particular, it is suggested that Zenobia's role in Aurelian's grand procession, her golden chains and her retirement to a villa at Tivoli are manufactured out of previous events and previous literary accounts, and so highly fictitious.[25] But I am not so sure. Roman triumphs were expensive and elaborately orchestrated affairs, propaganda aimed at the home front as well as at Rome's enemies, a gaudy display of Roman power and invincibility. Accounts of how Julius Caesar forced Cleopatra's half-sister Arsinoe to walk behind his chariot in his triumphal parade at Rome in 46 BC, laden with heavy chains, and then spared her life, may have provided a literary precedent for the author of the *HA* – but it may also have provided a practical precedent for Aurelian, who will surely have known about this famous scene in his own empire's history.[26] As we have seen, he had a keen eye for theatrical effect. What better than to repeat a dramatic scene from his famous predecessor? If anything, the Arsinoe precedent proves rather than disproves the Zenobia story. That Zenobia's chains were golden may be taken as a literary reference to the golden chain mentioned by Juvenal in his sixth satire against women.[27] But that was a simple ornament, whereas many of the display objects on show at these gaudy military triumphs were made of gold and there is no reason why Zenobia's chains should have been any different.

Where Aurelian departed from the Julius Caesar precedent was rather in his treatment of the male partner in the procession. Arsinoe's partner Vercingetorix, the Gallic chief who opposed Julius Caesar, was killed once the triumph was over: Zenobia's partner Tetricus, who may well have worried whether precedent would be followed, was spared and promoted. So without pressing every last detail, the general sense of Aurelian's triumph as given in the *HA* may be accurate enough – accurate enough for it to be fair for writers and artists since Roman times to sense and interpret Zenobia's depth of feeling, caught between conquest and defeat, adventure and humiliation, an unconventional public past as a warrior queen and a conventional domestic future as a Roman matron. At a Roman triumph, it was not always clear who was the real star of the show, the victor or the victim, and in this case, by tradition Zenobia emerges as the star.[28]

She may also have had the last laugh. If she did retire to Tivoli and have more children, as seems likely, she would have lived to see Aurelian assassinated the very next year in a plot by his senior officers that was almost the mirror image of the plot that Aurelian had been implicated in to assassinate his predecessor-but-one, Gallienus. She could then, by a neat irony, have visited the commemorative statue of Aurelian placed by the next emperor Tacitus in the new temple at Rome built by Aurelian with her money to house the spoils of Aurelian's war against her. Aurelian's cult statue would have stood side by side with the very cult statues that Aurelian had looted from her magnificent temple at Palmyra, the famous Temple of Bel. It was a reversal of fortune worthy of any playwright. Zenobia's most lasting legacy to us may have been to provide Aurelian with the wherewithal for Rome's first if clumsy attempt at a monotheistic religion, a prototype for the eventual triumph of Christianity.

The sun-god – *Sol Invictus*

Aurelian's rich spoils from Palmyra enabled him to embark on the most controversial innovation of his short career as a 'puzzling' emperor, an innovation that marks him out as something more than a rough soldier. On his return from Syria he used much of the money seized from Palmyra to build an impressive new temple in Rome, a Temple of the Sun (*Sol*), which was not only decorated with magnificent trophies of his eastern conquest but also featured two cult statues from Palmyra, the statue of Bel itself and (says Zosimus) a statue of the Sun.[29] So whatever else it may have been, his new temple was certainly a celebration of his triumph over Zenobia. The new temple also became a way of sharing Aurelian's triumph with the people of Rome, since its porticoes became the centre for the storage and distribution of free wine to those of the population of the capital city who qualified for free handouts.

Precinct of the Temple of Bel at Palmyra.

The choice of this venue for this popular purpose can hardly have been by chance, and was therefore a political gesture. Aurelian had earlier suppressed severe rioting at Rome and made significant additions to the items of free food distribution as a tactic to keep the city quiet. This not only associated the people of Rome with his eastern triumphs but was also a clear reminder that he had regained from Zenobia the mastery of Egypt, the most vital link in the corn supply to Rome. The corn ships were sailing again, only now you got wine as well as bread, thanks (again) in part to Zenobia's money.

The exact location of Aurelian's new Temple of the Sun at Rome is not known. Some say it stood in the Campus of Agrippa. Much more controversial is the question of what Aurelian intended in building his new temple. Was it just another piece of public architecture to adorn the city, in the grand Augustan tradition of imperial show-off? Or did it have real religious significance in his mind, and if so, what? Was Aurelian just a conservative traditionalist re-affirming the ancestral place of the Sun in the 'pagan' Graeco-Roman pantheon, or was he aiming at a new type of monotheism, a sort of prototype or dummy run for the victory of another monotheism, Christianity? If so, his was a ground-breaking experiment. Or was he aiming rather at what is known in the trade as henotheism, the promotion of one god to be the chief god around whom all others cluster? Or was he experimenting with syncretism, the gradual merging of gods and faiths into one? Or was he perhaps setting up a rival monotheism based on the Sun in a daring attempt to counter the rise of Christian monotheism?[30] By Aurelian's day the Christian church was already well-established, but was notoriously subject to periodic bouts of official persecution. Aurelian himself was about to initiate another bout of persecution when he was (providentially and justly, said the Christians) pre-empted by assassination. So his new temple must have been part of the religious politics of his day.

An ambitious reconstruction of Aurelian's religious programme is given by the French writer Robert Turcan:[31]

> the reform of Aurelian seems to have been inspired by a concern to base the imperial cult on a universal religious feeling and on some sort of cosmic evidence. In principle, solar theology offered the advantage of uniting together the philosophers and the worshippers of idols, the traditionalists of both west and east, even the Christian monotheists or Gnostics, around a common denominator: a religion of the life-giving and unfailing light, *Sol Invictus*.

Turcan points out that Sol Invictus was given the same titles as the emperor – *Augustus, Imperator, Dominus Imperii Romani*. Reciprocally, the emperor is *Invictus* and radiant like the sun. Turcan goes on:

> If the sun was physically the source of life, the life of men depended on the reigning Augustus, dispenser of terrestrial goods and guarantor of civil peace ... There was not just an analogy, but a close solidarity, not to say consubstantiality, between Sol and the emperor. They were like the coregents of the world, the two faces of the same sovereign power ... two aspects of the same *numen* simultaneously present in the sky and on earth.

Much of Turcan's interpretation of Aurelian's religious programme bears striking resemblance to Christianity itself as it evolved under Constantine and became the official religion of the empire with the emperor at its head. Constantine himself also used the banner of *Sol Invictus* when it suited him. Aurelian therefore stood close to a momentous turning point in Roman and European history, and for that we can acknowledge his debt to Zenobia and Palmyra.

But his import of the two statues from Palmyra to be the centre-pieces of his new temple has been met with contempt from some modern historians. Either, it is said, he showed his cultural ignorance as an ill-educated soldier because neither statue was really of a sun-god, so it was at best some sort of pretence; or it was a foolish move because it was not so long since the Syrian emperor Elagabalus (or Heliogabalus) had tried to import into Rome the sun-god of his native city Emesa, of which he was high priest, and was assassinated for his foolishness. The famous black stone that was the cult object of Emesa's sun-worship had been hastily returned to Emesa, where it belonged, and Elagabalus had suffered *damnatio memoriae* (retrospective official condemnation) for his alleged sexual and religious antics at Rome. How could an astute man like Aurelian possibly want to associate himself, however indirectly, with such a clown?

Sir Lawrence Alma-Tadema's famous painting, *The Roses of Heliogabalus*,
depicts the emperor smothering his guests under an avalanche of rose petals.

Aurelian's visions

Then there is the vexed matter of Aurelian's visions. According to the *HA*,
on his way to confront Zenobia Aurelian had not one, but two visions. The
first was at Tyana, the city at the gateway from Turkey into Syria. There
a certain Apollonius of Tyana, a noted sage long since passed away,
presented himself to Aurelian in a dream, urging him to spare the inhabitants of the city, not just out of mercy but also as a politically astute move
to encourage other cities which had similarly sided with Zenobia to surrender to him. It was after all common for rebel cities to be sacked, if only
to provide booty for the victorious soldiers, and the inhabitants might be
sold into slavery. Aurelian got the message, and the political tactic
worked.

The second and (if it happened) more influential vision happened at
Emesa. On visiting the temple there after his victory over Zenobia's army
Aurelian saw and recognized the self-same presiding deity that had shown
itself at the battle itself and aided his victory.[32] This triggered his desire
to build a Temple of the Sun at Rome and to restore the great Temple of
Bel at Palmyra. Many have dismissed these visions as either fabrications
by the author of the *HA* or an inept pre-figuration of the much more
famous Christian vision that the emperor Constantine claimed to have
had before the battle of the Milvian Bridge at which he defeated his rival
Maxentius in 312 for the throne of the western Roman empire. You may

think that such visions were invented, perhaps as convenient political propaganda. But before Aurelian's time the emperor Gallienus had been initiated into the Eleusinian Mysteries while on a visit to Greece to review its defences against invasion. Imperial interest in the mystical experience was not exceptional. In our age of disbelief it is temptingly easy to dismiss out of hand claims to have seen visions. But our ancestors thought otherwise.

Imperial morale

Vision or no vision, Aurelian could have had strong personal and political motives for creating his new temple. The morale of Rome, its self-belief as a conquering empire, had been rudely shattered by the capture alive by the Persian army of a full Roman emperor, Valerian. Even if Valerian had been captured by a trick during negotiations rather than in full battle, as some accounts maintain, nevertheless he was kept alive and humiliated at the Persian court by the victor, Sapor. His humiliation was also Rome's. Something needed to be done to restore Rome's self-belief, and Aurelian may have been feeling his way towards that. He may also have felt that the empire had by his time outgrown a religious system based on a miscellaneous collection of disparate gods that varied from city to city. This dissatisfaction had found its first expression in the attempt, most notably under the emperor Decius in the middle of the century, to create right across the empire a unified and uniform act of worship of the emperor, as a symbol of the moral unity of the empire. This unleashed the major persecution of Christians for which the emperor Decius is best known. Aurelian may have thought that the sun-god could represent some necessary new beginning or focus for Rome's moral unity. Support for this idea comes from his decision to set up a new college of priests to administer his new sun-worship, to rival and sit alongside the traditional centuries-old college of priests (the *pontifices*) that administered the rites of 'traditional' Roman religion. As himself automatically *pontifex maximus* (chief priest) by virtue of being emperor, Aurelian was of course the head of both colleges and therefore head of religion.

It is argued that by renaming the traditional college of priests the *pontifices maiores*, he was acknowledging that they were the 'superior' body of priesthood, and so he can hardly have been promoting sun-worship as the new orthodoxy. But this is to press the meaning of *maiores* too far – it can just mean ancestral, as in the famous phrase *mos maiorum*, the customs of our ancestors, or even just 'the old lot' as opposed to the new. Not long after, the name of the *pontifices maiores* was anyway changed to *pontifices vestales*, so defining their function simply as relating to the traditional rites of Vesta. No trace of superiority there. More likely, Aurelian was feeling his way towards a new orthodoxy but was cut short before he could develop it very far.

How to stay alive

Aurelian had another, more personal motivation for his religious reforms – one which was to prove a total failure. What was it to be a 'legitimate' emperor of Rome? What gave him (or anyone else) a better claim to be recognised as emperor than, for example, Zenobia's son Vaballathus? The traditional process of legitimising a new emperor was by vote of the Senate. But that tradition had long since been swept away during the long years of the successive soldier-emperors. Almost all of them seized power by a military coup or equivalent and had not died in their beds – it was 'dictatorship tempered by assassination'. Aurelian himself had seized supreme power by a more-or-less bloodless coup through acclamation by a part of the army. But did that make him legitimate, or more legitimate than anyone else? Perhaps, by the standards of the time, it did. But it did not solve the other and more pressing problem – how to stay in power and how to stay alive.

He may have thought that by promoting a new form of religious belief with himself at the middle of it as chief sponsor and head pontiff, he could distance himself from the common run of soldiery from which he had emerged and be so garbed in an aura of sanctity that he would be invulnerable to the assassin's sword. The aspiration to avoid that fate may also have lain behind his adoption of the regal trappings for which he was later so criticized, but which became characteristic of the so-called 'dominate' of later years, notably under Diocletian. This expressed itself in the diadem crown and the golden cloak and the habit of *proskynesis* (on which, coincidentally or otherwise, Zenobia had also insisted) whereby courtiers and visitors abased themselves by bowing to the ground or even kissing the feet of the emperor. The *Cambridge Ancient History* remarks that:

> We may safely suppose that Aurelian's Sol [sun] cult was intended to benefit the state as well as to promote and express Aurelian himself. The earthly autocrat needed, so Aurelian seems to have felt, a heavenly mirror-image; and once this heavenly autocrat was accepted, his earthly counterpart might expect to be still further magnified.[33]

In the event, it did him no good. Aurelian was cruelly assassinated a bare five years into his reign by a very ordinary military sword wielded by one of his own very ordinary generals, who was later tortured to death for his act of treachery. A statue of the assassinated Aurelian was posthumously put up in the same Temple of the Sun that Aurelian had built from the spoils of Palmyra. But it was made of silver, not the gold of Zenobia's chains.[34] Zenobia had won gold: Aurelian had to be content with silver. Zenobia, sort of, had the last hurrah.

11

Re-assessing Zenobia, 'a celebrated female sovereign'

It is hard not to be attracted to Zenobia. Generations of writers, painters, sculptors and historians, ancient and modern, have felt that attraction, and this historian is no exception. She does stand out as someone who did extraordinary things, not just for a woman – such a qualification would surely be patronising – but for any person caught up in the political struggles of her time. But in the context of the stressful third century, Zenobia's political position has been open to various interpretations. Just because the evidence is so scrappy, and just because the circumstances were so chaotic, but also because she was a woman, different hues and colours have been applied to the basic sketch of her life, some of them fanciful or idealised or implausible, others provocative about how we should expect a ruler of such a city as Palmyra at such a time of crisis in the Roman empire to react – and how, if at all, it mattered that the ruler was a woman. Given the gaps in the historical record, the very career of Zenobia, like her face and appearance, have become a sort of blank canvas onto which following generations could impose their own ideas of the exotic or the ideal female, their own 'inventions'.

But have those reconstructions, some in the name of art, some in the name of history, hindered rather than helped our understanding of women in positions of power and of Zenobia in particular? Zenobia has suffered over the centuries from being promoted as some sort of an ideal, in fact several differing, even incompatible ideals – an ideal of beauty, an ideal of chastity, an ideal of 'the feminine sublime', an ideal of female emancipation, a feminist icon, a glamorous Hollywood-style gun-toting warrior queen, a champion of the oppressed against the evil empire of Rome. But she is an altogether more interesting person if freed from all those idealisations and (frankly) falsifications. In short, recapturing the real Zenobia, or someone who may have been the real Zenobia, is no easy task, since it brings into play not just the imperfect historical evidence and our evaluation of it but also our contemporary and still evolving expectations about women's role in administration, politics and war.

That image of Zenobia, in chains but still regal and unbowed, has become the dominant image of the dethroned queen of Palmyra, as in the paintings by Herbert Schmalz and Edward Poynter as well as in Harriet Hosmer's statue and the much older literary tradition of Geoffrey Chaucer and Edward Gibbon. An artist is entitled to artistic licence. But does Hosmer's marble form distort our perception of the real Zenobia? Does it do any service to the cause of real female rulers or of real women active in the real and harsh world of national and international politics?

Unfit for the sceptre?

There was and perhaps still is a view that women are by nature not suited to supreme office. Zenobia has been cited as an example of this unsuitability, this weakness. Perhaps surprisingly, Anna Jameson, early champion of womens' rights and emancipation, friend to Harriet Hosmer and her close adviser in devising her statue of *Zenobia in Chains*, took this view. Jameson's 1831 book, *Memoirs of Celebrated Female Sovereigns*, devotes a chapter to Zenobia. In her Preface Jameson comes to a conclusion about female rulers generally that sits ill with modern ideas about gender equality:

> On the whole, it seems indisputable that the experiments hitherto made in the way of female government have been signally unfortunate; and that women called to empire have been, in most cases, conspicuously unhappy or criminal. So that, were we to judge by the past, it might be decided at once, that the power which belongs to us as a sex, is not properly, or naturally, that of the sceptre or the sword.

Zenobia did grasp the sceptre and the sword; the results for Palmyra were 'signally unfortunate'; and some Roman writers thought of her as little short of 'criminal'. But Zenobia and her advisers and supporters were building upon and extending the local and regional power base built up by her husband Odenathus in a highly uncertain political and military situation where to do nothing was not an option. However foolhardly Palmyra's bold venture may seem in retrospect, leading as it did to the demise of Palmyra as an important and wealthy trading city, it was a venture shared between man and woman, husband and wife. In the fraught conditions of the time, its progress and outcome had more the air of doomed inevitability, as in a Greek tragedy, that of female incompetence or 'criminality' as a ruler. Nor was Zenobia 'conspicuously unhappy' – though she may have been for all we know. The leading citizens of Palmyra presumably thought that Zenobia, when her turn came, was up to the task of wielding the sceptre, if not literally the sword. More interesting, if we could do it, would be to analyse how, if at all, the relationship between a female ruler of Palmyra and her advisers differed from the relationship between her male predecessor and his advisers. But we have no evidence at all for such an analysis. What is sure is that the citizens of Palmyra, and in particular its leading men, appear to have showed no reluctance to support a woman as leader. Jameson's verdict reflects the conventions of her own time rather than those of the Roman East.

146

Harriet Hosmer's statue of Zenobia.

Superbly regal?

Harriet Hosmer of course chose to see Zenobia differently to Jameson. Indeed she went to the other extreme. She arrived at a diametrically opposed conclusion about Zenobia. In doing so she imposed her own idealisation of her subject. She read widely but rejected any suggestion that her heroine was anything less than a great queen whose inbuilt nobility as a woman rescued her from the ignominy of defeat and captivity.

A close (female) friend of hers said that she was so much in love with her subject that she

> rejected as unworthy of belief the statement that Zenobia was ever shaken by her misfortune. To her imagination she was superbly regal, in the highest sense of the word, from first to last.[1]

For the sculptor, it was the moment of supreme tragedy that brought out the qualities of the female ideal.

> Hosmer's Zenobia is not a humiliated captive; her erect posture and royal jewels convey her majesty even in defeat ... the artist transformed the Queen of Palmyra from a symbol of woman's failings to an example of woman's courage and wisdom.[2]

Courage we may readily grant Zenobia. But the *Historia Augusta* and other authors make it clear that she was physically stressed by her harsh ordeal – who would not be? – and Hosmer's idealisation masks and betrays the grim realities of a Roman triumph.

Victimised woman?

The statue has come in for withering criticism on other scores. One writer says:

> Zenobia is, like Hosmer's other female subjects, a victim ... it is difficult to reconcile Hosmer's depictions of victimised women with her feminist orientations.[3]

Another says:

> Hosmer was popularly considered an exemplar of radically 'emancipated' femininity. It comes then as something of a surprise to see that her sculptural productions in the years 1850-60 consist almost exclusively of a series of traumatised or humiliated figures who meet a variety of unpleasant fates with expressionless equanimity ... her sculptures are anything but images of emancipation ... [her] female figures are, respectively, asleep, abandoned, turned into a tree, slaughtered, dead, on the eve of execution, being paraded in chains ... they constitute an eerily emotionless sorority, a zombie-like brigade of the living dead.[4]

Zenobia, we may conclude, was in reality no zombie and nobody's victim.

Sexless?

Several critics have, however, praised Hosmer's artistic decision not to exploit the erotic or sexual potential of Zenobia's captivity in the way that

148

representations of, say, Cleopatra almost always do at the hands of other neo-classical sculptors and painters. Sexy, in Hosmer's version, Zenobia is not. But the result is, says one writer, that in the statue 'the real woman is overpowered'.[5] Hosmer chose to represent Zenobia as weighed down, not so much by her chains (they are light wrist manacles rather than the heavier neck and ankle chains of classical accounts) as by the sheer volume of her drapery that descends in folds down to the floor. This renders it hard to detect the presence of any real body underneath those enveloping garments. What has been called the 'catatonic rigidity of the sublime'[6] reduces her statue to 'nothing but ridges and grooves', as the critic Lorado Taft said as long ago as 1903. There is nothing in Zenobia's story as far as we know it to warrant Hosmer's depiction of her in this way. Zenobia was not catatonically rigid – just the opposite. She was almost hyper-active, as was her opponent Aurelian, in a striking historical symmetry. She was not bereft of female characteristics. She seems to have been a fertile woman who had several children and also enjoyed jewellery and finery as much as anyone. There is no sign that she saw herself as a victim. Nor did she display any pretence at being an embodiment of 'the sublime'. Zenobia's chastity, even if that story about her is true, was strictly relative. Some have seen in it a suggestion that she was sexually frigid, seeking satisfaction in other, political pursuits.[7] On the contrary, she was, as far as we can tell, a sexually as well as politically active person. She was no nun.

Where being a woman probably counted positively in Zenobia's favour was at her trial after Palmyra's defeat. That Aurelian let her off comparatively lightly just because she was a woman, is certainly plausible. He would have known from literary sources that when Cleopatra's half-sister Arsinoe was led through the streets of Rome in chains, the great crowd took pity on her and were vocal about their feelings. Aurelian the showman would not have wanted a repetition of that. It would spoil his greatest piece of organised political theatre. He would also have known that Arsinoe was sent into exile at Ephesus rather than being executed but was killed not long after on the orders of Mark Antony but at the instigation of Cleopatra herself. Aurelian may not have wanted a repetition of that either, so placed her nearby at Tivoli where his minions could keep an eye on her.

The neo-classical imagination

The question is inevitably raised whether Hosmer's own unorthodox sexual orientation (as far as we understand it) had something to do with her decision to depict Zenobia in that eerily sexless non-erotic manner. Some neo-classical painting of the period appears today to be little more than an excuse to paint large pictures of good-looking young women (and some men) in far less than full dress but in a historical-literary context that made them (just) acceptable for public viewing. The painters Lawrence

Lord Leighton's *The Bath of Psyche*.

Alma-Tadema, Lord Frederic Leighton, John Waterhouse and Edward Poynter provide examples. Hosmer avoided that trap, but at the cost of falling into the opposite trap of denying sexuality altogether.

Admittedly it is hard these days to read neo-classical sculpture in general, and *Zenobia in Chains* in particular, with the eye of a mid-nineteenth century viewer, male or female. Artistic taste has changed drastically, and neo-classicism as an aesthetic was on the wane even in Hosmer's time, let alone in Schmalz's. If Hosmer's Zenobia is a Hosmer invention, still less was Zenobia the picture-postcard chocolate-box glamour puss of later neo-classical paintings like Schmalz's *Queen Zenobia's Last Look upon Palmyra*. Hosmer's own wry comment on one of her own works, a fountain, that it was so sweet that it ought to play sugar-water, is more appropriate to him than her. At least Hosmer was trying the express a notion of 'the sublime' that meant something to some of her contemporaries even if it means nothing today. Arguably, Hosmer herself and the life she lived out at Rome are more interesting to us today than the statue itself. The problem is that these neo-classical perceptions of Zenobia in paint and marble can and do rub off onto perceptions of Zenobia herself, just as the often lurid depictions of life at Rome in those neo-classical paintings and novels of the same period have coloured and warped perceptions of Rome ever since (orgies, nudes, banquets, marble halls, baths with naked women cavorting in the pools, and all that).

Variant readings of the *Historia Augusta*

The paradox is that the evidence for a more earthy, pragmatic, realistic polytonal view of Zenobia comes in the main from the very source that has been used to create an idealised picture of her – the enigmatic *Historia Augusta*. Hosmer may have rejected it as a source for her own idiosyncratic idealisation. But it has been the source of repeated versions of *the* or *an* ideal female since Boccaccio, most famously in Chaucer and in Gibbon, poet and historian creating much the same ideal, thus showing how in the case of Zenobia the line between literature and history, fiction and fact, is paper-thin. The *HA* has also been the source of an opposite negative view of Zenobia as an example of woman's weakness and vanity, as shown by her love of jewellery and personal ostentation. But it is in the *HA* that we can find, if we are alert to it, the evidence for Zenobia being a real ruler behaving, not as a woman who happens to be a ruler, but as a ruler who happens to be a woman.

The *HA* may owe something to Tacitus and to Juvenal's sixth satire in how it approaches Zenobia. But those literary precedents (if precedents they are) provide little of the detail that the *HA* gives us about Zenobia and which fleshes out, almost literally, the bare bones of what other authors tell us about the queen of Palmyra. Other authors tell us that she was bold, courageous and a good administrator, sharing the credit for the successes of her husband Odenathus. Starting from there, the *HA's* additional detail is often reasonable and must have come from some source or sources now lost, as for example when it says that she was a good horsewoman, careful with money, spoke three languages, and could hold her drink. The *HA's* portrait of a warrior queen also has within it many elements of the grimy realities of power and politics. The very text that has been used to paint a particular idealised portrait of Zenobia as a beautiful, intellectual, athletic but chaste queen in fact tells us that there was also a dark side to her, one which shows her behaving in the ruthless and morally suspect way that real people and real rulers so often do.

Wicked stepmother?

There are three charges that can be levelled against Zenobia. One is that she was a wicked stepmother, conniving in the murder of her husband in order to secure the succession to the throne of Palmyra of her son Vaballathus rather than of Haeranes, her step-son. This could be taken in two ways. It may be an easy cliché deriving from popular fiction – think of Cinderella, Snow White, Hansel and Gretel, Shakespeare's story about Cymbeline, or even the 1989 film *Wicked Stepmother* starring Bette Davis. The *saeva noverca*, the ruthless stepmother, was a stock character of classical Greek and Roman storytelling too: and of history telling. Livia, wife of the first Roman emperor Augustus, was said to have backed her own sons by a previous marriage, Drusus and Tiberius, to succeed Augustus and to have been connected with the deaths of rival family claimants. Tiberius did indeed succeed to the throne when Augustus died. There was also a story that Livia was implicated in the death of Augustus by poisoning some fresh figs.[8]

With Livia as with Zenobia, it is hard to know for sure whether this is a stock-in-trade of fiction being used to (mis)interpret events, or a case of life imitating art. But the joint assassinations of Odenathus and his son Hairan seem to have been due in the first instance to a family dispute of some sort, even if the Roman emperor Gallienus was lurking as a plotter in the background. If Zenobia was as close to Odenathus as the *HA* says (equal in administration, etc.) then in the context of the political machinations of the third century (and many other centuries), the allegation could just be true. It can never be proved either way. If true however, it would speak of an ambitious woman alive to the harsh realities of royal family politics, as real for an unscrupulous woman as for an unscrupulous man.

Betrayal

But it is her behaviour at that trial that has caused most dismay among Zenobia's admirers and cast most doubt on her probity, so creating the second charge against her. Zenobia did play the female card when it suited

Bust of Livia in the Louvre, Paris.

her. At her trial she blamed her advisers (all male) for her aggressive policy and got away with it, when the Roman soldiery were clamouring for her life. It appears that Aurelian ordered the deaths of many men in many cities, not only in Palmyra, who had supported Palmyra's ambitions, after Zenobia had helped to identify who they were. She in effect betrayed and denounced them. She was spared, they were not. This is the most contentious episode of her life, since it brings with it a moral obloquy that sits ill alongside all the various versions of Zenobia as an ideal and as a heroine, as an embodiment of the sublime and of female nobility.

And yet: think of Henry VIII, king of England, and how he sacrificed successive chief ministers – Thomas Wolsey, Thomas More, Thomas Cromwell – to his dynastic ambitions. Politics at the top level is a dirty business, and Zenobia showed that she could play dirty. Probably her advisers were doomed anyway, particularly Cassius Longinus, the intellectual who may have articulated the propaganda aspect of Zenobia's warfare, particularly the grafting onto Vaballathus of all those grandiose titles taken from

153

Roman practice. If Palmyra was aspiring to higher things in the east, it was only Longinus, after his long residence as a teacher at Athens, who could have articulated those wider ambitions. The rest of Zenobia's close regular advisers and generals were, as far as we know, local people with a local vision. That may be why Aurelian had it in for Longinus. If Zenobia's advisers were doomed anyway, why not survive?

Hubris or rebel?

The third charge against Zenobia is that of *hubris*, the overweening pride that goes before a fall. She aimed high and was brought low, humiliated. It is a favourite classical and neo-classical theme. Zenobia's venture into conquest brought in its train the impoverishment and destruction of Palmyra as a rich trading city with a highly distinctive Greek-semitic culture expressed in architecture, dress, iconography and religious practice. One website says that Zenobia was making a 'brazen claim to the imperial throne' of Rome itself, and some historians also incline to that interpretation of the grand titles that she claimed for her son and herself in the closing months of her independence.[9] If true, that would have warranted the charge of *hubris*, since Palmyra had nowhere near the resources or connections to make such a claim and there were few if any organised professional Roman legions still operational in the area whose switch of allegiance to Zenobia might have strengthened such a claim.

Rather, with the examples of the destruction of Hatra and Dura Europos in front of her, a realistic tribute to Zenobia is that she was trying, probably against the odds, possibly in desperation, to do what her husband Odenathus had been trying to do before her – to achieve what she could to safeguard the future of her city in perilous times. It was a gamble on survival that drove Palmyra's and Zenobia's actions at this time, not imperial ambition, not *hubris*. Zenobia was doing what a real ruler was supposed to do, and that was to fight for her city and its interests. The fact that she was a woman is, from that point of view, irrelevant, except only in the respect that it was a woman who was doing it in an era when women rarely held high office.

The titles claimed by or for Vaballathus in the closing stages of Zenobia's confrontation with Aurelian may have been intended to lay the rhetorical groundwork for some sort of a brokered deal with Rome, on the lines dubbed by historians 'co-regence', if that is not too grandiose a description of what was essentially kite-flying. But that is not the same as a claim to the throne of Rome itself. Nor does it make Zenobia into a 'rebel queen' like Britain's Boudica, a revolutionary hero (or heroine) rising up against Roman cruelty and oppression. Zenobia's case is not like Boudica's case at all. Calling Zenobia a rebel is just an easy headline. There is no evidence of Roman cruelty and oppression at Palmyra. On the contrary,

Palmyra prospered under the wing of Rome, and Rome gave Palmyra's merchants access to rich markets around the Mediterranean. There was no reason to rebel. The reasons why Palmyra took to arms were quite different. The fact that this eventually brought Palmyra into conflict with Rome does not justify explaining it in the simplistic terms of rebellion that more properly belong to the Star Wars narrative of Roman history. Rather, it was a dispute about who best could ensure the security of the Roman east, and how to do it.

Rome – or Persia?

If we accept that Zenobia was not a moral or feminist ideal but a real-life ruler who subordinated principle to power and survival, as rulers do, then it is easier to accept what the *HA* clearly tells us, that her husband Odenathus was not just a puppet or servant of Rome but an increasingly independent operator who kept open his lines of communications with Persia, Rome's enemy, as well as with Rome itself; and that Zenobia pursued this same independent policy of double-dealing between Rome and Persia, unsure of where Palmyra's best interests lay. There is a contrary view which holds that, first, Zenobia's husband Odenathus was acting within the formal Roman system of imperial government, with the approval and even delegated authority of the Roman emperor; and secondly, that Zenobia followed the same path and operated at first with the assent or connivance of Rome and with Roman officials moving easily between her rule and Roman rule as if between neighbouring open houses. But it is virtually impossible to square this interpretation with Zenobia's militant attacks on Arabia, Egypt, the rest of Syria and large parts of Asia Minor. It is striking how, from 260 onwards, first Odenathus and then Zenobia acted with increasing autonomy, and how that very independence came to look increasingly menacing from the standpoint of Rome and from the standpoint of the unity of the empire. Rome clearly signalled its intention to put an end to Palmyra's increasing autonomy, sooner or later, and Zenobia's policy was not personal megalomania, as some have suggested, but a calculated attempt to shore up its position against the day of reckoning. The policy of territorial expansion was a logical extension of her husband's achievements, driven by the certain knowledge that Rome had Palmyra in its sights.

There is also a possible third dimension to this story, the Arab dimension. Evidence from Arab writers suggests that Zenobia's aggressive policy may have been directed at rival Arab tribal groupings as well as, or as much as, at Rome. But the Arab evidence makes no mention of Rome, and there can surely be no doubt that the main confrontation was destined to be between Palmyra and Aurelian's Roman legions.

The third-century crisis

How you view Zenobia and Palmyra has direct relevance to how you view that whole stormy period of Roman history. Was the third century 'the age of crisis', even 'the age of anarchy'? Or was it a transition period in which the empire was experimenting with new forms of distributed government? Because they were short-lived, it has been fashionable to interpret the Gallic and Palmyrene ventures as just an early experiment in Diocletian-style decentralised government of the empire. On this theory, both Postumus and Tetricus in Gaul, and Odenathus and Zenobia in the east, by nobly acting as regional bastions of order under licence from Rome, made it easier to put the Roman empire back together again, Humpty-Dumpty-like, when circumstances allowed. They did Rome a favour. Perhaps indeed they foreshadowed Diocletian's administrative reforms instituted only a few years later in which he altered the governance of the empire by means of a limited decentralisation of authority to his famous Tetrarchy, a college of four emperors who divided up the empire between them, a college in which some were naturally more equal than others. Perhaps Diocletian was only formalising the division of power that Zenobia and her counterparts in the west were groping towards. In geographical terms, Zenobia's brief empire based on Syria did indeed look remarkably like the Diocese of the East later created by Diocletian.

But the Gallic empire at its height encompassed no fewer than four of Diocletian's dioceses (Galliae, Viennensis, Britanniae, Hispaniae). Perhaps the fashionable view is a serious case of the *post hoc ergo propter hoc* fallacy. To write off the crisis of the third century as just an experiment in decentralisation is to ignore the real danger of the collapse of the empire as a unified political entity. The Roman empire was surely in existential crisis in the middle of the third century. It might have split into three (or perhaps more) successor states as these secession movements drained away tax revenues and military resources, while Rome's external enemies, the 'barbarians', broke open the central hinge provinces of the empire in Italy and the Balkans. It was a critical moment in the history and survival of the Roman empire, and that is why Postumus and Zenobia matter in the grand scheme of Roman and European history. If the break-up had happened, then Palmyra's ultimate fate might have been vastly different. That is the key to understanding why Zenobia's aggressive expansionist policy was not just foolhardy, as some suggest, but a political gamble that just might have come off, but did not. Aurelian for one did not see it just as an experiment in decentralisation of power: nor of course did Diocletian's later successor, the famous Constantine, who fought hard and successfully to end Diocletian's experiment and restore a unified single monarchy for the whole Roman empire.

156

The Tetrarchs: statue set into the side of St Mark's Cathedral in Venice, looted from Constantinople by the Crusaders.

Despite some useful similarities and analogies between Gaul and the Roman east, they were anyway different cases. The Gallic emperors (so-called) did defend the Rhine frontier as their main priority, but repeated attempts were made from Rome to dislodge them. Rome and its emperors clearly did not like them. Contrarily, Palmyra under Odenathus and Zenobia did not concentrate on defending the Euphrates frontier, but set its sights elsewhere, on control of much of the rest of the eastern

Roman empire. Rome however did not like the Palmyra venture either, and made attempts to dislodge its regime. If Rome had a view, it was surely that its empire was in transition to dissolution. The empire was under attack all along its extended Rhine, Danube and Euphrates frontiers, and the continued existence of the Gallic and Palmyrene secessions was just one more ominous symptom of impending catastrophe. To call it 'the age of anarchy' may be an exaggeration. There was a strong continuity of military government provided by men from the central Balkan provinces with shared ethnic and probably political outlook. But what these soldier-emperors faced was indeed an empire in existential crisis, the crisis of the third century.

Assessing Aurelian

In confronting that crisis, Aurelian emerges as a particularly striking example of a man from a very ordinary background in the Balkans who proved to be anything but ordinary in his achievements and ambitions – like him or not. He seems to have recognised that the Roman empire of his day was passing through not just a military crisis – which he more than any other single emperor managed to repair – but also a crisis of ideology, self-belief and religious identity. He made moves to repair that damage too, with results that are still controversial. His new Temple of the Sun at Rome, built with Zenobia's money and peopled by statues and treasures looted from Zenobia's city, has been characterised variously as simply a reaffirmation of traditional Roman worship of the sun; as a foolish attempt to resurrect the Syrian religious practices that his Syrian predecessor as emperor, Elagabalus of Emesa, had attempted to introduce into Rome with disastrous results; or as an imaginative even bold attempt at a new monotheistic religion for Rome, a sort of prototype for Christianity – all courtesy of Zenobia's money and the seized assets of Palmyra.

Aurelian was cut short by assassination before his intentions could be made clear beyond doubt. But whichever view you take – and I am inclined to the third option – Aurelian emerges as a capable and complex emperor with his hand on the hilt of his sword, certainly, but also with his mind on fundamental questions about what holds together a multi-cultural empire like Rome's. That same concern for imperial unity also drove him towards a more extreme form of emperor worship that stuck in the gullet of some of his contemporaries and of many of those who write about him, but which became characteristic of the Roman imperial regime in later decades and centuries, especially when the capital shifted from Rome to Constantinople. So puzzling Aurelian was and is: but also impressive. He was a far more complex and thoughtful ruler than his rough soldier's background might suggest.

11. Re-assessing Zenobia, 'a celebrated female sovereign'

Assessing Zenobia

Zenobia's venture, on the other hand, is best seen as an opportunistic secession movement whose aims were made up as she went along, as an answer to highly specific circumstances of uncertainty and turmoil. If Odenathus her husband was a local warlord with an ill-defined but expanding sphere of influence and pretensions to set up some sort of local ruling dynasty at Palmyra, then Zenobia followed on from that in an attempt to become, in an uncertain world, a regional Syrian warlord whose future relations with Rome were open to negotiation – if Rome would negotiate. Only by building up a formidable regional power base could Rome be forced to negotiate, and only in this light do Zenobia's military conquests and claims to grand titles for her son make sense. In the event, Aurelian wouldn't play ball. Zenobia's career of conquest was nipped in the bud before anything like a fixed frontier could develop for Palmyra's sphere of influence, which was even more imprecise and more temporary than the equivalent sphere of influence of the Gallic secession. Rome also saw the frontier line problem, but answered it differently. After the collapse of Palmyra, a new desert frontier defence system was constructed by the emperor Diocletian, the Strata Diocletiana, which left 'outside the walls' large areas once controlled by Palmyra.

Such an interpretation of the careers of Odenathus and in particular of Zenobia may seem messy, imprecise, something less dramatic than the rebel warrior queen challenging the evil empire of the Star Wars version of Roman history, something less glamorous than the exotic beauty clad in regal finery that fascinated Chaucer and Gibbon, something more prosaic than the tragic heroine of a real-life grand opera. But Zenobia acted as a ruler would, any ruler, not as a woman would. The worst insult to her is to suppose that as a ruler she should be judged differently to any other ruler, just because she was a woman. Her actions may have been good or bad, vain or justified, morally sound or morally wrong, politically sound or politically wrong. At certain junctures, it mattered that she was a woman. She may have owed her life, her second life in enforced retirement, to her sex. But in general her actions were the actions of a ruler, doing what rulers do, for good or ill.

Oddly enough, the perception of Zenobia that seems most warranted by her career freed of moralistic baggage is that which puts her onto the face of so many Syrian banknotes. For Syrians, she is something of a hero of independence, that independence that came to the country only in 1945, after centuries as part of the Ottoman Turkish empire and after being handed over against its will to the French in the post-First World War territorial carve-up between the imperial powers of Europe. If Zenobia was not strictly a Syrian or Arab nationalist, she came somewhere near it, like her husband before her. By carving out and expanding a sphere of influence in what today we call the Middle East, based on a city of Syria, she

159

drew attention to a different potential boundary line of power and rule than the traditional Roman-Persian divide, and gave Syria a potential identity different from its immediate Greek-Hellenistic past. As a trial run for an independent Syrian nation, Zenobia's bold venture passes muster. The Arab world seems to agree. Zenobia was the subject of stage musical and dance events in Dubai in 2007 and Bahrain in 2009.[10]

Perhaps today we can finally discard all attempts to interpret the life of Zenobia as a neo-classical embodiment of the sublime in women; as that other neo-classical invention, a bastion of Roman rule; as a romantic desert queen of the fabled east; as a feminist icon with emancipation in mind; or as a victim of men and circumstance. Perhaps instead we can just relax and see her as a ruler and head of state of a remarkable city at a remarkable period of history who won praise from her natural enemies for some of her qualities and odium among her admirers for some of her faults, and who just happened to be a woman.

Odenathus' (alleged) titles:
what did they mean?

Many titles have been attributed to Odenathus in an effort to establish what exactly his status was, both at Palmyra and within the wider Roman empire, especially within the eastern parts of that empire. Was he a Roman office holder? With regional authority granted to him by Rome? Or was he just a leading citizen of Palmyra from a distinguished local family and a local war-lord with pretentions to founding a ruling dynasty at Palmyra? The answer depends on how you interpret those titles. They can be divided between those that derive from inscriptions, and those that derive from literary texts.

A. Titles deriving from inscriptions

1. Senator. Odenathus is frequently described by the Greek term *lamprotatos* (but of course in Greek letters) normally taken as the equivalent of *clarissimus* in Latin. At that period this meant that he held the rank and title of 'senator' as a hereditary right, perhaps dating back to the time of the emperor Septimius Severus (emperor 193 to 211) since Odenathus had as his first name 'Septimius'. It is assumed, reasonably, that the family had rendered service to that emperor, perhaps when he was fighting for his supremacy in the east against other contenders. It was an honorary title, as indicated by the adjective 'adlected' or 'co-opted' (*synkletikos* in Greek) often added to the title. In itself, it implies prestige rather than power, social status rather than military or administrative authority.[1]

2. Consul. Odenathus also enjoyed the title of *hupatikos* (again in Greek letters) normally taken as the equivalent to the Latin *consularis,* meaning 'of consular rank'.[2] Does this indicate that he held or had held some job reserved for men of consular rank? If so, then some scholars have speculated that the only job he could have held, given his known activities, is governor (*legatus*) of his own province, that is, Syria Phoenice, one of the two administrative provinces into which Syria was at that time split. That in turn would mean that he was, at that time, part of the official Roman system of government. But there is one fatal objection to this. That objection is that since the time of the proclamation of the usurper Avidius Cassius in 175, it had been an iron rule that, to minimize the risk of rebellion, a man could not be appointed as governor of the province from which he came. Instead, it is most likely that in Odenathus' case it was another honorary title, meaning that he had the right to the *ornamenta consularia*, the trappings of an ex-consul.[3] We do not know how he got this title. But once again, it implies prestige rather than power.

3. *Exarch*. This was a Greek title, and the equivalent to this in Palmyrene was RS', or Ras Tadmor. It was a local title, local that is to Palmyra, and may have been unique to that city. It indicates that Odenathus was a leading citizen with authority in the city. It was often coupled in inscriptions with the honorific title 'senator'. It belonged to the earlier part of Odenathus' career, before the great Roman military debacle of 260, and was a title shared with his first son Haeranes.[4] It was a title indicating the wielding of power in the city, but it says nothing about Odenathus' status outside Palmyra, and in the form of Ras Tadmor it corresponded to no known formal Greek or Latin administrative office.[5]

4. *Despot(es)*. This again is a Greek title, with the Palmyrene equivalent of MRN. It is used only once in the evidence, in an inscription already referred to, put up in Odenathus' honour by the local gold and silver workers.[6] It is an old word meaning, in the era of classical Greece, autocrat or absolute ruler (hence the English pejorative term 'despot'). This has been taken as evidence that Odenathus was, or sought to be, ruler or king of Palmyra, perhaps as the self-appointed founder or continuer of a royal dynasty. Malalas does indeed refer to him as 'king (or emperor) of the Saracen barbarians'. But the objection to taking this title at face value, again fatal, is that in three other inscriptions put up by local trade guilds, he is referred to explicitly as their patron, using exactly that word.[7] If he really had been a king, these other guilds would surely not have dared to downplay his status. In other words, *despotes* in this context means, not king, but 'patron', perhaps exaggerating for effect.[8] It does not signify a political or military office.

5. *King of Kings*. This title looks more serious. It belonged to the period after the Roman debacle of 260, and is expressed as *basileus basileon* in Greek and MLK MLK' in Palmyrene.[9] It was a Greek or local title, not a Roman title. It was a title claimed for Odenathus' first son Haeranes. But it was claimed for Odenathus himself only after his death. On the one hand, it is hard to understand why the son should have it, and not the father. On the other hand, it must be suspect as being posthumous propaganda by Zenobia. More importantly, because it was not a Roman title at all, even if he held it, it implies nothing about Odenathus' status in the eyes of the Roman authorities. If anything it was a Persian title – Sapor had it – and no doubt familiar to anyone in the Near East. It is speculated that Odenathus adopted it (if he did) for his son as well as for himself as a sort of challenge to Sapor, a sort of 'Yah Boo' after Odenathus had pursued that Persian monarch down the Euphrates and reclaimed some of his war booty. It could hardly have been a claim to the Persian throne, as some have supposed.[10] Odenathus had nowhere near the military strength to enforce such a claim. It might have been part of Odenathus' propaganda effort to build up his personal prestige in the area. But he may never have claimed that title in the first place.

6. *Corrector* or *restitutor*. These possible titles for Odenathus are hugely controversial – but wrongly so, I believe. They are Latin titles, so do not in themselves appear on Palmyra's inscriptions (very few of which contain Latin). Instead, they appear in a Greek equivalent *epanorthotes*, either in Greek letters or in a direct Palmyrene transliteration as PNRTT', or in a Palmyrene equivalent title of MTQNN'.[11] If you accept that these Greek and Palmyrene titles are the equivalent of *corrector* in Latin, then *corrector* could indeed be used as a formal title indicating a senior office within the Roman imperial hierarchy. That *could* make Odenathus a formal representative of Rome and Roman power, with wide and legitimate (in imperial terms) authority. However, the Greek term is a slippery one. It means, at its basic level, someone who puts to rights or restores to order. Similarly, the Palmyrene root TQN means 'to set right, arrange, set in order'.[12] So the title could be the equivalent of *restitutor* in Latin, which is much more of an honorary or laudatory title commemorating past achievements and indicates nothing about formal office-holding. It is a vacuous title.[13] As if that was not objection enough to reading into this term some formal bestowal of legitimate Roman authority and powers, the term *corrector* itself is not without ambiguity, and may not necessarily bear the weight sometimes put upon it.[14]

However, the fundamental objection is that these terms, on either interpretation, were applied, not to Odenathus at all, but to his son by Zenobia, Vaballathus, after the assassination of Odenathus and of his first son, at a time when Zenobia and her supporters were trying to build up a new or expanded position for Palmyra. The supposition that these titles – whatever they meant – were also applied to Odenathus himself, is entirely based on the notion that Vaballathus would not, could not, have claimed titles that he had not inherited from his father. This is nonsense. They could just be an act of retrospective invention. By the time Vaballathus was laying claim to these and many other titles, the whole political ball-game had changed. There is neither evidence nor historical justification for 'reading backward' these titles to Odenathus. Like King of Kings, they were most likely posthumous propaganda.

7. *Dux Romanorum* and *Imperator*. These are Roman titles, and top titles at that, implying in each case the virtual or actual power of the Roman emperor himself, or of one sharing that supreme power. But the objection to attributing either of these titles to Odenathus is that on coins, milestones and inscriptions they were claimed by his son Vaballathus after the assassination of Odenathus, and there is no direct evidence that Odenathus himself ever held or claimed them, except on the same mistaken basis as *corrector/restitutor*, namely that Vaballathus must have inherited such titles from his father.[15] But, to repeat, the political ball game changed, and to read back such titles from son to father is a questionable assumption, another retrospective invention. (The similar title *dux orientis* is discussed below.)

In summary, the titles attributed to Odenathus in inscriptions turn out to signify local authority and prestige but do not necessarily imply anything at all about Odenathus' rank or status within, or in the eyes of, the Roman regime. This is a classic case of inscriptions not being the hard objective evidence that some experts would like them to be, but being subject to interpretation according to what you already think, from other sources, was going on. In other words, far from the inscriptions being basic evidence to amplify an unstable literary record, your interpretation of the literary record influences what you think the inscriptions may tell us. It is assumptions built upon the literary texts that have been allowed to colour the interpretation of the inscriptions.

B. Titles deriving from literature

1. Augustus. There is one reference in the fragile *Historia Augusta* to Odenathus being given the title *Augustus,* but in default of any other evidence whatsoever for this title relating directly to Odenathus, this unlikely suggestion is generally rejected.[16] Coins issued in the name of Vaballathus, his son, do claim this title. But as before, that is not evidence for the father, and the son was operating in quite different circumstances.

2. Dux Orientis. This is a potentially important title which could imply overall military authority exercised over a wide geographical area within the Roman system of government. The title *Dux Orientis* is however more problematic than the title of *Dux Romanorum* (above). It all depends on how you choose to interpret the Greek word *strategos* in the literary evidence and how you rate the authors who use it.

3. Strategos. Generally, *strategos* in Greek meant a general in charge (hence English words like 'strategic'). So it could be a simple reference to a man appointed to take charge of a military group, or in later use it could mean one of the two *duumviri* who were in overall charge of a city in the normal system of Roman urban government. Festus calls Odenathus a *decurio* at Palmyra, a loose term meaning foreman or member of a ruling committee.[17] So it was not necessarily a very significant description. One inscription tells us that a certain Julius Aurelius Oge was acting as *strategos* at Palmyra, possibly at the same time as Odenathus was also said to be a *strategos*, so there may have been nothing unique about the title.[18] But both Zonaras (twice[19]) and Syncellus appear to be more precise, and say that Odenathos was made *strategos* of the East, or indeed of the whole East, and this title may be equated with the formal Roman title of *Dux Orientis.* If that were indeed Odenathus' proper title and role, that would be a high office in the Roman imperial system, implying command over all Roman troops on the eastern frontier, answerable only to the emperor himself, Gallienus. On the other hand, it could have been an unfortunate anachronism.

Both these Roman authors were writing a long time after the event. Both wrote in Greek in the time of the Byzantine empire. Syncellus lived at the turn of the eighth and ninth centuries, Zonaras in the twelfth century, that is, 500 and 800 years after the events they are describing. More specifically, the Latin term *dux*, equated with the Greek term *strategos*, began life as a general informal term, came to signify a special command over some sort of task-force under the Severan emperors, but was only fully formalized as the title of a military man put in charge of an entire frontier zone by the emperor Diocletian, that is, some decades after Odenathus' time. Only in the time of the emperor Constantine, in the next century, did each frontier zone get its own *dux* (duke). So Zonaras and Syncellus may have been using a term familiar to them and to later times, but wrongly attributed to the mid-third century. But that does not entirely rule out the possibility that there was some content to this attribution even in the 260s. How you view that possibility depends on how you read our old friend, the *HA*, on the matter of the alleged *imperium* granted to Odenathus by the Roman emperor Gallienus.

4. Imperium. *Imperium* in Latin could take on several shades of meaning. Centrally it meant the supreme authority wielded by the Roman emperor, or delegated by him to a senior military or other figure in his administration. It could therefore indicate an office or function of command exercised over a nominated geographical segment of the empire. But *imperium* could also mean, in a much looser and less formal sense, simply power. It could be used, for example, of the power exercised by the head of a family over the members of that family, or of the dominion or sway held by any ruler.[20] The *HA* in several places refers to the *imperium* gained by Odenathus in the East. But how did he gain it? The Latin of the *HA* has been pressed into meaning that Gallienus formally granted him that *imperium*, as emperors could – in other words, a formal appointment by the emperor. But the Latin need not mean that at all.

Nor can it be inferred that what the *HA* writer meant was *imperium maius*, a more formal term indicating over-riding authority, i.e. over provincial governors and military commanders, such as was granted to

Germanicus in 7 and to the great general Corbulo in 63 – in both cases, in the East. One reference in the *HA* says (in its original Latin) that *Odenathus rex Palmyrenorum obtinuit totius orientis imperium* (Odenathus king of the Palmyrenes obtained command of the whole east).[21] It does not say *how* Odenathus obtained it. It could as well have been obtained by the force of his own armed intervention as by appointment, with *imperium* used in its looser sense (as it could be) to indicate power rather than an office.

Another *HA* reference, already mentioned, says that Gallienus gave him the title Augustus *participato imperio* – because he was participating in power. We have seen that the grant of the title *Augustus* has no other evidence to support it. The accompanying phrase could be taken as equally false, or as simply acknowledging the brute fact that Odenathus was in fact wielding power in the East. It does *not* say that *imperium* was granted or bestowed by the emperor. The *HA* uses the term *imperium* freely of all pretenders and usurpers who claimed authority or power. Eusebius says that Zenobia *tenebat imperium* – certainly not, in her case, by formal grant of the Roman emperor.[22]

The third reference says bluntly that Odenathus had seized power in the East.[23] The Latin says *sumpsisset*, a stronger term than *obtinuit*, but with the same sense of grabbing something – not being given it. In this context, it is also worth noting a phrase used in another part of the *HA*, where it says that Odenathus acted 'as if taking the side of Rome', a very suitable caution by the *HA* author.[24] Elsewhere, Zosimus simply says that Gallienus asked Odenathus to come to the help of the Roman armies – hardly an order to a subordinate.[25] In short, the *imperium* attributed to Odenathus was not a formal imperial grant or delegation of authority, but a simple statement of the obvious – that in his day he gained and wielded considerable power in the Roman East.

Once *imperium* is taken to mean simply 'power' and not a formal grant of Roman high office, and once titles used only after his death are eliminated, then Odenathus was not a duke (*dux*) of anything or anywhere but reverts to being an eminent and ambitious local civilian and military leader with distinguished honorary titles operating adroitly in a dynamic and dangerous political environment.

Appendix B

The Zenobia-Aurelian coalition
theory and P.Wisc. 1.2

As related in Chapter 6, there is an intriguing theory, taken by some as
proven fact, that during her brief spell in the political and military
limelight of Roman history Zenobia ruled Egypt in some sort of agreement
with Rome, some sort of coalition or co-regency arrangement in which
Zenobia's under-age son Vaballathus and the Roman emperor Aurelian
were co-rulers of Egypt, with Zenobia of course still acting as queen-regent
in the name of her son and so in effective control on the Palmyra side.
Coins and documents issued in Egypt and elsewhere after Zenobia's
military annexation of Egypt in late 270 and during the period of Zenobia's
control of Egypt appear to lay claim to such a coalition. Vaballathus is
styled by grand Roman titles such as *vir clarissimus, rex, consul, imperator, dux romanorum* (senator, king, consul, general, Roman military commander) and later *augustus, imperator* or *imperator caesar*. He is given
equal billing with Aurelian. What is going on?

In this book I have chosen to interpret these titles as political propaganda, at most offering from Palmyra's side a possible deal between
Palmyra and Rome in that period of uncertainty before Aurelian arrived with
his legions to put a stop to Palmyra's secession by force. In themselves, I
suggest, the titles and the claims they imply are empty of real practical
content. However, there is a directly contrary interpretation, one which
would radically alter the picture of what the politics of the Roman east were
at this period. It would drastically modify the picture presented in this book
of a systematically hostile relationship between Zenobia and Rome from the
death of Odenathus onwards, and by implication would retrospectively modify the picture also presented in this book of a wary arms-length relationship
between Odenathus and Rome. In short, if correct it would tend to restore the
theory of a co-operative even formalised friendly relationship between
Palmyra and Rome over the whole period from 260 onwards up to 272
spanning both Odenathus and Zenobia – the coalition theory. The proof, or
suggested proof, of this coalition theory raises fascinating questions about
how history comes to be written, which is why it is important.

The matter at issue is whether four well-known Roman officials held
office *both* under the command of Odenathus or Zenobia *and* under the
command of the Roman emperor of the day, offering allegiance to both at
the same time or at least switching seamlessly between one allegiance and

the other. The most important of these men are Statilius Ammianus and Julius Marcellinus, both of them in relation to Egypt, to Zenobia's period of control of Egypt, and so to the emperor Aurelian. The other two men are Virius Lupus and Salvius Theodorus. If this 'contrary' interpretation of the careers of these four men is correct, it would indicate a very cosy political relationship between the Roman high command and the regime in Palmyra. Let us look at these men in turn.

1. Statilius Ammianus

The test case is Statilius Ammianus. Was he appointed as governor (prefect) of Egypt by Zenobia? Did he then negotiate the handing back of Egypt to Roman control? And did he then continue in that high office under Aurelian? The most interesting and provocative statement of this version of events and of the politics of the period is given by Potter in his excellent book on Rome. Referring backwards from the eventual recovery of Egypt by the Aurelian in 272, Potter says:

> Aurelian's campaign in the east is far more complex than the straightforward tale of war and re-conquest that has come down to us through the narrative sources ... first and foremost there was the recovery of Egypt, seemingly as the result of negotiation with the prefect whom Zenobia left in charge. This man was Statilius Ammianus, who was appointed prefect in 270 and would remain in office until at least July or August 272, if not indeed until May 273 ... he is one of a number of figures who appear to have been able to move between the two camps.[1]

Southern suggests that as Ammianus had previously been governor of Arabia during the time of Odenathus, without any sign of hostility between them,

> it may be that Zenobia had more or less inherited him and that he was a trusted ally ... At least three Roman governors, all of equestrian rank, were compliant or even actively supported her ... To all intents and purposes normal Roman administration was still functioning and Zenobia did not insist on constant acknowledgement of her status or equal rank with the Roman emperor.[2]

The noted papyrologist Alain Martin states baldly that the evidence shows

> Statilius Ammianus taking charge at the finest hours of the Palmyrene regime. So there can be no question of making this prefect into a creature of Aurelian, arriving in Alexandria in the baggage of the soldiers coming to subdue the partisans of Zenobia and Vaballathus.[3]

A more conventional view of Ammianus is given by Watson in his excellent biography of Aurelian. He believes that Ammianus was appointed prefect of Egypt only in the wake of Aurelian's reconquest in 272, and so was not an appointee or ally of Zenobia at all but part of the reaffirmation of central government by Aurelian. He says that

> it is therefore highly likely that Ammianus was installed as the new prefect by Aurelian's counter-invasion force in the late spring [of 272].[4]

So here is the disagreement. Statilius Ammianus was indeed beyond doubt in office in Egypt after the fall of Palmyra when Aurelian was in full control. So what is the strength of the evidence for saying that this man was in office before that, and so under both regimes? To find an answer to that question means delving into the highly specialist world of papyrology – the interpretation of papyrus fragments found largely in Egypt. For the non-specialist, this is dangerous territory. But here goes.

The evidence is based mainly on one papyrus fragment only, a 46-line half-papyrus known in the trade as P.Wisc. 1.2, so-called because it is held in the Memorial Library of the University of Wisconsin, one of a bundle of papyri bought in Egypt in 1920. It is torn down the middle, and only the left-hand half survives. The question is, what was written on the right-hand side? The process by which the missing part of the text of this torn papyrus, plus the missing part of a brief related papyrus fragment known in the trade as P.Mich. 5478a, have been extensively reconstructed so as to become the suggested proof that Statilius Ammianus was in office under Zenobia as well as under Aurelian went in seven cumulative add-on stages, which we need to examine. Did we here have the Seven Pillars of Wisdom on this matter – or something else?

Stage One. The great weight placed upon this one papyrus fragment P.Wisc. 1.2 makes it surprising that the text of this papyrus as first published contains no reference to Ammianus, no reference to Aurelian, and indeed was dated by its editor, the distinguished expert P.J. Sijpesteijn, to the reign of the emperor Septimius Severus, that is, some 60-70 years before the events we are interested in and so irrelevant to them. His dating depended on the reference in the surviving portion of the text to an emperor called Lucius [something]. Sijpesteijn thought this could only mean Lucius Septimius Severus.[5] Overall, Sijpesteijn thought that 'an interpretation which could have any claim to exactitude cannot be provided, neither can a translation'.

Stage Two. The noted scholar Naphtali Lewis then pointed out that the dating to Severus was not water-tight. Aurelian also had the forename Lucius, and the Egyptian office-holders referred to in the papyrus did not, he said, exist in the earlier period but did exist in the time of Aurelian. Ergo, he said, the papyrus dates to the time of Aurelian. But Lewis still dismissed the papyrus as 'too fragmentary to tell us anything of consequence'.[6]

Stage Three. The distinguished Oxford papyrologist John Rea then re-examined the papyrus and suggested that the letters]amiano[that

Sijpesteijn had found in it could 'plausibly' be changed to]mmiano[– and so could indicate Statilius Ammianus if the new dating of the document to the reign of Aurelian was correct.[7] The photograph of P.Wisc. 1.2 provided by Sijpesteijn in his original publication is impossible for a non-specialist to decipher.

Stage Four. Rea later firmed up his view that the text 'should be corrected' in this way, and pointed out that this textual restoration would confirm Ammianus as in office under Aurelian as sole emperor, therefore after the defeat of the Palmyrenes. But given the different dating systems between Egypt and Rome he left somewhat open the question of whether this papyrus also places Ammianus in office earlier, during the time of Zenobia's occupation of Egypt.[8] It may be noted that Rea uses the term 'coalition' in his discussion as if it were a fact, and refers to Vaballathus and Aurelian as 'co-rulers' of Egypt. He says that this coalition lasted 'at least until 11 March' of 272.

Stage Five. The noted Italian papyrologist G. Bastianini, noting that this papyrus fragment was the only serious evidence on the matter, then argued that the text, if closely read, also showed that Ammianus did indeed become prefect sometime in the summer of 271, therefore in the time of Zenobia. This interpretation rests upon reading the Greek letter and numeral Beta in line 22 as meaning Year Two, and therefore as Year Two of Aurelian, and not as part of a quite different Greek word *Bouleutai*, as Sijpesteijn had supposed.[9]

Stage Six. Commenting on that other fragment of papyrus known as P.Mich. Inv. 5478a, discovered in 1928/29, Sijpesteijn suggested that after suitable restoration this fragment confirmed Ammianus as in office in the later years of Aurelian's reign, but accepted the notion that he was already in office in 271 perhaps up to 274/5.[10]

Stage Seven. Alain Martin then developed this scenario still further. Noting that the last document to associate the names of Vaballathus and Aurelian is dated to April 272,[11] and on the basis of an extensive suggested restoration of the text of P.Mich. Inv. 5478a different to that of Sijpesteijn, he argued that it shows that Ammianus was in place during that previous period when papyri and coins refer to a joint rule of Egypt by Vaballathus and Aurelian. He dates P.Mich.Inv. 5478a to between August 271 and spring 272. By this means Martin dates Ammianus' initial tenure of the job to the time of Zenobia's occupation of Egypt, and says that this confirms the evidence from P.Wisc. 1.2. He also points out that by the end of June 272 this curious episode is all over, and Aurelian is in sole charge of Egypt, as shown by other papyrus evidence.[12]

So there we have it. To question this cumulative pyramid of textual reconstructions of two tatty fragments of papyri is to question the methodology of a whole set of distinguished papyrologists. But I find the pyramid shaky. Of course these textual reconstructions, however extensive, are not impossible. But does the conclusion arrived at survive that crude but useful tool, the reality check? Are these textual reconstructions, rather than proving that there was a real-life coalition in place between Rome and Palmyra, actually based upon a prior presumption that such a coalition existed? To base a radical (re)interpretation of this period of history on a reconstruction of two bits of paper (or papyrus) that do not in the last analysis even exist, seems to me a step too far.

Even more challengingly, is it historically plausible that such a political coalition could have existed in the months and years after Zenobia's army and supporters had forcibly taken control of Arabia and Egypt by violent military means, ending with the suicide of the then Roman governor of Egypt, Tenagino Probus? Surely it is quite implausible. That is of course a matter of historical judgement. But even apart from events in Egypt itself, the earlier background of an attempted military strike by Rome against Palmyra itself and the possible involvement of the Roman emperor in the assassination of Odenathus, plus the speed with which Aurelian swooped on Palmyra as soon as his hands were free, make the coalition/ co-ruler hypothesis for Egypt most unlikely. If that is so, the only plausible explanation for the battery of titles claimed for Vaballathus in Egypt is that it was outright political propaganda aimed at a possible future arrangement that Aurelian chose to ignore.

2. Julius Marcellinus

This man is a real puzzle, again in relation to Egypt. There is substantial evidence that this Roman official acted as vice-prefect of Egypt in the year 271 (*agens vice praefecti*). That puts him in office, albeit a junior office, at a period when Zenobia had gained control of Egypt. His rulings while in that office seem to have remained in force under Aurelian, so he seems to have come to no harm later as a result of his holding that office.[13] So did Zenobia appoint him? Was he an example of an official moving easily between camps?[14] If Ammianus is parked in the doubtful category, then unanswerable questions arise about what was going with Marcellinus. Why was he only acting governor (vice-prefect)? Was he in office for the whole period from the Palmyrene take-over of Egypt to the arrival of Ammianus, whenever we think that was, or only for part of that time? Was Palmyra only in control of parts of Egypt, so that normal Roman administration continued in the other parts?

As a possible explanation, it seems to me most likely that after his boss, the full prefect Probus, had committed suicide after his defeat by the pro-Palmyra forces, this Marcellinus, who was already there as his deputy prefect, may have felt that the wisest thing to do was to stay on and offer at least token service to Zenobia until the situation clarified itself – an offer presumably accepted, since Zenobia had no administrative officials of her own to run the place. If anyone eased the eventual restoration of Roman control of Egypt, I suspect that it was Marcellinus rather than

Ammianus. But that is my speculation. It is a muddy situation certainly. But in default of the main evidence for a coalition arrangement based on Ammianus, Marcellinus offers not so much a further proof of officials moving easily between the two camps as of some adroit political manoeuvring by this man in a tight situation – an adroitness perhaps recognised by Aurelian. On inspection, the remaining two men turn out to offer even less support for the coalition theory.

3. Virius Lupus

This man was governor of the province of Asia in 271-72, at a time when Zenobia had occupied at least parts of that region. Previously, he had been governor of Syria Coele (a division of Syria) in around 265 under Gallienus at a time when this would have placed him under the authority of Odenathus *if* Odenathus had held high Roman office, as some suppose.[15] But if, as this book argues, Odenathus made only local claims to authority, it is not surprising that Gallienus appointed a governor of that part of Syria in the normal way. As to this man's office as governor of Asia, Antioch did not fall to the Palmyrenes until 271/2, and parts but only parts of Asia fell to them soon after. But large parts of the province of Asia never fell under even the temporary control of Zenobia. Also, by that period, Aurelian was preparing to move on Palmyra. So again it is not surprising that a Roman governor was appointed for Asia in the normal way. Virius Lupus is therefore not evidence for Roman officials moving between the two sides. For both his known jobs, his was a normal and unsurprising Roman appointment.

4. Salvius Theodorus

This man was prefect of Syria Coele after Virius Lupus, under the emperor Claudius, and so a contemporary (probably) of Zenobia.[16] But if Zenobia was not yet claiming any great status for herself or her son but was beginning from the strictly local authority and titles inherited from her husband Odenathus, and if she had not yet begun her career of conquest, then it totally unsurprising that normal Roman administration was still functioning at this time – whatever happened later.

In summary, the careers of these four men do not provide incontrovertible support for the counter-intuitive idea of a 'coalition' in Egypt between Palmyra and Rome or of easy movement of officials between the two rival camps, either during the time of Odenathus or during the time of Zenobia. The case of Julius Marcellinus is certainly a puzzle. But in default of the other three alleged suspects, he does not by himself stand up the case for this supposed coalition. Of course, dear reader, *lector amice*, you may check the sources for yourself and conclude otherwise.

Notes

1. Inventing Zenobias: pen, brush and chisel

1. The painter's father was German, and in German the word 'schmalz' means dripping, the fat that runs off meat while cooking, and so comes to mean also 'slushy sentimentality', which sums up what some critics think of Schmalz's work. Schmalz later changed his name to Carmichael.

2. Information courtesy of Judith Weingarten at www.zenobia.tv.

3. See R. Hingley and C. Unwin, *Boudica – Iron Age Warrior Queen* (Hambledon, 2005).

4. Fergus Millar, *The Roman Near East* (Cambridge, 1993), 172-3.

5. G. Bowersock, 'The Hellenism of Zenobia', in J.T.A. Koumoulides (ed.), *Greek Connections* (Notre Dame, 1987), 21.

6. Eugenia Equini Schneider, in *Moi, Zenobie, Reine de Palmyre* (Centre Culturel de Pantheon, 2001), 23.

7. O. Hekster, *Rome and its Empire AD 193-284* (Edinburgh, 2008).

8. See Ernest Will, *Les Palmyréniens: La Venise des Sables* (Armand Collin, 1992).

9. Sources for Hosmer's life include Margaret Thorp, 'The White Marmorean Flock', *New England Quarterly*, June 1959; Susan Waller, 'The Artist, the Writer and the Queen: Hosmer, Jamieson and "Zenobia" ', *Woman's Art Journal*, Spring-Summer 1983; Cornelia Carr, *Harriet Hosmer, Letters and Memories* (1913); Mara Witzling, *Voicing our Visions: Writings by Women Artists* (Universe Books, 1991); and Gabrielle Gopinath, 'Harriet Hosmer and the Feminine Sublime', *Oxford Art Journal* 28 (2005).

10. According to the account of Hosmer at www.glbtq.com/arts, accessed July 2009.

11. A. Watson, *Aurelian and the Third Century* (Routledge, 1999), 87.

12. *Historia Augusta (HA) The 30 Pretenders* 30.12. *Zenobia*, tr. D. Magie (Loeb Classical Library).

13. *HA The 30 Pretenders* 30.

14. *London Review of Books* (23 October 2008), 23: review of K. Ellis, *Star of the Morning: The Extraordinary Life of Lady Hester Stanhope* (HarperPress, 2008).

15. Joan Haslip, quoted in M. Kociejowski (ed.), *Syria through Writers' Eyes* (Eland, 2006) 107.

16. E.g. Alexander Baron's *The Queen of the East,* Beatrice Small's *Beloved* and Judith Weingarten's *The Chronicle of Zenobia, the Rebel Queen.*

17. See Wikipedia, for example, or the Women's History site, or the excellent account at www.roman-emperors.org.

18. Quoted from www.otto-graph.com, as at 04/10/2008.

19. *HA The 30 Pretenders* 30.27.

20. Syncellus, *Chronography* 470.

21. Zosimus 1.59 and Zonaras 12.27.

22. John Malalas, *Chronographia* 12.299.

23. Malalas again.

24. B. Dignas and E. Winter, *Rome and Persia in Late Antiquity* (Cambridge, 2007), 162.

25. *HA The 30 Pretenders* 17 (*Maeonius*), perhaps supported by Orosius, *Histories* 7.23.4. Eutropius 9.13 leaves the matter open.

26. *HA Aurelian* 30.

27. The phrase is Mary Beard's.

28. Zosimus 1.55.

29. See the excellent discussion of Roman triumphs in Mary Beard, *The Roman Triumph* (Cambridge, 2007).

30. Aurelius Victor, *About the Caesars* 28.2, Epitome 28.3, *HA Gordian* 33, 1-2.

31. His successor Tacitus pursued the conspirators (*HA Tacitus* 13) as did Probus (*HA Probus* 13).

32. The German scholar Hermann Dassau first raised doubts about the *Historia Augusta* in 1889, calling its author 'a forger'. It took many more decades for his view to be generally accepted.

33. Ernest Will, *La Venise des Sables,* 167.

34. D. Burgersdijk, 'Zenobia's Biography in the Historia Augusta', *Talanta* 36-7 (2004-5).

35. *HA The 30 Pretenders* 30.20.

36. See G. Bowersock, 'The Hellenism of Zenobia', in *Greek Connections*, ed. J.T.A. Koumoulides (Notre Dame, 1987).

37. The Younger Pliny, *Letters* 2.20.

2. Zenobia – 'a brigand, or more accurately, a woman'

1. Geoffrey Chaucer, *Canterbury Tales: The Monk's Tale: Zenobia*, tr. D. Wright (Oxford World's Classics, 1985).

2. Zosimus 1.39.

3. John of Antioch, fragment 152.2.

4. *HA The 30 Pretenders* 30.5-18.

5. Aurelius Victor, *The Caesars* 33.3.

6. Burgersdijk, 'Zenobia's biography in the Historia Augusta', *Talanta* 36-7. The fact, also cited, that Tacitus mentions another Zenobia in his *Annals* bk.12 is surely irrelevant – it was probably a common name.

7. *HA The 30 Pretenders* 30.15.

8. There are several examples of Zenobia coins in the Cabinet des Médailles, part of the Bibliothèque Nationale de France, Paris, especially inventory numbers 3645, 3646, 3647, 3648 and 3649. See also K. Emmett, *Alexandrian Coins* (2001).

9. The Latin is *limbo purpureo*, where a *limbus* means an ornamental border or fringe on a robe, or a girdle. But I assume that Zenobia would not have let gems drag along the floor.

10. *HA The 30 Pretenders* 30.13.

11. See excellent photographs in the 1998 catalogue issued by the museum *The Palmyrene Inscriptions*.

12. E. Equini Schneider, *Moi, Zenobie, Reine de Palmyre*, 25, for the Arab tradition about Zenobia.

13. See the excellent short summary in T. Cornell and J. Matthews, *Atlas of the Roman World* (New York, 1982), 180-1.

14. *HA The 30 Pretenders* 30.12.

15. Cassius Dio 62.1.1 and 2.2-4.

16. Hingley and Unwin, *Boudica – Iron Age Warrior Queen*, 58.
17. *HA The 30 Pretenders* 30.7.
18. See D.F. Graf, *Rome and the Arabian Frontier* (Ashgate, 1997), 356-7.
19. Malalas 26 and 28.
20. Graf, 351-4.
21. See R. Alston and S. Lieu, *Aspects of the Roman Near East* (Brepols, 2007), 4 and 11. Alston writes: 'I assume that the involvement of the Palmyrenes was a function of their expertise in dealing with Eastern markets'.
22. *HA The 30 Pretenders* 30.22.
23. See for example the inscription at *CIS* 2.3971, a milestone found west of Palmyra and giving the distance of 14 miles (from Palmyra presumably) with that form of her name and the Palmyrene version SPTYMY' BTZBY.
24. For Zabbai, see the inscription at *OGIS* 648 (also *IGR* 3.1030 and *Inv.* 3.20), in which Zabdas and Zabbai (or Zabaios), generals both, honour Septimia Zenobia.
25. See Khaled As'ad and J. Yon, *Inscriptions de Palmyre* (Institut d'Archéologie du Proche Orient, 2001), 69-70.
26. M. Sartre, *The Middle East Under Rome* (English translation Harvard, 2005), 551 n. 105.
27. See *Inv.* 3.22 (also *OGIS* 2.640, *IGR* 3.1033 and *CIS* 2.3932) with 19 lines of Greek and only 8 of Palmyrene.
28. Sartre, 352, says Zenobios' claim is 'not substantiated' and (551 n.105) 'the argument is extremely weak'.
29. As'ad and Yon, *Inscriptions*, 69-70.
30. *HA The 30 Pretenders* (*Zenobia*) 30.2.
31. *HA The 30 Pretenders* 30.2
32. Accessed on 04/10/2008 and 25/06/2009.
33. For example, *IGR* 3.1027 and 3.1028 (also found at *OGIS* 647 and 649).
34. See *IGR* 3.1029 (also found at *OGIS* 650) which refers to an Antiochus whose mother was Zenobia.
35. Zosimus 60: 'they placed the purple robe around Antiochus'.
36. Continuator of Cassius Dio fragment 7. For Hairan, and an extended discussion of the sons of Odenathus, see D.S. Potter, *Prophecy and History in the Crisis of the Roman Empire* (Oxford, 1990), appendix 4, 386-8. Potter concludes he had two by his first wife, two by Zenobia, namely Hairan and Vaballathus. I remain to be convinced.
37. *HA The 30 Pretenders* 27 and 28, and *Aurelian* 38.1.
38. Syncellus, *Chronography* 470, with Zonaras 12.27.
39. Eutropius 9.13.2 supported by Jerome, *Chronicle* 274, Eusebius, *Chronicle* 263.2-5 and *HA The 30 Pretenders* 30.27.
40. Zonaras 12.27.
41. See U. Hartmann, *Das Palmyrische Teilreich* (Franz Steiner, 2001), 112-16, for a discussion of whether there were one or two sons of Odenathus' first marriage, concluding that there was 'probably' just one, with variant names, Hairan or (in Greek) Haeranes (HYRN in Palmyrene) and Herodianus (Herodianos in Greek). For Hartmann's complete stemma for Odenathus' family, including an Antiochus as a son of Zenobia, see his p. 128.
42. The *HA Gallienus* 13.1 and *The 30 Pretenders* 15.5 (about Odenathus) says that his cousin Maeonius killed him, but at 17.2 (on Maeonius) adds a report that Maeonius was in conspiracy with Zenobia. Zosimus 1.39 confirms that Odenathus' death was the result of treachery, as does Syncellus 467, and Zonaras 12.24 agrees it was a cousin. The Continuator of Cassius Dio, fragment 7, says Odenathus was

executed with the agreement of Gallienus, and John of Antioch, fragment 152, calls it a conspiracy of Gallienus. Malalas 12.298 also blames Gallienus for the killing of Odenathus, but in battle.

3. Bride of the desert: deliberately inventing Palmyra

1. T. Kaizer, *The Religious Life of Palmyra* (Franz Steiner, 2002), 17 for population.
2. The phrase is J. Teixidor's. Palmyra has also been termed 'the bride of the desert'.
3. D.L. Kennedy in *The Roman Army in the East* (*JRA* Supplement 18, 1996), 11.
4. Appian, *Civil Wars* 5.1.9.
5. For India, Strabo 2.5.14, with 17.1.13. For Palmyrene ships, *Inv.* 10.91, 10.95 and 10.96.
6. M. Hammad, 'An Amphitheatre at Tadmor-Palmyra?', *Syria* 85 (2008).
7. This tax or tariff law, found cut into stones 1.75 metres tall and 4.8 metres wide, and now in the Hermitage Museum in St Petersburg, is well discussed in I. Browning, *Palmyra* (Chatto, 1979) and by J.F. Matthews, 'The Tax Law of Palmyra', *JRS* 74 (1984). For the text see *OGIS* 629 and *IGR* 3.1056. The *Periplus of the Erythraean Sea* (tr. L. Casson, 1989) also lists goods brought in from India.
8. *Caravan Cities* (Oxford, 1932).
9. See F. Millar, 'Caravan Cities: the Roman Near East and Long Distance Trade by Land', *BICS* Supplement 71 (1998), and R. Alston and S. Lieu, *Aspects of the Roman Near East* (Brepols, 2007), 2.
10. At 2 Chronicles 8.4 and 1 Kings 9.18.
11. Malalas 18.2.
12. Josephus, *Jewish Antiquities* 8.153-4.
13. Palmyra is extensively but somewhat differently treated in G.K. Young, *Rome's Eastern Trade* (Routledge, 2001); M. Sartre, *The Middle East under Rome* (English tr., Harvard, 2005); B. Isaac, *The Limits of Empire* (Oxford, 1990); D.S. Potter, *The Roman Empire at Bay* (Routledge, 2004); *Prophecy and History in the Crisis of the Roman Empire* (Oxford, 1990); F. Millar, *The Roman Near East* (Cambridge, 1993); E. Will, *Les Palmyréniens: La Venise des Sables* (Armand Collin, 1992); and K. Butcher, *Roman Syria and the Near East* (British Museum Press, 2003). For any beginner in this complex area, I recommend Butcher's book, which has excellent maps.
14. Millar, *Roman Near East*, 319.
15. Quoted in M. Kociejowski, *Syria Through Writers' Eyes* (Eland, 2006), 101.
16. Pliny, *Natural History* 5.88.
17. Kaizer, *Religious Life*, 17.
18. Butcher, *Roman Syria*, 156.
19. Strabo, *Geography* 16.1.27.
20. Will, *Les Palmyréniens*, 20-1.
21. Appian, *Civil Wars* 5.1.9.
22. For Palmyra's bowmen, see also *HA Claudius* 7 and *Aurelian* 26.
23. Appian 5.1.10.
24. Herodian 6.4.5.
25. Pliny, *Natural History* 5.88.
26. Will, *Les Palmyréniens*, 10.
27. Butcher, *Roman Syria*, 277.

28. As noted previously, Aurelius Victor speaks of the Roman East falling 'under the dominion of brigands and a woman' (*The Caesars* 33.3). Malalas refers to 'barbarian Saracens' (12.297) and the continuator of Cassius Dio refers to 'the barbarian horde' (*FHG* 4 p. 197). *HA Aurelian* twice refers to 'the brigands of Syria' (26 and 27).

29. See Wikipedia, under 'Aramaic', accessed Jan 2009.

30. *HA The 30 Pretenders* 30.21.

31. Isaac, *Limits of Empire*, 143.

32. See e.g. *Inv.* 9.6 (Seleucia) and *Inv.* 9.11 (Babylon).

33. Dignas and Winter, *Rome and Persia in Late Antiquity*, 156.

34. See especially Young, *Rome's Eastern Trade*, 137-8 and 149.

35. M. Gawlikowski in 'Palmyra as a Trading Centre', *Iraq* 56 (1994) lists 34 Palmyrene inscriptions relating to the caravan trade.

36. See inscription no. 15 in Gawlikowski, 'Palmyra as a Trading Centre'.

37. Strabo, *Geography* 16.1.27.

38. *Synodiai* are the caravans in Greek. The *synodiarchs* are sometimes called *archemporoi* in the inscriptions. See *Inv.* 3.7 (bringing home a caravan safely), *Inv.* 3.13 (*archemporos*), *Inv.* 3.28, 9.14 and 9.30 for *synodiarchs*. Refer also to *OGIS* 2.632 and 2.633, and *IGR* 3.1050, 3.1052 and 3.1053.

39. The existence of wealthy 'patrons' as a separate activity was for long the received opinion, but I here follow Young in *Rome's Eastern Trade*, 151-4.

40. Young, *Rome's Eastern Trade*, 158, distinguishes between the full-time militia employed by the city and the ad hoc escorts put together for each caravan: but they must have been much the same men.

41. See Millar, *Roman Near East*, 328.

42. P. Erdkamp, *A Companion to the Roman Army* (Blackwell, 2007), 262.

43. Procopius, *On the Persian War* 1.1, tr. A. Cameron.

44. Isaac, *Limits of Empire*, 144.

4. Persia resurgent: the crisis of the third century

1. His name is variously transliterated into English as Sapur, Sapor, Shapor or Shabuhr. Similarly, their dynasty is variously referred to as Sasanian, Sassanian, Sassanid.

2. See B.C. MacDermott, 'Roman Emperors in the Sassanian Reliefs', *JRS* 44 (1954). The date of 260 is generally used for Valerian's capture, but some scholars have suggested 259 or even 258.

3. Specifically by M. Rostovtzeff.

4. For text and translation, see A. Maricq, 'Res Gestae Divi Saporis', *Syria* 35 (1958).

5. Herodian 6.4.5.

6. Two sackings of Antioch are attested by various Roman-era authors, including Zosimus 1.27 ('immense plunder'), Syncellus and Zonaras 12.23 ('a multitude of prisoners'). It was an obvious target for a Persian in search of booty. The second sack may have been in 260. Valerian had rebuilt Antioch in 254 (Zosimus 1.32.2), about the time when minting of coins began there after the first sack.

7. For a detailed exposition of the events of this period, see Millar, *The Roman Near East*, esp. 159-73; Potter, *The Roman Empire at Bay*, 3-69; and Sartre, *The Middle East under Rome*, 348-58.

8. Zosimus 12.36.

9. *On the Deaths of the Persecutors* 5.

10. For a non-Roman and more pro-Persian view of these events, see the online *Encyclopedia Iranica*, under 'Sapor'.

11. Zosimus 37.

12. See L. de Blois, *The Policy of the Emperor Gallienus* (Brill, 1976).

13. Aurelius Victor 33.

14. *HA The Two Gallieni* 26.1.

15. Dignas and Winter, *Rome and Persia in Late Antiquity*, 19.

16. See Millar, *Roman Near East*, 168, with *Inv.* 3.21 (for the year 247), *Inv.* 3.7 and 3.13 (for the 250s and 260s).

17. See *Oxford Classical Dictionary* entry on Hatra.

18. Herodian 3.9

19. Ammianus 25.8.5.

5. Just another usurper? The political legacy of the first Mr Zenobia

1. I use this transliteration of his name as being the simplest to pronounce in English: others use Odaenathus, or Odainathos – the Greek spelling – or Odainat or even Enathos, or of course 'DYNT as transliterated from the Palmyrene.

2. M. Gawlikowski, 'Les Princes de Palmyre', *Syria* 62 (1985). Also see Hartmann, *Das Palmyrenische Teilreich*, 128.

3. Zosimus 1.39; *HA The Two Valerians* 4 and *The 30 Pretenders* 15.

4. Odenathus' harassment of the withdrawing Persians is described in Zonaras 12.23, Eutropius 9.10 and Festus, *Breviarium* 23. His siege problems are in *HA The Two Gallieni* 10.

5. Festus, *Breviarium* 23.

6. Zosimus 12.36.

7. M. Sprengling, *Third Century Iran* (Chicago, 1953), 108.

8. Zosimus 1.29 says there were two campaigns by Odenathus against Persia, getting as far as Ctesiphon.

9. See A. Schmidt-Colinet (ed.), *Palmyra: Kulturbegegnung im Grenzbereich* (Mainz, 2005), 31, contribution by Professor M. Gawlikowski.

10. For the Quietus incident, see *HA The Two Gallieni* 2.2, *The 30 Pretenders* 14.1 and 15.4, and Zonaras 12.24.

11. *HA The Two Gallieni* 10.

12. *HA The Two Gallieni* 10.3; Zosimus 1.39.

13. See nn. 6 to 9 appended to Hebrew quotation reproduced at item 4.3.1 in M.H. Dodgeon and S.N.C. Lieu, *The Roman Eastern Frontier and the Persian Wars AD 226-363* (Routledge, 1991).

14. Quoted as item 4.3.3 in Dodgeon and Lieu, *Roman Eastern Frontier*.

15. Millar, *Roman Near East*, 169.

16. *HA The Two Gallieni* 12.6, confirmed by George Syncellus (quoted in section 4.5.1 of Dodgeon and Lieu, *Roman Eastern Frontier*).

17. See discussion and suggestions by L. de Blois, 'Odaenathus and the Roman-Persian War of 252-264 AD', *Talanta* 6 (1974).

18. Malalas 12.26.

19. Udo Hartmann in his introductory chapter to *Das Palmyrenische Teilreich* (Franz Steiner, 2001) 10.

20. G.K. Young, *Rome's Eastern Trade* (Routledge, 2001), 235 and 238.

21. Sartre, *The Middle East under Rome*, 354.

22. Dignas and Winter, *Rome and Persia in Late Antiquity*, 25 and 160.

23. Zonaras 12.24.

24. The titles held or attributed to Odenathus and to his son by his first wife Haeranes, have fascinated several scholars. See Potter, *The Roman Empire at Bay*, 259-61; Potter, *Prophecy and History in the Crisis of the Roman Empire*, appendix 4; B. Isaac, *The Limits of Empire*, 220-8; Millar, *Roman Near East*, 165-73; and Young, *Rome's Eastern Trade*, Appendix 4. A health warning – much of the discussion is based on a prior presumption of Odenathus as a loyal ally of Rome.

25. Millar, *Roman Near East*, 171.

26. Agathias 4.24.

27. *HA The Two Gallieni* 56.

28. *HA The Two Gallieni* 10.4.

29. *HA The Two Gallieni* 21.5.

30. *HA The Two Gallieni* 10.5.

31 Malalas 12.27.

32. The Continuator of Cassius Dio, fragment 7, says Odenathus was executed with the agreement of Gallienus, and John of Antioch, fragment 152.2, calls it a conspiracy of Gallienus.

33. *HA The Two Gallieni* 13.5.

34. Peter Patricius, fragment 10.

35. See D. Schlumberger, 'Vorod l'Agoranome', *Syria* 49 (1972), with *Inv.* 3.6, 3.7, 3.8, 3.9, 3.10 and 3.11.

36. See *HA Aurelian* 27-8.

37. Millar, *Roman Near East*, 168

38. Sartre, *The Middle East under Rome*, 355.

6. Arms and the woman: Zenobia goes to war

1. Herodian 2.7.9 and 2.10.7.

2. Hartmann, *Das Palmyrenische Teilreich*, ch. 1.

3. The view supported by Eutropius 9.13.2 and by John of Antioch fragment 152.

4. *HA Galllienus* 13. 4-5.

5. Potter, *Roman Empire at Bay*, 266 thinks that the failed expedition took place under Claudius on chronological grounds because Heraclianus had previously been too busy plotting the assassination of Gallienus.

6. *HA Claudius* 4.3-4.

7. D. Magie, Loeb edition of *Historia Augusta, Claudius* 1, n. 1.

8. See G.S. Aldrete, *Gestures and Acclamations in Ancient Rome* (Johns Hopkins University Press, 1999).

9. R. Winsbury, *The Roman Book* (Duckworth, 2009), 116.

10. *HA Tacitus* 4.1-4, 5.1-2 and 7.1, and *Probus* 11.6-9 and 12.8.

11. *HA The 30 Pretenders* (Zenobia) 30.11. Interestingly, there is an alternative reading of the text which provides 'secretly' instead of 'deliberately', which might suit the context better and be a more interesting comment. The Latin variants are *consulte* (deliberately) or *occulte* (secretly).

12. Zosimus 1.43 and 45.

13. Zosimus 1.39 and John of Antioch fragment 152.2.

14. The positions of the two generals are given in two inscriptions *Inv.* 3.19 and *Inv.* 3.20, where they are called (or call themselves) 'eminent men'.

15. D. Nappo, 'The Impact of the Third Century Crisis on the International Trade with the East', 242, in O. Hekster et al. (eds), *Crises and the Roman Empire* (Brill, 2007).

16. Young, *Rome's Eastern Trade*, 181.
17. Zosimus 1.44-6.
18. *IGLS* 9107, cited at Dodgeon and Lieu, *Roman Eastern Frontier*, 4.6.4.
19. Malalas 12.
20. Hartmann, *Das Palmyrenische Teilreich*, 281, repeated by Southern, *Zenobia*, 109.
21. Continuator of Dio, *FHG* 4.
22. See discussion in Watson, *Aurelian*, 238.
23. Zosimus 1.44.
24. *HA Claudius* 11 refers to him as Probatus. Zosimus 1.44 calls him Probus, as does Syncellus.
25. The phrase used by Zosimus 1.44 and Orosius 7.22.12.
26. Zosimus 1.50.
27. Referred to by Procopius, *The Persian War* 2.5.
28. Zosimus 1.51.
29. Zosimus 1.50.
30. *HA Aurelian* 22.5.
31. See milestone cited at *CIS* 2.3971 and Dodgeon and Lieu, *Roman Eastern Frontier*, 4.5.5.
32. See Egyptian papyrus documents *P.Oxy.* 1264 and *BGU* 946, cited at Dodgeon and Lieu, *Roman Eastern Frontier*, 4.7.5, where their date is given as March 272. There is an extended discussion of this complex matter by Sartre, *Middle East under Rome*, 551 n. 109.
33. These titles are found on coins and milestones. See *ILS* 8924 (Imperator Caesar Augustus), *IGR* 3.1027 and 1065 = *OGIS* 647 (both in the Greek form, *despotes autocrator*).
34. Equini Schneider in *Moi, Zenobie, Reine de Palmyre*, 23.
35. J-P Rey-Coquais, 'Syrie Romaine', *JRS* 68 (1978).
36. This striking phrase is Potter's.
37. *HA The 30 Pretenders* 30.23.

7. The French connection: guardians of the Rhine

1. I am particularly indebted to J.F. Drinkwater and his extensive account in *The Gallic Empire*, Historia Einzelschriften 52 (1987), with input from R.J. Bourne, *Aspects of the Relationship between Central and Gallic Empires in the Mid to Late Third century AD with Special Reference to Coinage Studies* (BAR International Series 963, 2001) and (in French) J. Lafaurie, 'L'empire Gaulois. L'apport de la numismatique', *ANRW* 2.2 (1975).
2. My translation of the *HA's si facultas locorum pateretur* (*The 30 Pretenders* 30.23).
3. Among Roman era authors, Eutropius, Orosius, Zonaras and Zosimus all refer, if briefly, to these events in the western provinces, as well as Aurelius Victor and the *Historia Augusta*. In the background are also Dexippus and a supposed common source for some of these other authors, the hypothesised 'Kaisergeschichte' or KG.
4. '[Gallic Empire coin hoards] taken en masse do impart a more or less consistent sum of information, but it is information that is hard to assess. For that situation to change, a reliable method of translating numismatic data into historical language would have to be developed – at present unlikely.' C. Cheesman, cited by Bourne.
5. Orosius 7.22.10.

6. Eutropius 9.11.

7. See Aurelius Victor, *De Caesaribus* 33.8, Zosimus 1.38.2 and Zonaras 12.24.

8. Eutropius 9.1 says ten years, backed by coin evidence. See T.D. Barnes 'Some Persons in the Historia Augusta', *Phoenix* 26 (1972).

9. See description in P. Van Gansbeke, 'La mise en état de la defence de la Gaule au milieu de IIIe siècle après J-C.', *Latomus* 14 (1955).

10. A.R. Birley, 'Britain during the Third Century Crisis', 49, in Hekster et al. (eds), *Crises and the Roman Empire*.

11. Zosimus 1.41 and Zonaras 26.1.

12. *HA The 30 Pretenders* 5.4 with Gansbeke, 'La mise en état'.

13. Bourne, *Coinage*, 6, remarks that 'even during the period of the Gallic regime there is little evidence of an improvement of military sites, somewhat surprising if one considers a nationalistic tendency and fear of barbarian invasion as being motives for the revolt of Postumus'.

14. Eutropius 9.9.

15. Drinkwater, *Gallic Empire*, 53.

16. Bourne, *Coinage*, 1.

17. Bourne, *Coinage*, 4-5. See Chapter 5 on the pretender list in the *Historia Augusta*.

18. See Drinkwater, *Gallic Empire*, 19.

19. For Gaul see Drinkwater, 20.

20. See e.g. Hekster, *Rome and its Empire*, 83.

21. See e.g. *Cambridge Ancient History*, 2nd edn, vol. 12.

22. Hekster, *Rome and its Empire*, 25.

23. Watson, *Aurelian*, 90 argues for containment.

8. Warrior and showman: the 'puzzling' emperor Aurelian

1. *CAH* vol. 12, p. 61 and Potter, *Empire at Bay*, 268.

2. Orosius 7.23.4; Eutropius 9.13.

3. Malalas, *Chronicle* 12.30: *polemicos*.

4. Eutropius 9.13.

5. Lactantius, *On the Deaths of the Persecutors* 6.

6. *HA Aurelian* 34.2: *severus, truculentus, sanguinarius princeps*.

7. *HA Aurelian* 44.2: *nimia ferocitas*.

8. *HA Aurelian* 44.1.

9. *Epitome* 35.4-5: *ultima crudelitas*.

10. *HA Aurelian* 8.3.

11. *HA Aurelian* 44.2.

12. Eutropius 9.14.

13. *HA Aurelian* 37.1.

14. Malalas 12.30.

15. Ammianus 30.8.8.

16. See excellent discussion in Watson, *Aurelian*, esp. 159-63.

17. *HA Aurelian* 3.

18. *Epitome* 35.1.

19. *HA Aurelian* 4.2.

20. *HA Aurelian* 6.1, Malalas 12.30.

21. *HA Aurelian* 6.4.

22. *HA Aurelian* 10.

23. *HA Aurelian* 7.4.

24. Eutropius 9.1.

25. Potter, *Empire at Bay*, 264.

26. The phrase used by the Russian historian M. Rostovtseff.

27. P. Cosme, 'A propos de l'édit de Gallien', 109, in Hekster et al. (eds), *Crises and the Roman Empire.*

28. *HA Claudius* 11.6-8, *Aurelian* 18.1. We cannot be sure exactly what forces that command consisted of at this time.

29. For detail see the finely argued chronology proposed by Watson, *Aurelian*, especially his Appendix B on 'Problems of Chronology'. Zosimus 39 for attack on Athens.

30. Aurelius Victor 33.

31. Ammianus 16.12.36.

32. *HA Claudius* 11.3-9 and Zosimus 1.45.

33. Zosimus 1.42-3.

34. L. De Blois, *The Policy of the Emperor Gallienus* (Brill, 1976), 214.

35. Zosimus 1.40.

36. Aurelius Victor 33.19-21 'a plan of Aurelian'. Victor is the only author to finger Aurelian by name.

37. Eutropius 9.12 for this account of Quintillus.

38. Malalas 12.30.

39. Zosimus 1.48.

40. See R.T. Saunders, 'Aurelian's Two Iuthungian Wars', *Historia* 41 (1992) and J.F. Drinkwater, *The Alamanni and Rome* (Oxford, 2007). Drinkwater argues that the names used by Roman authors for invading Germanic forces may be somewhat arbitrary and not reflect any organised ethnic group or 'gens' with distinct ethnic identity. See also analysis in Watson, *Aurelian*, 216-21.

41. Saunders, 'Aurelian's Two Iuthungian Wars', 72.

42. See Dexippus fragment 6 = *Fragmenta Historicorum Graecorum* 3, 682-5. See also *HA Aurelian* 18.6 and Epitome 35.2

43. See Drinkwater, *Alamanni,* esp. 74-8.

44. Dexippus uses the Greek word *strateusantes* which his modern editor equates with *educimus* in Latin, both of which can fairly be translated in this way.

45. Drinkwater, *Alamanni*, 77 and 360-1.

46. For a good discussion of the wall, with excellent diagrams and pictures, see N. Field, *The Walls of Rome* (Oxford, 2008).

47. Zosimus 1.49.

48. Saunders, 'Aurelian's Two Iuthungian Wars', 78.

49. Aurelius Victor 35, with *Epitome* 35.4-5 and Eutropius 9.14.

50. Zosimus 1.49, with *HA Aurelian* 21 and 38, and Eutropius 9.14.

51. Malalas 30.

52. *HA Aurelian* 39.5.

53. Aurelius Victor 33.

9. Showdown: Aurelian *versus* Zenobia's cooking-pot men

1. *HA Aurelian* 26.5: *timet quasi femina, pugnat quasi poenam timens.*

2. Zosimus 1.39-56.

3. Orosius, *Histories* 7.22.12; Festus, *Breviarium* 33; Jerome, *Chronicon*; Jordanes, *Historia Romana.*

4. Festus, *Breviarium* 24.

5. Livy 35.48 (Antiochus); (Carrhae) Dio 40.22 and Plutarch, *Crassus* 24.

6. Ammianus 16.10.
7. Ammianus 16.12.
8. *HA Alexander Severus* 56.5.
9. Heliodorus 9.15, tr. W. Lamb (Dent, 1997).
10. *HA Aurelian* 22.5.
11. Orosius, *Against the Pagans* 7.23.4: *magis proelii terrore quam proelio.*
12. Festus, *Breviarium* 33-4.
13. Zosimus 50.
14. A complex debate about the exact order and location of battle was summarised (and settled) by G. Downey, 'Aurelian's Victory at Immae AD 272', *TAPA* 81 (1950).
15. *HA Aurelian* 11.4.
16. *HA Aurelian* 25.1.
17. *HA The 30 Pretenders* 30.3.
18. *HA Aurelian* 26.1-6.
19. *HA Aurelian* 26.6-27.5.
20. *HA Aurelian* 27.2.
21. M. Gawlikowski, 'Inscriptions de Palmyre', *Syria* 48 (1971); *Inv.* 9.28.
22. I have drawn here upon P. Erdkamp (ed.), *A Companion to the Roman Army* (Blackwell, 2007) and J.W. Eadie, 'The Development of Roman Mailed Cavalry', *JRS* 57 (1967).
23. *HA Aurelian* 35.4.
24. *HA Aurelian* 35.4, 41.9.

10. The end of the affair: golden chains and silver statue

1. Zosimus 1.56.
2. *HA Aurelian* 30.
3. *HA Aurelian* 30.
4. Southern, *Empress Zenobia*, 146.
5. John of Antioch, fragment 155.
6. Eunapius, *Lives of the Sophists* 456. Plotinus apparently said Longinus was a scholar but no philosopher (Porphyry, *Life of Plotinus* ch. 14, 19-20).
7. Libanius, *Letters* 1078 for panegyric to Odenathus.
8. Athanasius, *History of the Arians* 71 says that Zenobia was a Jewess (she was semitic) and supporter of Paul of Samosata. Other church writers also connect him with Palmyra, but Eusebius in his *Ecclesiastical History* does not.
9. *HA The 30 Pretenders* 30.22. See also Millar, *Roman Near East*, 169 and Potter, *Roman Empire at Bay*, 267-8.
10. *HA Aurelian* 30.
11. Zosimus 1.61.
12. *HA Aurelian* 32 and *Firmus* 3-5.
13. Eutropius 9.13 and *HA The 30 Pretenders* 24, supported by Aurelius Victor 35 and Zosimus 1.61.
14. Virgil *Aeneid* 6.365
15. Zonaras 12.27.
16. Zosimus 1.59.
17. Zonaras 12.27.
18. Malalas *Chronicle* 12.299.
19. Jerome, *Chronicon* s.a. 274; Jordanes, *Historia Romana* 291; Festus, *Breviarium* 23; Eutropius 9.13; *HA The 30 Pretenders* 30.24.
20. Syncellus, *Chronography* 470.

21. While differing in detail, the *HA*, Eutropius and Aurelius Victor all agree on this.

22. *HA The 30 Pretenders* 30.24-7. Translations are from the Loeb edition of the *HA*.

23. *HA Aurelian* 34.

24. *HA Aurelian* 33.

25. As for example by Burgersdijk, 'Zenobia's biography in the Historia Augusta', *Talanta* 36-7.

26. For Arsinoe see Cassius Dio 43.19.

27. Juvenal 6.589.

28. See Beard, *Roman Triumph*, 128-42.

29. The temple is mentioned by Zosimus 1.61, Aurelius Victor 35, *HA Aurelian* 35. There is dispute about exactly what these cult statues were.

30. For extended discussion of religion at Palmyra, see T. Kaizer, *The Religious Life of Palmyra* (Franz Steiner, 2002). For sun worship, see G.H. Halsberghe, *The Cult of Sol Invictus* (Brill, 1972) and R. Beck, *The Religion of the Mithras Cult in the Roman Empire: Mysteries of the Unconquered Sun* (Oxford, 2006).

32. See *ZPE* 2.16.2 'Le Culte Imperiale au IIIe Siècle', esp. 1071-3.

33. For both visions see *HA Aurelian* 24 and 25.

34. *CAH*, 2nd edn, vol. 12, 557.

35. *HA Tacitus* 9.

11. Re-assessing Zenobia, 'a celebrated female sovereign'

1. Lydia Maria Child, writing in 1865, quoted by Waller (see next note), 25.

2. Susan Waller, 'The Artist, the Writer and the Queen: Hosmer, Jameson and Zenobia', *Woman's Art Journal* 4:1 (1983), 22-6.

3. Mara Witzling in *Voicing our Visions* (Women's Press, 1991), 44.

4. Gabrielle Gopinath, 'Harriet Hosmer and the Feminine Sublime', *Oxford Art Journal* 28 (2005) 64-69.

5. Margaret Thorp in *New England Quarterly* (June 1959), 158.

6. Gopinath's phrase.

7. See I. Browning, *Palmyra* (Chatto, 1979), 47.

8. See Cassius Dio 55 and Tacitus, *Annals* 1.3, 1.5 and 1.6.

9. The quotation is from Judith Weingarten's extensive website about Zenobia and Palmyra at www.zenobia.tv and judithweingarten.blogspot.com, accessed September 2009.

10. Information: Judith Weingarten's website.

Appendix A

1. For *lamprotatos*, with or without *synkletikos*, see for example *Inv.* 3.16 (= *IGR* 3.1035 = *CIS* 2.3944) for Odenathus' son, and for Odenathus himself *Inv.* 3.17 (= *IGR* 3.1031 = *CIS* 2.3945) and *Inv.* 8.55 (a family burial monument = *OGIS* 2.642 = *IGR* 3.1034 = *CIS* 2.4202) and *OGIS* 2.643.

2. See for example *Inv.* 3.17 and the trade guild inscriptions discussed in Gawlikowski, 'Les Princes de Palmyre', *Syria* 62.

3. See Young, *Rome's Eastern Trade*, 234; Potter, *Prophecy*, 389-90; Millar, *Roman Near East*, 165.

4. See *Inv.* 3.16 for the son; and *OGIS* 2.643 with Gawlikowski, *Syria* 62 (1985), 251-61 for the father.

5. Young, *Rome's Eastern Trade*, 232.

6. *Inv.* 3.17 = *CIS* 2.3945.

7. These trade guild inscriptions are discussed by Gawlikowski, 'Les Princes'. In his list, number 9 refers to 'despotes' but numbers 5, 7 and 8 refer to Odenathus as patron.

8. Millar, *Roman Near East*, 165.

9. *Inv.* 3.3 = *IGR* 1032, for Herodianus receiving the title at a ceremony on the Orontes river, perhaps after some victory over Persian forces: and *Inv.* 3.19 and *CIS* 2.3971 (a milestone) for posthumous references to Odenathus as King of Kings.

10. Young, *Rome's Eastern Trade*, 237.

11. *Inv.* 3.19 = *CIS* 2.3946 (again) and *CIS* 2.3971 (that milestone again).

12. Potter, *Prophecy*, 391.

13. See Millar, *Roman Near East*, 170; Young, *Rome's Eastern Trade*, 238; and Isaac, *Limits of Empire*, 221.

14. Millar, *Roman Near East*, 171.

15. The milestones and coins are discussed by Millar, *Roman Near East*, 171-2. Coins call Vaballathus 'DR' = Dux Romanorum, and 'Imperator'.

16. *HA The Two Gallieni* 12.1.

17. Festus 13.

18. *Inv.* 3.4 = *CIS* 2.3934

19. Zonaras 12.23 and 24.

20. For the full range of meanings, see the *Oxford Latin Dictio*nary.

21. *HA The Two Gallieni* 10.1

22. Eusebius 29.

23. *HA The 30 Pretenders* 15.1.

24. *HA The Two Gallieni* 3.5.

25. Zosimus 1.39

Appendix B

1. Potter, *Roman Empire at Bay*, 270. See also J. Rea in *Chronique d'Egypte* 87 (1969) for the 'coalition' and 'co-ruler' theory.

2. Southern, *Empress Zenobia*, 88, citing Hartmann and Rey-Coquais as sources.

3. A. Martin, 'P.Mich.Inv. 5478a et le préfet d'Egypte Statilius Ammianus', *Latomus* 59 (2000).

4. Watson, *Aurelian and the Third Century*, 169.

5. P.J. Sijpesteijn in *Papyrologica Lugduno-Batava (Pap. Lugd. Batava)* 16 (1967).

6. N. Lewis, 'Noemata legontos' (but in Greek letters) *BASP* 4 (1967), 34. His reading also means substituting the Greek capital letter D in the place of the Greek capital letter S which appears in Sijpesteijn's original reading, since Aurelian's full name was Lucius Domitius Aurelianus.

7. J. Rea, 'Two Notes', *BASP* 5 (1968), 40.

8. J. Rea, 'The Date of the Prefecture of Statilius Ammianus', *Chronique d'Egypte* 87 (1969).

9. G. Bastianini, 'P. Wisconsin 2 e la Prefettura di Statilius Ammianus', *ZPE* 32 (1978), 81-4.

10. P.J. Sijpesteijn, 'Known and Unknown Officials', *ZPE* 106 (1995), 203-34, but esp. 210-11.

11. *P.Oxy* XL 2904.

12. *P.Oxy* XL 2902.

13. See discussion of this man by J. Rea in *Chronique d'Egypte* 87 (1969), 135 commenting on the papyri *PSI* (*Papiri greci e latini della Società Italiana*) 10.1101 and 1102, which are the main evidence for Marcellinus, with Watson, *Aurelian*, 169 and 264 n. 28.

14. 'most likely Zenobia's choice' – Southern, *Empress Zenobia*, 115.

15. See Potter, *Empire at Bay*, 271.

16. J-P. Rey-Coquais, 'Syrie Romaine de Pompée à Dioclétien', *JRS* 68 (1978) for both Virius Lupus and Salvius Theodorus.

Bibliography

Place names refer to the university press of that name.

Abbreviations

ANRW = *Aufsteig und Niedergang der Römischen Welt*
BASP = *Bulletin of the American Society of Papyrologists*
BICS = *Bulletin of the Institute of Classical Studies*
CIS = *Corpus Inscriptionum Latinarum*
HA = *Historia Augusta*
IGR = *Inscriptiones Graecae ad Res Romanas Pertinentes*
ILS = *Inscriptiones Latinae Selectae*, ed. H. Dessau
Inv. = *Inventaire des Inscriptions de Palmyre,* ed. J. Cantineau
JRS = *Journal of Roman Studies*
OGIS = *Orientis Graeci Inscriptiones Selectae*
P.Oxy. = *Oxyrhynchus Papyri*
Pap. Lugd. Batava = *Papyrologica Lugduno-Batava*
TAPA = *Transactions of the American Philological Association*
ZPE = *Zeitschrift für Papyrologie und Epigrafik*

Main classical sources for Zenobia

For a more comprehensive and detailed list of authors relevant to the period, please consult Dodgeon and Lieu, *The Roman Eastern Frontier and the Persian Wars AD 226-363*, to which I am also indebted for the following.

Ammianus Marcellinus. Soldier turned historian, from Antioch. Fought against Persia. His surviving history covers the years 353-78.
Aurelius Victor. From Africa. Around 360 published a brief account of the Roman empire down to his own day.
Cassius Dio. Greek historian and senator (consul 205 and 229). Wrote large-scale history of Rome from foundation to his own time, only part of which survives.
Epitome des Caesaribus. A summary by an unknown author of the history of the Roman Empire from Augustus to Theodosius.
Eunapius. Greek scholar of the fourth century who wrote a history of the period 270-404.
Eusebius. Greek churchman and theologian who lived about 260 to 340 and wrote an *Ecclesiastical History* from the Apostles down to Constantine.
Eutropius. Probably from Bordeaux, he published not later than 380 a summary of Roman history from the start to the emperor Jovian.
Festus. Latin writer who published a brief outline of Roman history in about 370.
Herodian. Greek historian whose work covers the period 180-238.

Bibliography

Jerome (a.k.a. Eusebius Hieronymus). Theologian, translator and Bible scholar who lived about 340 to 420 and continued the historical work of Eusebius.

John of Antioch. Wrote a chronicle of events from the Creation to 610.

Jordanes. Latin historian who lived about 550 and wrote about Gothic and Roman history.

Lactantius. Latin church propagandist who lived about 240 to 320 and wrote *De mortibus persecutorum* (*About the Deaths of our Persecutors*).

Libanius. Greek scholar and orator from Antioch, an influential pagan. Lived about 314 to 393.

Malalas. Greek lawyer from Antioch who wrote a world survey from the Creation to 563.

Orosius. Spanish priest who wrote *Historia adversus Paganos*, a history of Rome from its beginning to 417, from a Christian viewpoint.

Peter the Patrician. Greek government official under the emperor Justinian who wrote several works of history only known from fragments.

Procopius. From Caesarea, he was military secretary to Belisarius, Justinian's great general, and served on the eastern frontier.

Scriptores Historiae Augustae. Collection of biographies of Roman emperors purporting to be by six authors but probably by one, written after 360.

Syncellus, Georgius. Latin form of Greek name of an eighth- to ninth-century author of a chronicle of events from early times to 284 which drew on Eusebius.

Zonaras. Byzantine historian of the twelfth century who wrote a universal history down to 1118 which is a summary of previous works.

Zosimus. Greek historian and government official who wrote his *Historia Nova* (*New History*) covering the period 180 to 410, relying much on Eunapius.

Modern authors

Alcock, S., *The Early Roman Empire in the East* (Oxbow, 1997).

Alston, R and S. Lieu (eds), *Aspects of the Roman Near East* (Brepols, 2007).

Armstrong, D., 'Gallienus in Athens, 264', *ZPE* 70 (1987).

As'sad, Khaled and Jean-Baptiste Yon, *Inscriptions de Palmyre* (Institut Français d'Archéologie du Proche Orient, 2001).

Augé, C. and J.M. Dentzer, *Petra, the Rose-red City* (Thames and Hudson, 2000).

Baldini, A., 'Discendenti a Roma da Zenobia?', *ZPE* 30 (1978).

Ball, W., *Rome in the East* (Routledge, 2000).

Barnes, T.D., 'Some Persons in the Historia Augusta', *Phoenix* 26 (1972).

Bastianini, G., 'P.Wisconsin 2 e la Prefettura di Statilius Ammianus', *ZPE* 32 (1978).

Bauer, G.C., *The Age of the Soldier Emperors* (Noyes Press, 1975).

Beard, M., *The Roman Triumph* (Cambridge, 2007).

Beck, R., *Religion of the Mithras Cult in the Roman Empire* (Oxford, 2006).

Bouchier, E.S., *Syria as a Roman Province* (Blackwell, 1916).

Bourne, R.J., *Aspects of the Relationship between the Central and Gallic Empires*, BAR International Series 963 (2001).

Bouzou, T., in *Moi, Zenobie, Reine de Palmyre* (Exhibition catalogue, Paris 2001).

Bowersock, G., 'The Hellenism of Zenobia', in J.T.A. Koumoulides (ed.), *Greek Connections* (Notre Dame, 1986).

Bowersock, G., *Roman Arabia* (Cambridge, 1983).

Bowman, A.K., P. Garnsey and A. Cameron (eds), *Cambridge Ancient History*, 2nd edn, vol. 12: *The Crisis of Empire AD 193-337*.

Bibliography

Browning, I., *Palmyra* (Chatto, 1979)

Burgersdijk, D., 'Zenobia's Biography in the Historia Augusta', *Talanta* 36-7 (2004-5)

Butcher, K., *Roman Syria* (British Museum Press, 2003).

Caubet, A., *Aux Sources du Monde Arabe* (Louvre illustrated catalogue).

Christol, M., *Essai sur l'Evolution des Carrières Senatoriales* (Nouvelles Editions Latines, 1986).

Christol, M., *L'Empire Romain de 3me Siècle* (Editions Errance, 1997).

Cizek, E., *L'Empereur Aurelian* (Paris, Les Belles Lettres, 1994).

Cohen, H., *Medailles Impériales* (Leipzig, 1930).

Constantine, D., *Friedrich Hölderlin: Selected Poems* (Bloodaxe, 1996).

Crawford, M., 'Finance, Coinage and Money from the Severans to Constantine', *ANRW* 2.2 (1975).

Cronin, P., *Harriet Hosmer, Lost and Found* (Catalogue Raisonné, Charta, 2009).

De Blois, L., 'Odenathus and the Roman-Persian War of 252-264', *Talanta* 6 (1974).

De Blois, L., *The Policy of the Emperor Gallienus* (Brill, 1976).

Dignas, B. and E. Winter, *Rome and Persia in Late Antiquity* (Cambridge, 2007).

Dixon, K.R. and P. Southern, *The Roman Cavalry* (Batsford, 1992).

Dodgeon, M.H. and S.N.C. Lieu, *The Roman Eastern Frontier and the Persian Wars AD 226-363* (Routledge, 1991).

Downey, G., 'Aurelian's Victory over Zenobia at Immae', *TAPA* 81 (1950).

Drinkwater, J.F., *The Alamanni and Rome 213-496* (Oxford, 2007).

Drinkwater, J.F., *The Gallic Empire* (Historia Einzelschriften 52, 1987).

Eadie, J.W., 'The Development of Roman Mailed Cavalry', *JRS* 57 (1967).

Emmett, K., *Alexandrian Coins* (Wisconsin, 2001).

Equini Schneider, E., in *Moi, Zenobie, Reine de Palmyre* (Exhibition catalogue, Paris, 2001).

Equini Schneider, E., *Septimia Zenobia* (L'Erma di Bretschneider, 1993).

Erdkamp, P. (ed.), *A Companion to the Roman Army* (Blackwell, 2007).

Fields, N., *The Walls of Rome* (Oxford, 2008).

Gansbeke, P. Van, 'La Mise en état de la defence de la Gaule au milieu du IIIe siècle après J-C', *Latomus* 14 (1955).

Gawlikowski, M., 'Inscriptions de Palmyre', sub-section 'Aurélian et le temple de Bel', *Syria* 48 (1971).

Gawlikowski, M., 'Palmyre et l'Euphrate', *Syria* 60 (1983).

Gawlikowski, M., 'Les Princes de Palmyre', *Syria* 62 (1985).

Gawlikowski, M., 'Palmyra as a Trading Centre', *Iraq* 56 (1994).

Gibbon, E., *Decline and Fall of the Roman Empire* (Penguin, 1995).

Gopinath, G., 'Harriet Hosmer and the Feminine Sublime', *Oxford Art Journal* 38 (2005).

Graf, D.F., 'Zenobia and the Arabs', in D.H. French and C.P. Lightfoot (eds), *The Eastern Frontier of the Roman Empire* (Oxford, 1987).

Graf, D.F., *Rome and the Arabian Frontier* (Ashgate, 1997).

Halsberghe, G.H., *The Cult of Sol Invictus* (Brill, 1972).

Hanson, W.S. and I.P. Haynes (eds), *Roman Dacia*, *JRA* Supplement 56 (2004).

Hartmann, U., *Das Palmyrenische Teilreich* (Franz Steiner, 2001).

Hekster, O. et al. (eds), *Crisis and the Roman Empire* (Brill, 2007).

Hekster, O., *Rome and its Empire AD 193-284* (Edinburgh, 2008).

Hingley, R. and C. Unwin, *Boudica – Iron Age Warrior Queen* (Hambledon, 2005).

Hornblower, S. and A. Spawforth, *Oxford Classical Dictionary* 3rd rev. edn (Oxford, 2003).

Bibliography

Hughes-Hallett, L., *Cleopatra – Queen, Lover, Legend* (Pimlico, 2006).
Hvidberg-Hansen, F.O., *The Palmyrene Inscriptions in the Ny Carlsberg Glyptotek* (Ny Carlsberg Glyptotek, 1998).
Isaac, B., *The Limits of Empire* (Oxford, 1990 rev. 1992).
Jameson, A., *Memoirs of Celebrated Female Sovereigns* (Elibron Classics reprint, 2005)
Jones, T. and A. Ereira, *Terry Jones' Barbarians* (BBC Books, 2006).
Kaizer, T., *The Religious Life of Palmyra* (Franz Steiner, 2002).
Kennedy, D. and D. Riley, *Rome's Desert Frontier* (Batsford, 1990).
Kennedy, D.L., 'Syria', in *Cambridge Ancient* History, 2nd edn, vol. 10 (1996).
Kennedy, D.L., *The Roman Army in the East*, *JRA* Supplement 18 (1996).
Kociejowski, M., *Syria: Through Writers' Eyes* (Eland, 2006).
Lafaurie, J., 'L'Empire Gaulois. L'apport de la numismatique', *ANRW* 2.2 (1975).
Levick, B., *Julia Domna* (Routledge, 2007).
Lewis, N., 'Noemata legontos', *BASP* 4 (1967).
MacDermott, B.C., 'Roman Emperors in the Sassanian Reliefs', *JRS* 44 (1954).
MacMullen, R., *The Roman Government's Response to Crisis 234-337* (Yale, 1976).
Maricq, A., 'Res Gestae Divi Saporis', *Syria* 35 (1958).
Martin, A., 'P.Mich.Inv. 5478a et le préfet d'Egypte Statilius Ammianus', *Latomus* 59 (2000).
Matthews, J.F., 'The Tax Law of Palmyra', *JRS* 74 (1984).
Millar, F., 'Caravan Cities', *BICS* Supplement 71 (1998).
Millar, F., 'Paul of Samosata, Zenobia and Aurelian', *JRS* 61 (1971).
Millar, F., *The Roman Near East* (Cambridge, 1993).
Parker, S.T., *Romans and Saracens* (American School of Oriental Research, 1986).
Potter, D.S., 'Palmyra and Rome: Odaenathus' Titulature and the Use of the Imperium Maius', *ZPE* 113 (1996).
Potter, D.S., *Prophecy and History in the Crisis of the Roman Empire* (Oxford, 1990).
Potter, D.S., *The Roman Empire at Bay* (Routledge, 2004).
Rathbone, D., 'The Dates of the Recognition in Egypt of Emperors from Caracalla to Diocletianus', *ZPE* 62 (1986).
Rea, J., 'The Date of the Prefecture of Statilius Ammianus', *Chronique d'Egypte* 87 (1969).
Rea, J., 'Two Notes', *BASP* 5 (1968).
Rey-Coquais, J-P., 'Syrie Romaine, de Pompée à Dioclétien', *JRS* 68 (1978).
Richmond, I.A., 'Palmyra under the Aegis of Rome', *JRS* 53 (1963).
Rostovtzeff, M., *Caravan Cities* (Oxford, 1932).
Sartre, M., 'Palmyra, Greek City', *Annales Archéologiques Arabes Syriennes* 42 (1996).
Sartre, M., *The Middle East Under Rome* (English translation, Harvard, 2005).
Saunders, R.T., 'Aurelian's Two Iuthungian Wars', *Historia* 41 (1992).
Schlumberger, D., 'Vorod l'Agoranome', *Syria* 49 (1972).
Schmidt-Colinet, A., *Palmyra: Kulturbegegnung in Grenzbereich*, 2nd edn (P. von Zabern, 2005).
Shahid, I., *Rome and the Arabs* (Dumbarton Oaks, 1984).
Sijpesteijn, P.J., 'Known and Unknown Officials', *ZPE* 106 (1995).
Sijpesteijn, P.J., *The Wisconsin Papyri*, *Pap. Lugd. Batava* 16 (1967).
Southern, P., *Empress Zenobia* (Continuum, 2008).
Starcky, J., *Palmyre* (A. Maisonneuve, 1952).
Stephenson, I.P. and K.R. Dixon, *Roman Cavalry Equipment* (Tempus, 2003).

Bibliography

Stoneman, R., *Palmyra and its Empire: Zenobia's Revolt against Rome* (Michigan, 1992).

Swain, S., 'Greek into Palmyrene: Odaenathus as Corrector Totius Orbis', *ZPE* 99 (1993).

Todd, M., *The Walls of Rome* (Elek, 1978).

Turcan, R., *The Cults of the Roman Empire* (Blackwell, 1996).

Vermaseren, M., *Mithras* (Barnes and Noble, 1960).

Waller, S., 'The Artist, the Writer and the Queen: Hosmer, Jameson and Zenobia', *Woman's Art Journal* 4.1 (1983).

Watson, A., *Aurelian and the Third Century* (Routledge, 1999).

White, J.F., *Restorer of the World: The Roman Emperor Aurelian* (Spellmount, 2005).

Will, E., 'Marchands et chefs de caravans à Palmyre', *Syria* 34 (1957).

Will, E., 'Pline l'Ancien et Palmyre', *Syria* 62 (1985).

Will, E., *Les Palmyréniens: La Venise des Sables* (Armand Collin, 1992).

Witzling, M. (ed.), *Voicing Our Visions: Writings by Women Artists* (Universe Books, 1991).

Young, G.K., *Rome's Eastern Trade* (Routledge, 2001).

Websites
Google 'Zenobia' and there are a lot of websites, often of poor quality if not positively misleading or fanciful. But Judith Weingarten's site at www.zenobia.tv is lively and well-informed, along with judithweingarten.blogspot.com.

Index